ENTERPRISING STATES
The Public Management of Welfare-to-Work

This book explores two fundamental shifts in the paradigms of governance in Western bureaucracies. They
are the widespread use of privatisation, private firms
and market methods to run core public services, and
the conscious attempt to transform the role of citizenship from ideals of entitlement and security to new
notions of mutual obligation, selectivity and risk. In this
work Mark Considine undertakes an examination of
the most important universal service of the modern welfare state – unemployment assistance – to explain and
theorise the nature of these radical changes. He has
undertaken extensive interview and survey research in
the United Kingdom, the Netherlands, Australia and
New Zealand. In each case Considine finds there has
been a significant break from the standards of legal-
rational bureaucracy. He identifies a new corporate-
market regime at the core of new governance arrangements in the four different systems.

Mark Considine is an Associate Professor in the Depart-
ment of Political Science at the University of
Melbourne. With Simon Marginson, he is co-author of
*The Enterprise University: Power, Governance and Reinven-
tion in Australia* (Cambridge University Press, 2000) and
author of *Public Policy: A Critical Approach* (1994). With
Jenny M. Lewis he was awarded the Marshall E. Dimock
Award for the best lead article published in *Public
Administration Review* in 1999.

ENTERPRISING STATES

The Public Management of
Welfare-to-Work

MARK CONSIDINE

University of Melbourne

CAMBRIDGE
UNIVERSITY PRESS

PUBLISHED BY THE PRESS SYNDICATE OF THE UNIVERSITY OF CAMBRIDGE
The Pitt Building, Trumpington Street, Cambridge, United Kingdom

CAMBRIDGE UNIVERSITY PRESS
The Edinburgh Building, Cambridge CB2 2RU, UK
40 West 20th Street, New York, NY 10011–4211, USA
10 Stamford Road, Oakleigh, VIC 3166, Australia
Ruiz de Alarcón 13, 28014 Madrid, Spain
Dock House, The Waterfront, Cape Town 8001, South Africa

http://www.cambridge.org

First published 2001

Printed in Australia by Brown Prior Anderson

Typeface New Baskerville (*Adobe*) 10/12 pt. *System* QuarkXPress® [DOCUPRO]

A catalogue record for this book is available from the British Library

National Library of Australia Cataloguing in Publication data
Considine, Mark, 1953– .
Enterprising states: the public management of welfare to work.
Bibliography.
Includes index.
ISBN 0 521 80598 8.
ISBN 0 521 00052 1 (pbk.).
1. Unemployed – Services for. 2. Insurance, Unemployment –
Management 3. Public administration. 4. Civil service. I. Title.
354.96

ISBN 0 521 80598 8 hardback
ISBN 0 521 00052 1 paperback

Contents

Tables

Acknowledgements

Large projects incur large debts. This one is no exception. The Australian Research Council provided the funds which made the fieldwork in these four countries possible. The National Public Administration Research Fund (Australia) helped fund the very first round of élite interviews in Australia. Jan Carter and Deakin Human Services Australia provided ongoing interest and support for the project. The Deakin connection also led to my collaboration with Dr Michael White at the Policy Studies Institute in London where, with the assistance of Jane Lakey, I was able to launch the United Kingdom and Netherlands studies. Michael provided invaluable advice and support throughout the four years it took to bring the project to this stage.

Theo Keulen in the Netherlands Employment Service, Tony Gavin in the New Zealand Employment Service, Steve Sedgewick in the Australian Department of Employment, Education and Youth Affairs and John Fletcher in the UK Employment Service gave permission for me to conduct interviews and surveys and I thank them and their organisations for their willingness to support independent research. The same can be said for the many officials who gave time and the benefit of their experience to answer questions and educate me in the complex work they do. Thanks also to the Commonwealth and Public Sector Union in Australia for their support.

My colleagues Ann Capling and Michael Crozier at the University of Melbourne were unstinting in their interest in the project and in reading drafts of chapters and articles along the way. Joel Aberbach and Zeke Hasenfeld at UCLA, Bert Rockman at the University of Pittsburgh, Colin Campbell at Georgetown University, Adrienne Heretier and Colin Crouch at the European University Institute, Anna Yeatman at Macquarie University, Ewe Becker at the University of Amsterdam, Jan

Carter at Deakin University and Bob Goodin at the Australian National University provided welcome assistance, sometimes in the form of comments on drafts, and sometimes in discussions of the new governance process as a more general phenomenon. Jenny Lewis at the University of Melbourne helped with aspects of the design, collaborated on the development of the governance scales and co-authored the *Public Administration Review* article which informs an important part of Chapter Seven. Catherine Smith and the Statistical Consulting Centre at the University of Melbourne assisted with the discriminant analysis and with a number of interpretation problems associated with the comparison of the four country data. Rita De Amicis my Departmental Manager found a way around countless obstacles associated with the funding, travel and teaching relief elements of the project. Hans Lofgren and Anne Ellison helped with bibliographic research. Wendy Geekie and Natalie Maddafri assisted with preparation of the questionnaires and manuscript. Peter Debus, Gillian Fulcher and Paul Watt saw the manuscript through its various incarnations and were enthusiastic and helpful throughout. The four anonymous Cambridge readers also added valuable insights and suggestions.

My wife Genevieve gave space and support for all that can be found in the pages that follow, read drafts, and endured my absences and preoccupations with rare generosity. I dedicate this book to her.

CHAPTER 1

Enterprising the State

Perhaps there once was a time when the terms 'state', 'market' and 'bureaucracy' had settled meanings and when the institutions which they helped define had standard, widely understood purposes. If so this is certainly a book about the closing of that era and about a radical set of changes that now seeks to alter the nature of governance in many advanced capitalist states. The particular reform strategies I will identify in four countries map the contours of wider changes in the nature of contemporary governance. Their front-line reinventions spell out the central characteristics of a process of change which can be defined as the *enterprising* of the state.

This transformation is something less than a final accomplishment. Process is often more revealing than structure. The enterprising activity takes root in forms of managerialism, contractualism and reinvention within programs aimed at both the work of officials and the identity of citizen-clients. As such it constitutes a new transition model for systems of public action which are seeking ways to meet the challenges of globalisation and the imperatives of new levels of cultural diversity (Jessop, 1991; Lash and Urry, 1987). At stake is the inheritance these countries share in their common foundation as liberal democracies. Liberalism's debt to the idea that public power is best understood as a system of subordinate functions, carefully layered beneath the sovereignty of the state and neatly separated from the private realm, is now being called into question. A new configuration of independent subsystems is taking up the role of providing and controlling public goods, and thus ordering the lives of citizens outside the direct control of state agencies. As Hutton and Giddens (2000, p. ix) put it, 'Governments and states everywhere are less confident about the merits of the public domain and the effectiveness of public action, and

1

increasingly abdicate initiative to the private sector or seek out the private sector as a partner.'

While expressing common ideas concerning the virtue of an enterprising form of governance, these new roles of public agencies and actors nevertheless will be seen to impact differently in each of our four countries. At the level of actual plans, technologies and tactics this general enterprising mode builds new forms of political and organisational coherence out of three common repertoires. To distinguish the levels of this transformation dynamic I will refer to these three institution-level types as *governance strategies* or *models*. In some cases the three appear as stages in a path of sequential development, in others as points of departure by reformers seeking to accommodate their own institutional histories to a common set of competitive pressures. Each has an encompassing desire to plot a path away from an older notion of procedural or bureaucratic governance. And the enterprising imperative driving all three alternatives involves a common performance ambition and a shared interest in applying the lessons learned from neo-liberalism and its offspring, the various economic theories of organisation.

Each of the three reform strategies – the corporate, the market and the network – aim to reinvent governance as something different to hierarchy and functional specialisation. The new field of public power is constituted through systems of interdependence among public and private actors, sometimes including citizens mobilised as co-producers. This will be most obvious in the programs described below as a decisive turn away from universal state services and standardised responses to social problems. In short the enterprising process includes a new interest in flexible, reciprocal relationships and shared responsibilities expressed not as democratic theory or the world of rights familiar to liberals, but as chains of contracts and brokered exchanges between self-enterprising actors. New questions of agency and autonomy challenge older certainties based on the power of rules and a previous sovereignty expressed through the hierarchical arrangement of public and private roles and their careful distinction.

The new enterprising dynamic involves the state in a huge and self-conscious project of reinvention. First, in place of legal-bureaucratic action based on entitlements and universal treatments, the new rationality seeks to found government upon a code of specific performance. Second, the tenets of organisational economics have been mobilised to define governance as the judicious creation of any contract between parties able to effect an efficient manufacture of outputs. Third, the public interest is released from any privileged idea of public service and instead resides mainly in the calculation and the distribution of risks. Fourth, universality is jettisoned in favour of new forms of program selectivity in which clients are provided with those services most likely to set them 'free' of any habitual or continuing use of the state's assistance, a condition now defined and stigmatised as dependence. Finally, these chosen interventions are provided within new relationships which ask officials and those they serve to practise and mimic within their interactions the same strategies they expect to meet outside in an emerging social world. And they are asked to do this without the old, clear pathways into work, education and prosperity, not least because the state itself no longer defines itself as a guarantor of any standard measure of civilised comfort.

The book examines the practice of this form of enterprising governance from the perspective of just one central set of public services – the welfare benefits and programs delivered to unemployed people. Although central to the historic role of the welfare state in all Western democracies, these services are hardly a full picture of modern government. Health, education and criminal justice would also vie for attention in any complete survey. Yet in the case of employment services we see the state's largest non-professionalised commitment and one which bears directly upon post-industrial society's most important project – the transformation of work. This offers a unique view of a critically important intersection of internal governmental reform and the larger processes of social reinvention which evidently preoccupy the advanced societies.

These processes of organisational transformation have been taking place in each of these national systems for at least a decade. The various forms of New Public Management (NPM) which Hood (1995, p. 96) identified have variously sought to empower managers, improve efficiency and incorporate private agencies into the delivery of public services. But as Ingraham (1996, p. 249) has shown, these more general paths to reform have in practice expressed more than one imperative. The one road carries several forms of traffic. Some observers have sought to emphasise the role of political constraints, while others have focused more upon managerial and economic preoccupations. In practice we find both researchers and practitioners caught up in a complex array of changes and claims. Consequently we know more about what has been left behind than about what lies ahead.

The *ancien régime* is by now very familiar, both in its virtues and its vices. Our image, appreciation and critique of industrial society is of a century defined by large, legal-rational organisations rolling in formation towards standardised ends (Blau, 1956; Touraine, 1988). Political parties, welfare systems and private corporations have each been viewed as manifestations of this common system for imagining and producing mass society (Poggi, 1978; Rose, 1996).

Theories of democratic governance developed during the heyday of mass industrial societies spent much of their effort upon devising better means to order and direct these large organisations from above. Most of last century is therefore marked by efforts to improve and strengthen executive authority within states, mass parties and big corporations. All invested heavily in the extension of what Chandler (1977, p. 483) has called 'the visible hand' of managerial power. With the accretion of all important forms of decision-making to a new class of managers in ever larger corporations, institutions found that 'administrative coordination proved more profitable than market coordination'. This is not to deny a smaller tradition of local participation and citizen action, but instead to recognise that it did not often manage to define the terms of social innovation.

Specialisation of official roles and technical skills had become the standard organisational response to demands by citizens and to the new opportunities created by advanced capitalist economies. A tradition of scholarship starting with Max Weber (1947) and including Blau (1956), Etzioni (1964) and Simon (1957) established the generalised power of this set of theorems. At its high point after the Second World War this process of rationalisation saw a common model of service delivery emerge across the public spheres of the advanced capitalist world.

Employees in public organisations were appointed into a career system based on hierarchical co-ordination, promoted on technical merit and granted a discretion to act only within a defined field of competence. Law, precedent and a knowledge of the files guaranteed (in theory, if not always in practice) that citizens would receive equal treatment, be subject to due process and enjoy a common opportunity to be served. Our understanding of the role of the modern state has been entirely dependent upon our confidence in the ability of mass public bureaucracies to deliver everything from a fair system of voting to a common aged pension. It was also within this framework of procedural rights that civil servants were encouraged to define the ethical treatment of the public as the practice of impartiality and even indifference towards their individual identities, including class, religion or gender. It was widely assumed that to open the door to any special treatment threatened a return to the invidious world of nineteenth century patronage.

This double-play of specialisation and standardisation also mirrored and mimicked many of the organisational strategies of private corporations such as the larger banks and bigger car manufacturers, where routines and technical skills guaranteed replicant products to a vast market. The T-model Ford became the emblem of everyone's individual right to share a commoners' capitalism. That the image of a mass society that underpinned this vision was always something of an exaggeration did not prevent its popularity among decision makers. All social institutions exist first and foremost as exaggerations.

The certain grasp of this industrial model is now enfeebled by a new reality. Premised upon diversity and driven by a new scarcity of public resources, a reinvented ideal of public service seeks to substitute standardisation with selectivity. Consequently in government services in countries in the Organisation for Economic Cooperation and Development (OECD) there has been a proliferation of 'new governance' models. These are also grouped under the heading of New Public Management, although there are now so many successors to the first radical gestures of the mid-1970s that 'new' has lost its meaning. A more variegated orthodoxy now claims the ground once occupied by the old state-bureaucratic paradigm. Whether we call it postmodern (Fox & Miller, 1995), post-bureaucratic (Barzeley, 1992) or just 'neo-liberal' (Rose, 1996), the common commitments of this reform movement are found in the spread of privatisation, decentralisation and individual-centred responses to public needs. These adopted strategies suggest nothing less than a major strategic and cultural shift in the way advanced societies now seek to define the public sphere and the roles of citizens and officials within it (Hasenfeld, 1992; Handler, 1996, p. 3).

The seeds of this revolutionary change are found in the turn from bureaucracy. Despite its central place in all accounts of responsible government, public bureaucracy now has few advocates and many critics. At all points of the political spectrum there is a litany of complaints coming from social democrats, liberals, postmodernists and neo-conservatives – the state has become too big, too costly, too rigid, too standardised, and too insensitive to individual identities. This remarkable consensus appears to be a consequence both of actual deficiencies and of the emergence of anti-government ideologies associated with the new cultural power of business. As Fournier and Grey (1999, p. 108) put it, the new vision 'seeks to stigmatise and marginalise bureaucracy, in general, and public bureaucracy in particular, as being outmoded and as functionally and morally bankrupt'.

Bureaucracy is viewed as a pejorative characteristic of all publicly-run services and thus of the modern welfare state itself. As we know, the classical exposition of the bureaucratic type came from Max Weber (1947). His model of modern governance emphasised rational-legal distinctions between the different classes of officials wielding authority, clear rules for guiding the actions of those occupying these various ranks, and a strong form of supervision:

> The authority to give commands . . . is distributed in a stable way and is strictly delimited by rules concerning the coercive means . . . The principles of office

hierarchy and of all levels of graded authority means a firmly ordered system
of super- and subordination, in which there is supervision of the lower office
by the higher ones (Weber, 1947, p. 331).

This impersonal service by a legal-rational technocracy is being
replaced a governmental system which embraces the normative world of
the entrepreneur and the organisational imperative of the polycentric
corporation. The tools of reform are often those of the management
consultant or the recently hired senior executive from a large bank or
car manufacturer. But to make sense of this change we need to distinguish carefully between the act of reform, its strategy and its ultimate
object. The process of enterprising the state may well be one which
favours private sector methods and models, but the object of the process
is still the state itself.

Using private sector methods does not, of itself, change government
institutions into a private sphere. It is both premature and unnecessarily
reductionist to equate the enterprising spirit with mere privatisation.
The state organisations drawn into the new reform paradigm remain
actors in their own right. Indeed the enterprising process often empow-
ers executive actors within public organisations in new ways. These also
typically remain organisations funded by taxes and they continue to seek
ways to provide services for citizens. There is no act of social magic that
can cause the state to vanish simply by calling those who fund and
receive its services 'customers' or 'stakeholders'.

This enterprising logic certainly speaks with a corporate and market
vocabulary, but this may be its means rather than its end. Central
government purposes are evidently deployed though contractors, temporary commitments and private forms of implementation. But the
state itself is also enterprised, strengthening its managerial and strategic power. Nowhere is this more evident than in the welfare state
institutions of advanced capitalist societies. The nineteenth and early
twentieth century struggles to centralise and regularise forms of
assistance under the banner of citizen rights is now being disassembled
into a world of different, partial and non-standard interventions. The
virtues of a universal, industrial model of citizenship are now hedged
and mediated by an interest in variation, experimentation and new
forms of self-responsibility which advocates have called 'the new paternalism' (Mead, 1997). The new administrative competence required
to individualise services in a manner capable of creating such self-
mobilisation by welfare clients implies a state organisational system
which has achieved 'entrepreneurial governance' (Osborne & Gaebler,
1992). Enterprising the clients turns out to be a similar process to
enterprising the service providers.

The justifications for the deliberate dismantling of key parts of the old bureaucratic system highlight different aspects of its previous inadequacy and of its technological obsolescence. Mass institutions such as the public service have been variously pilloried for their 'Yes Minister' arrogance and their 'one size fits all' inflexibility. Which critique is selected in each reform episode depends on where the observer sat during the rule of the *ancien régime*. In other words the end of the bureaucratic model is an achievement of overlapping complaints, not all of them imaginary. Politicians attack the unwillingness of senior officials to adopt new political programs and the tendency of civil servants to stick to 'tried and true' methods for solving problems. Budget managers and business think-tanks attack the 'tax and spend' approach to treating new issues with more and more programs. Citizen groups point out that large public agencies shield the powerful from legitimate community demands. And in the most surprising assault of all, bureaucrats in central agencies complain of the 'capture' of their colleagues by unions and others who, they say, make the public sphere an all too easy target for 'rent seekers'.[1]

Whether or not we accept these arguments in the terms presented, there can be no doubt about the new terms of debate. Global pressures on the advanced economies have intensified rapidly. Countries wishing to attract capital and secure their standard of living must shave costs at every possible level, including the level of government. But there is more going on than simply an energetic economy drive. Cost-cutting has opened the door to new ways of defining the public purpose. This has generated widespread interest in ways to do 'more with less' and to meet existing demands through cost shifting to other levels of government, to private organisations and back onto the shoulders of citizens themselves. An enterprising governance implies less government in some fields, reregulation in others and greater self-governance in all (Kooiman, 1993; Aucoin, 1990; Boston et al., 1991; Caiden & Seidentopf, 1982; Knott & Miller, 1987).

These pressures signify both risks and great possibilities for advanced societies and their citizens. They promise a different world for the governed and a new power structure for the governors. We can no longer read the roles of public servants from a constitutional grid established from above, nor one driven uniformly through a bureaucratic code. Enterprised states are now constructed or 'made up' by the efforts of intersecting authorities seeking greater influence at ground level. The older focus upon basic legal and material rights has been joined by the efforts of states seeking to alter and mobilise the cultural power of new hybrid public-private institutions. Groups of citizens are selected for special treatments that seek to define their self-identity or subjectivity as a far more precise object of official attention.

Sometimes this implies the surprising empowerment of consumers and sometimes the sudden withdrawal of their public rights. But everywhere it involves a greater interest in specifying and exacting measured performance, comparing the achievements of agents and increasing the flexibility and mobility of public resources. More than ever before the motivations and personal norms of actors are critically important to these questions of performance. Managers, professionals, clerical workers and clients are invited to enterprise themselves according to an ideal of improvement that shifts the risk of investment and consumption down closer to the level of the individual.

This new diversity has one critical anchor. Personal and organisational changes converge regarding the importance of comparing and measuring one's own actions and achievements against ideals of self-responsibility and of self-enterprise. In its most extreme form this implies a state role which is closer to that of the management consultant or the small business than to the older model of paternal insurer and provider. Social protection gives way to risk management. Security is replaced by a calculus of the entrepreneurial possibilities of running one's life, career or household as a solitary accomplishment. Government becomes less a matter of providing things and more a question of managing incentives (Yeatman, 1995; Rose, 1989).

The term 'enterprising state' employed here derives from two research traditions. The first, most obviously, is the new management literature which for nearly twenty years has sought to apply private sector organisation theory to problems of state administration. Starting with Chandler's (1977) path-breaking study of the managerial revolution of the early twentieth century and culminating in Drucker's (1992) work on the 'new society of organisations', entrepreneurial ideals have been linked to broader conceptions of social development. In both industrial and post-industrial management revolutions the state has been identified as the recipient, not the initiator of social innovation.

In a second research tradition popularised by Rose (1989), Gordon (1991) and du Gay and Salaman (1992), the concept of enterprise is extended and radicalised to include not just organisational innovations but also ideas about the revised role and responsibility of subjects. The movement to increase flexibility, to embrace innovative information technologies and to decentralise social systems is here associated with new notions of agency and citizenship. As Almond and Rubery (2000, p. 281) point out, the more general forms of decentralisation associated with the governance reform movement suggest different forms of state agency in each country. In the UK for example, the Thatcher period is recognised as one in which a pro-market regime actually led to significant increases in the state's power over such things as industrial relations, training and other labour market programs. Yet there is little doubt, even among antagonists, that the result of these more general movements has been the emergence of a new rationale for state action which is based upon commitments to individual choice, risk-taking and self-direction.

As King (1995, p. 211) argues, this has created a new 'version of social citizenship, promulgated by New Right pressure groups and conservatives' which seeks 'to match any rights to assistance a citizen holds with a corollary set of duties which must be satisfied as a condition of the former'. In a project which is openly defined as cultural, motivational and personal, the state seeks to change the character of the citizen, to re-make him or her as a self-enterprising agent. Nor is this ambition confined to neo-conservatives. Exponents of the 'Third Way' and other social democratic parties have also embraced the commitment to the new risk-taking entrepreneurship (Perri 6, 1997; Giddens, 1999).

In practice these more general forms of institutional change involve uncommon implementations. Politicians and public officials seek to blend and hybridise new strategies aimed at stimulating the performance of agencies and individuals. They invent new relationships with one another, replacing single-purpose agencies with short-term, conditional relationships with suppliers, competitors and collaborators. This new flexibility in the definition of public services stimulates a complex power structure in which old hierarchies of state, market and civic agencies are forced to reconsider their relationship to government and to match the state's own self-enterprising dynamic by reinventing themselves in radical ways.

The book takes the enterprising dynamic as its theme, not its conclusion. The impact of a more generalised logic of governmental reform is found in the three different reform types or models, each of which takes some common performance commitments and welds them into a precise strategy of institutional reinvention. The models for enterprising the state therefore express an imperative and a normative structure, not a single institutional accomplishment. Three pragmatic types have emerged as competitors of the old bureaucratic approach with its focus upon law and procedure. Just as the postwar welfare state was expressed as liberal, conservative and social democratic regimes in different societies, so too the enterprising state allows more than one trajectory (Esping-Andersen, 1990). Each is driven by the historical commitments and established political deals between interests. This too suggests disjuncture, adaptation and hybridity (Young, 1995, p. 163).

In four countries with proud records of social reform these different strategies blend and exploit the instruments of the new public management in order to enterprise state organisations. Some seek to empower private contractors, some to bind public servants with new forms of performance management. All strive to change the role of citizens from one of entitlement to something involving new obligations and new forms of self-mobilisation, and perhaps of self-enterprise. One of our primary analytical challenges is to investigate the extent of convergence and re-standardisation. Is the new set of relationships a different kind of governance system, or the end of any settled idea about the role of government?

In the 'Welfare-to-Work' reforms in these four different countries there are two processes at work. The first involves organisational change within the public service itself. Bureaucrats find themselves having to define their roles according to new demands and strict objectives. Outcomes, targets, commercial codes and private agreements govern more and more of what they are asked to do. Management science takes centre stage and legal rules appear less potent as the measure of what needs to be done and how it is to be achieved.

The second process involves new relationships with other public and private agencies and with the citizens who receive services. Here we expect brokerage, selectivity and risk to assume a bigger share of the work to define public goods. This at least is the expectation with 'best fit' between the claims of proponents and the arguments of theorists. As an empirical claim this 'new governance' appears to require a dramatic empowerment at the front line where officials, contractors and clients take on more individualising roles. This may also come hand-in-hand with a new potential for impoverishment. Solutions to problems are less likely to involve the guarantee of resources and more apt to require new forms of administration and motivation.

The enterprise tool-kit can be recognised as a number of familiar devices, each of which has its own role in these national systems. Each of the following instruments will be seen to contribute to the formation of more cumulative processes of change in the four country studies which follow. But first it is worth summarising their more generic features:

Performance Management

In place of a public service which was criticised as overly interested in controlling the input side of the budget, and in building public programs as a means to satisfy the strategic needs of bureaucrats or those of their allies, reformers insist upon output measurement. The performance revolution that took place in the 1980s saw public organisations subjected to a host of management techniques aimed at convincing them to focus upon the specific results governments wanted. Program budgeting, corporate planning, the introduction of performance indicators and performance pay each contributed to this movement.

Managers, and particularly senior managers, sought to develop the skills necessary to construct performance schedules and methodologies by which their organisations would now be measured. They looked to business schools to provide training and to private consultants to model the organisational structures needed. Driving the changes from above were central agencies such as Prime Minister's offices, Treasury bureaucrats and a few enthusiastic politicians who saw the performance system as a way both to increase control and cut costs.

Entrepreneurial Action

In place of the view of public agencies that held standardised implementation as a primary virtue, governments now see public organisations as having a responsibility to create their own means of addressing problems and meeting demands. To be entrepreneurial is to invent a range of different implementations, experiments and innovations. For example, the US commitment to 'entrepreneurial governance', embodied in Vice President Al Gore's National Performance Review, has favoured bureau cutting at the top of the civil service and flexible innovation at the bottom (Gore, 1993).

An existing tradition of 'contracting out' services has been strengthened, but now with fewer rules about which activities need to stay within the public service and which are to be given back to citizens, shared with private markets or abandoned altogether. Citizens in one part of a program no longer need to expect the same service as those elsewhere and far greater value is placed upon risk-taking as a means to locate and create efficiency.

Principal-Agent Separation

In order to protect a new role for public policy makers, reformers frequently seek to distinguish between the functions of the 'principal' and those of their 'agents' (Donaldson, 1995). Often this split is expressed in an attempt to divide the public sector into executive organisations and those that invent an appropriate management system to produce the agreed set of outcomes.

In the UK the process of civil service reform associated with the Thatcher and Major governments is perhaps best exemplified by the Next Steps initiative. By separating policy-making departments headed by bureaucrats from service delivery agencies headed by Chief Executive Officers, and by linking the two through public performance agreements, the UK reformers enacted one notable form of 'principal-agent separation'.

A similar logic informs efforts to bind contractors in both the public and private sectors into performance agreements in which the executive arm accepts a new role for itself as 'governing at a distance'. With fewer burdens at the service delivery end, government sees itself as liberated from the industrial relations and the direct management costs associated with program implementation. Shifting resources around the system is therefore viewed as far easier, since cuts and cost shifts are now embedded in private agreements with firms and semi-independent public organisations. Even the employment contracts with public servants may come to resemble private agreements, provided unions and arbitration institutions can be weakened.

Meanwhile the division of management expertise into either steering or rowing rather than both promises a new specialisation (Osborne & Gaebler, 1992). Enacting public programs now becomes an act of purchasing rather than a skill at day-to-day administration. Non-executive politicians are implicated in the new division between steering and rowing and find themselves distanced from both the patronage opportunities afforded by a single public service and from the chance to represent their constituents inside the service.

Quasi-Markets

A further step in the process of institutional de-coupling sees central government actors empowering more than one agent to bid for and then produce a defined set of outputs. This serves not only to improve the agent's skills in producing a defined output, but also puts new pressures on them to measure their costs (or prices) against another agent's willingness to take their place at the front line.

In the New Zealand and Australian health systems the use of 'quasi-markets' has placed service delivery organisations in direct competition for both resources and clients. Armed with standard methods for measuring the cost of similar procedures, hospitals and health centres engage in efforts to win a larger share of services previously allocated by regional and political methods. Choices about which services to offer the 'principal' government authority therefore rest upon decisions about local competitive advantage and the wise use of spare capacity.

For the policy makers at the senior executive levels of public organisations the creation and active shaping of quasi-markets offers a new form of rationality. Under older notions of deliberative action organisations were thought to test and compare different means to reach any given goal. Cost benefit analysis and the application of utilitarian principles for selecting programs provided the much debated basis of this rational actor model. But the real life demands of the model were almost always too heroic for cost-strapped public organisations under political pressure to make quick decisions.

The competitive contracting-out of programs substitutes a new, equally powerful rationale for decision making. The different approaches used by contractors become the alternative (experimental) implementations of the program and by shifting new business towards the agents with the best performance, policy makers can promise new forms of efficiency.

Citizen Responsibility

The final common theme informing the contemporary reform move-ment is the idea that those receiving services should become more active on their own behalf. This has two related, but not altogether consistent, manifestations. The benign part is a concept of consumer sovereignty borrowed directly from activism in the private economy. To curb the inflexibility and stubbornness of the old fashioned bureaucracies governments may attempt to give clients more choice in the selection of their services. In some departments this takes the form of requiring bureaucrats to consult with their customers, to gather customer satisfac-tion data and even to include customers on advisory panels or 'user boards' (Considine, 2000). At its strongest this pro-consumer stance also identifies increased choice as a key means to empower clients. Rather than 'one size fits all' and the other parodies of bureaucratic service, a new approach sees officials responding to customer demands by fashioning individual programs. In other words choice becomes the motor to drive a new appreciation of diversity.

The second element of this consumer responsibility theme is the idea that those receiving services from government should contribute more. This is both a financial and a normative strategy. The first is simply a means to raise charges on service users. User payments, co-payments and vouchers provide a way to raise the funds needed to provide a service. These devices offer a means to shift costs back onto citizens, clients and their families. However the active involvement of clients may also include requiring them to provide part of their own service. This is often represented by reformers as a way to personalise the service.

Self-service is viewed as a means of activating or mobilising clients and thus reducing their dependence on government. But changing the service may also require an attempt at changing the identity of those involved. Rather than stay in hospital, patients could recover at home. Parents and children then become carers and nurses. In place of social security payments more people may be encouraged to take out private insurance for unemployment, sickness and old age. In place of pensioners governments are actively creating new identities for self-funded retirees and self-risk managers.

Four Model Strategies

While these common themes and justifications suggest the workings of a single 'enterprising' imagination driving the definition of public service, in practice, the organisational reforms produced according to these various imperatives are fashioned from local institutional material and born of political compromise. The same enterprising urge can beget different offspring, even if the gene pool is much the same. So between a single realised model of the newly enterprised state and the host of untidy accommodations of old and new techniques of organisation are some important choices for reformers. I will define these choices as ones which reflect four different narratives or images of governance, and as thus embodying four possible types of authoritative action. One is the old bureaucratic types, the other three are the 'new governance' types.

In other words, the themes of public sector reform that have emerged across these advanced capitalist systems in the past ten years actually allow a variety of possible realisations of 'new governance' in practice. In selecting these four basic types this study does not insist that they are the only models which can be imagined. Indeed, every individual plan for reforming a program or agency usually extols its own version of the 'new governance' repertoire.

But to compare the major Welfare-to-Work reforms in these countries it's first necessary to identify what it is that they may hold in common. I will sift for their core elements, using the ideal-types as a standard and as a means of calibrating the distance between pure principle and the messy world of actual achievements. The strategy types are therefore a means of opening up the problem of defining and explaining the new public sector and its primary purposes. Finally, where actual practices combine elements of different types, the process of hybridisation itself can be compared with the strength or weaknesses in the original types.

These four models are the 'procedural', 'corporate', 'market' and 'network' models of public action. They are discussed at greater length in the next chapter where their historical origins and central claims are compared. The first, the 'procedural', is the older form of public organisation run by laws, rules and precedent. Although its last rites have been frequently performed it's necessary at least to check its vital signs. The second type, the 'corporate', conforms to the managerial initiatives and their interest in performance. Here rules are less important than plans.

Precedent is replaced with output targets and program measures. This is the model world of managerialism that offered to save hierarchical systems of command from the first complaints of costly inflexibility.

The third type, the 'market', places contracting at the centre of the organisational system and seeks to define value through the competitive allocation of tasks among a world of independent agents. The contracting state therefore embodies the idea that market mechanisms do better than older forms of co-ordination. The fourth, the 'network', imagines a set of public and private agencies taking over the joint delivery of public services. Using enhanced communication and negotiation to bridge the gaps between organisations involved in bringing services to the same populations, network governance expresses the reformer's hope that co-production might become the alternative to divisive markets and rigid hierarchies.

Comparing Welfare-to-Work Institutions

To explain the enterprising of these states the book looks in detail at the same set of public institutions in Australia, the Netherlands, New Zealand and the United Kingdom. Welfare-to-Work is a shorthand description for a complex mix of public institutions, rights and entitlements. In a wider debate it also suggests the decline of 'entitlement' programs and the rise of forms of assistance which are more conditional. For present purposes these Welfare-to-Work institutions may be defined as programs which involve the granting of income support to those who undertake to search for work. These programs originate in a public mandate established by legislation, and may include the use of ancillary services such as training, counselling or health care. These are dynamic and controversial services that sit at the very centre of the welfare state's modern purpose. In reforming the way these services are organised in four different systems the study will examine far more than the routine treatments meted out to unemployed people, important though that task may be. It will inquire into new forms of public service, a different power structure in the public sphere, and perhaps even a radically different means for understanding the role of the state in the postindustrial era.

Why these four countries? Since the study aims to explain and theorise new forms of public organisation it was important to choose systems with an obvious interest in, and commitment to, governance reform. Australia, the Netherlands, New Zealand and the United Kingdom each have a well deserved place at the top of the OECD's list of the most energetic public sector reformers. Starting at different points each has worked to fashion new programs and new techniques for meeting the challenges of global competition and a revised state role. And while arguably the vanguard of the OECD 'new governance' movement, these four are not necessarily representative of anything but those seeking major change. As Shand (1996, p. 64) puts it, New Zealand and the United Kingdom are considered 'radicals', while Australia and the Netherlands are classified as more 'measured' in their embrace of the new models. Less enthusiastic are the civil law countries, Japan and the federal level in Germany. A different book would be needed to explain why some countries rapidly embraced change while others dragged their feet or shielded themselves from such pressures. My purpose is to understand the dynamics and choices for those who sought the pioneering path.

Since reform is always built within institutions with distinctive histories, it was important to have some variation in institutional context. This provides a means to judge the extent of generalised change and the degree of path-dependence. Australia and New Zealand are post-colonial societies with imported institutions and vulnerable economies. They also own reputations for social innovation, including controversial affections for the neo-liberal model of reinvention. The Netherlands and the UK are mature capitalist societies with long traditions of public service.

All four countries have Welfare-to-Work institutions that are run by the national level of government. In 1996 when these four were selected for study they had unemployment rates within the middle band of OECD rates. The Netherlands was lowest with 6.8 per cent, New Zealand had 7.3 per cent, the UK had 8.7 per cent and Australia had the highest rate at 8.9 per cent (OECD, 1996). Further, the choice of countries was made with different forms of public-private involvement in mind. Two countries (Australia and the Netherlands) had recently reformed their bureaucracies by bringing private organisations into the centre of the service delivery role. The other two had reformed an existing set of public service organisations to make them more responsive to the 'new governance' agenda. Clearly there would have been advantages in choosing a larger group of countries. For instance, it might be thought that any attempt to investigate the impact of New Public Management without including the USA is rather like staging Hamlet without the prince. But as most readers will understand, the US case is too diverse and complex to allow easy comparison. Its federal government mandates employment programs but then cedes responsibility for implementation to the states, and in some cases to the counties. Consequently there is no single US case but more than fifty different forms. A plausible case could also be made for including a Scandinavian example, perhaps Denmark where Welfare-to-Work reforms have been energetic and comprehensive. In the end the choice of the four was determined by the limits of one person's capacity to undertake detailed fieldwork in different countries during the same period. It will be for others to explore the extent to which the enterprising dynamic and attendant governance strategies might be a competent framework for the analysis of these other systems.

The study focuses upon one single field of reform – public welfare and employment assistance. This was chosen because it is both a major commitment of all these systems and because it is a service which links government directly to its citizenry and to labour and capital. Why study this one policy field? There are no methodological imperatives for choosing one field rather than a number. Other fields such as health or agriculture might have shown different manifestations of the new governance changes, but limited resources compel us to selective efforts.

But if one major sector is to be used to explore these issues then this one has many merits. Whatever else might be said about unemployment and the welfare state's response to it, these services cannot be viewed as marginal to the public sector's historical role. As a point of entry into the wider realm of governance relations this single vantage point therefore has more advantages than many others. It is a primary function in all advanced systems, it uses considerable funds and it employs hundreds of thousands of public servants. Indeed the combined total of employment service and social security staff makes this the largest in many countries. More than this, the plight of the unemployed holds a mirror to the new organisational systems being developed in advanced societies. As Beck (1986) argued in the German case, the unemployment crisis questions the social contract between citizens and the state. The restructure of public welfare and employment services, particularly where that involves more market-oriented, post-bureaucratic systems, therefore grants insight into both the cause and effect sides of one of the most important questions of our time. It allows us to reverse the usual question 'What are governments doing about the nature of unemployment?' by also asking, 'What is persistent unemployment doing to the nature of government?'

How front-line staff do it, who helps them, what resources they have available and how they devise strategies to overcome obstacles and resolve conflicts are the questions to answer. In the answers lie the best clues we have for understanding the new architecture of politics. The big questions about public authority, governmental purpose, accountability, discretion and performance all rest upon the strategies and achievements of these front-line officials working with new forms of governance. We need to know more about the way they tackle their jobs, how they interact with suppliers, supervisors, competitors and clients.

Then it may be possible to explain how and whether a new governance system constitutes a break from the more universal system of rules and procedures which characterised the old order. How far have these systems travelled towards flexible, competitive, self-enterprising or co-produced services of the type imagined in 'new governance' aspirations?

An important omission from the study concerns the experience of the job seekers. They were not interviewed and neither were they surveyed. Again, this would have required another study of even greater complexity. Job seekers cannot be ignored, however. Much of what the advisers talk about is their interactions with these clients. When officials recount their experiences of their jobs they also say quite a bit about the way unemployed people use the service and battle to achieve things they value. But there is no avoiding the fact that this is second-hand testimony and therefore somewhat partial. While all those spoken to or surveyed expressed commitment to their clients, there is no getting around the fact that these officials have their own stake in the system and that this often involves differences and conflicts with clients. So in drawing conclusions about the interactions that take place at the front line, the book will mostly try to describe only the reality that exists for officials and their organisations. The final chapter examines some of the implications which these have for clients, but as to their own reactions and strategies? – they will have to await a different study.

Summary of the Argument

In the following chapters I will discuss how services are shaped by the new ideals of governance. The broad thrust of the enterprising dynamic will be shown to shape the changes which each system has enacted in the late 1990s. For each, I will outline their commitments to the de-coupling of public organisations, the use of private agencies to deliver public services, the greater reliance on contracts, the employment of performance targets and the new demands upon staff to be selective and flexible in their interactions with clients. I will show how this set of commitments overshadows and often supplants the norms of the older bureaucratic code: how proceduralism, universal treatment and standardised interventions are on the wane.

Using interviews and surveys of front-line staff the book will identify the emergence of the three hypothesised strategies – the corporate, market and network. The core values and tools of these new approaches are robust, measurable and distinctive. Far from being mere catchwords or transitory rhetorical flourishes deployed only by ministers and consultants, these types emerge as very real engagements enacted within the core of these services, touching staff members, agencies and clients alike.

At the outset it seemed more probable that each system would tend towards one or other of the four strategies. I expected the UK to lie closest to the traditional procedural type because on the surface its Employment Service had retained most of the universalist norms of the Westminster bureaucracy. The New Zealand case I presumed would lie closest to the corporate type because in that country reformers had apparently done most to borrow a unified 're-engineering' model direct from the private sector and had avoided the resort to competition among public and private agencies. On the other hand, the Australian case appeared at the outset to own all the necessary attributes of the market, or quasi-market, type. It had replaced a single public service system with a multi-agency system in which competitors struggled to fashion local business plans which reflected the price government paid for successful outcomes for job seekers. And in the Netherlands case the long history of corporatist institution building I expected to have led to a powerful imperative towards networking. This I drew from the extensive literature on Dutch consensualism and from the official justifications for the inclusion of private recruitment companies in the public employment services system (Lijphart, 1968; Visser & Hemerijck, 1997).

Each of these expectations proved open to challenge once the general model of governance was viewed as a practical achievement at the ground level. And among a number of important surprises was the fact that a new hybrid strategy emerged as heir to the traditional governance type. This new type was generalised across the four countries: it was a strong form of coherence and certainly more impressive than many of the things which distinguished national systems from one another. Although expressing distinctive, measurable differences in the way agencies organise their power, the corporate and market types actually expressed a single dimension composed of a powerful hybrid set of commitments. Termed 'corporate-market governance', this hybrid emerged from the study as the new form of organisation now replacing traditional commitments to bureaucratic treatment and legal-rational authority. It shows the more general enterprising dynamic to be *both* a broad normative structure and a practical, robust strategy. Target-setting and central control cohabit with price-sensitivity and competition. Flexibility is conditioned by a strong commitment to specific performance obligations, and various forms of discretion and risk-taking are found to work within, not against, the state's power to compel certain common outcomes, including cultural ones.

Note

1 A term used in organisational economics to describe those who distort programs for their own economic advantage.

CHAPTER 2

Governance in Fours

To notice that an enterprising spirit has taken hold of the official imagination in many advanced systems is not to say that each acts upon this imperative by following precisely the same path. Changes in institutional structures are necessarily filtered by local lessons of the past. If institutions 'gain intelligence from cumulative experience' they also shed commitments by a similar process. So different, discrete systems often avoid arbitrary fixes and dead-end adjustments by engaging 'networks of imitation' (March & Olsen, 1989, pp. 54–5). Countries with broadly similar institutions facing similar pressures make choices from within a defined range (OECD, 1995; 1992). And as Cameron (1992, p. 167) points out, such 'organisation is not merely a technical arrangement of work, authority, resources and relationships. Alternative ways of organising an institution represent choices among competing values.'

In seeking to understand how a general cultural shift in favour of enterprising the state establishes itself in a defined value-set and strategy for reforming Welfare-to-Work programs, I develop two themes. The first argues that important aspects of the older bureaucratic order are now in terminal decline among officials, contractors and managers. The procedural type, with its roots deep in the classical bureaucratic tradition no longer appears to have the commitment of politicians, consultants and executive managers. I discuss the extent to which this erosion of confidence in the procedural, bureaucratic tradition has penetrated the workings of actual state institutions in these four countries. The second theme suggests the emergence of a more variegated, even hybridised role for these same institutions, which is represented in three different strategies of governance. These are defined as the practical methods for ranking priorities, setting service delivery norms and co-ordinating action among agencies. They take the broad ambitions of the enterprising spirit and turn it into real techniques and reform methods. Corporate governance, market governance and network governance are identified in the research and practice literature as the currently popular organisational models for ordering and directing public commitments. I describe the extent of their internal coherence and the strength of their purchase on the actual practices and work orientations of local agents of the state.

I begin by exploring the normative, or ideal-type, foundations of these four governance strategies. My purpose is not to canvass the intellectual histories of these organisational positions, for that would require a book in its own right. Instead, I seek to distil the common reference points, rules, super rules, tactics and norms of three different conceptions of public governance, in order to show how their ambitions impact upon the practical organisation of public services, officialdom and the world of contractors, vendors and consultants. I use the central notion of governance type or model as a way to ask after the forms of social organisation and the degree of coherence underpinning the reforms of these states. In other words these four governance strategies are but ideal-types drawn from the work of protagonists, consultants, commentators and managers. First then how might they suggest distinctive visions of a post-bureaucratic order (Barzeley, 1992)?

As Chapter 1 suggests, a common self-enterprising dynamic establishes the broad intent or meta-narrative of a new governance movement in many OECD countries. This common cause involves a new commitment to output measurement, to performance improvement and to a greater focus on the client's contribution to success. But it is clear that this spirit may manifest itself in a number of possible institutional ensembles. Each system changes its governance structures by filtering the lessons of the past through newly dominant ideals of enterprise, entrepreneurship and institutional reinvention. In the process, choices emerge and a different cast of players influences how such questions are decided.

The research strategy seeks to ground these normative decisions and strategies in a study of pragmatic new forms of state organisation. Consequently, the book's empirical focus is directed at those public agencies, bureaucracies, contractors, firms and non-profit agencies which seek to participate in the work of the state. More precisely, do different forms of restructure create new relationships at the front line, and do they have common properties? The public officials and contractors who deliver these welfare-state programs are central players in a new game of flexible, intensive and selective service delivery.

My central hypothesis is that if the new governance reform rhetoric is to result in actual regimes of power and choice then this should be evident at the front line, otherwise restructures might be seen as simply part of an older, prosaic game of budget cuts and bureaucrat-politician manoeuvres. Exploring the four strategy types as complex organisational ensembles raises questions about the extent to which the normative or symbolic enterprise of consultants and senior policy makers actually results in the emergence of new systems.

The book shows that the four ideal type regimes have different claims in the four countries. The procedural type is shown to be in rapid decline everywhere, but not to the same degree. Evidence from the front line shows that a limited repertoire of governance alternatives has emerged in practice. These presently involve attempts to mix or blend certain core elements of quite different organisational types. 'Corporate governance' shows the world of bureaucratic rules and entitlements the legal-rational world to be amended rather than replaced, by forms of organisation which rely upon targets, quotas and fixed throughput objectives. A second 'market' type involves an attempt to combine aspects of public service with quasi-market instruments, with competition for resources and the use of prices to govern the work of agencies or contractors. The third is a form of network governance involving a limited but interesting form of resource sharing across organisational borders. It defines a service in which co-operation with private organisations is stronger than competition, flexible work practices and discretionary behaviour flourish, and the time commitments of officials are spread across a wider matrix of possible engagements.

The Four Types: Procedural, Managerial, Market and Network

A review of recent public sector reform movements in the OECD describes four ideal-type realisations of public institutions and the place of bureaucracy in the overall system of state-society relations (Kooiman, 1993; Kettl, 1997). The first three frameworks correspond broadly to contemporary phases in the development of public bureaucracy from its postwar past to its current period of transformation between 1980 and the late 1990s. These three are termed the procedural, corporate and the most recent form, market governance. Each has different legislative enactments of public service regulations, different expectations about the roles of public managers, together with alternative strategies for resource allocation, organisational dependency and interdependency, and accountability.

The literature also identifies a fourth framework – 'network governance'. While some indications exist to suggest that the network type is beginning to enter the minds of reformers, the other three types have thus far dominated the thinking of those framing legislation and fashioning new organisational designs. Networking enters the debate as a

Table 2.1   Four governance types

	Source of rationality	Form of control	Primary virtue	Service delivery focus
Procedural governance	Law	Rules	Reliability	Universal Treatments
Corporate governance	Management	Plans	Goal-driven	Targets
Market governance	Competition	Contracts	Cost-driven	Prices
Network governance	Relationships	Co-production	Flexibility	Brokerage

synonym for multi-agency co-ordination, reciprocation, lateral communication and discretionary bargaining by local actors. But is it only a gesture towards a future organisational form? The study draws on detailed empirical research to estimate its impact. First I identify the core properties of this framework and outline the study's methods.

Each of these governance ideals can be described as having a recognisable organisational character. Table 2.1 summarises, for each, its form of rationality, form of control, primary virtue, and the nature of its service delivery focus. The source of rationality is the administrative logic through which each governance type defines its core means for organising itself and its own characteristic definition of value. Secondly each type has a characteristic method of control and co-ordination, a standard requirement in all forms of organisation and one that always points to a characteristic modus operandi.

The third dimension is the primary virtue each type has in the minds of its proponents, including policy makers. For present purposes I take such virtues at face value and use them to explain the attraction of a particular approach to organisation to partisans, and to give insight into larger social questions such as the role played by equity and economic performance (Connor, 1992). Whether such claims actually materialise as practical accomplishments must be left to the evaluators to decide. For now it is enough to know how its proponents imagine a system's appeal. The fourth element concerns how reformers define the typical method for delivery of an actual program through supervision, planning and disciplinary intervention.

The Procedural Type

Procedural bureaucracy can be defined as a typical resort to any recognised system of universal rules and ranks. It is widely accepted that the first forms of modern public administration were modelled on military and church lines (Beer, 1970; Bendix, 1968, p. 208), the twin attractions being a unified chain of command populated by a specialised layering of expert, subordinate ranks.

In the US, for example, following the Civil War, the modern administrative system experienced a revolution when military principles of organisation travelled into the civil bureaucracy (Stone & Stone, 1975). The *Pendleton Act* of 1883 expressed the core elements of this system: a central agency established a standardised system of public employment, impartial hiring based on merit, and a near universal classification system for government jobs. This 'procedural governance' aimed to separate policy and administration, as in Woodrow Wilson's (1887) hopeful insistence that 'administrative questions are not political questions'. In Britain and its Westminster dependencies these same sentiments had already emerged most forcefully in the Northcote-Trevelyan inquiry of 1853. And the 'Rhenish' systems had the Weberian model to thank for a carefully articulated set of technical grades and distinctions (Peters, 1993).

In these new administrations, public servants were considered to be employees of a special kind. They were either Crown servants or, in the republican vocabulary, held an equivalently high status which specified their particular vocation as employees of the public interest. This reserved status was widely recognised in law in these countries and was sanctioned by a regulatory system which required public servants to give fair and judicious treatment to the public.

Within the procedural governance type co-ordination is achieved by a system of rules and statutes, public servants' professional training and their specific experience with each local system of protocols and accepted practices. Strong managerial authority prevails, but the system allows senior staff to 'stand behind' the regular work, and to concentrate their attention on appeals and difficult cases (Beer, 1970).

Being rule-bound, such public organisations require layers of checking and auditing, so as to reduce the likelihood of large errors, including those engendered by patronage. Even given relatively low levels of technological development, these systems are relatively inexpensive, frequently delivering standard services to millions of citizens at minimal per-unit cost.

However, by the end of the 1970s reformers had found many of these organisational arrangements to be inadequate in serving a more dynamic public sector environment. New circumstances demanded faster changes in programs and greater sensitivity on the part of officials in their action on cases. The dense layers of protocol and standard procedure buttressed by a career structure were a shield against external pressures and some internal pressures from above. For example Roger Douglas (1993, p. 220), the former New Zealand Finance Minister, described his agenda of quantum leaps as one requiring active support from bureaucrats. Not surprisingly, Douglas favoured replacing people who would not 'adapt to the new environment', a feat only achievable if the procedural system were first opened up to direct political management.

The Corporate Type

Proponents of corporate governance imagined this to be a planned synthesis of government objectives and the modern resource allocation methods of large firms. They viewed planning instruments as a source of political management through which the executive branch and its appointed senior officials could more actively direct resources towards groups and outcomes determined by government policy (Halligan & Power, 1992). The first experiments with this framework were in the 1950s and early 1960s in the US where Robert MacNamara and the RAND Corporation attempted to develop comprehensive program budgeting. In Britain the first gestures were found in the Fulton Report (1968), which argued for 'accountable management', driven by a system of defined sub-units with their own objectives and performance criteria, and linked to central strategic planning (Garrett, 1980; Zifcak, 1994).

A second, more comprehensive wave of corporate bureaucratic reforms began with President Carter's *Civil Service Reform Act* of 1978 which strengthened the role of managers and was accompanied by efforts to improve budget planning through Management by Objectives (MBO) and Zero Base Budgeting (ZBB). This same trio of interests (management improvement, goal-oriented planning and budget reform) is found in the other systems which moved toward the corporate bureaucratic ideal in the 1970s and 1980s. These include the Thatcher Government's Financial Management Initiative (FMI), its Financial Management Unit (FMU) and management information systems (MINIS) initiated in the mid-1980s; the Australian Labor Government's Financial Management Improvement Program (FMIP), program budgeting, and corporate planning initiatives of 1984–86; and New Zealand's *State Owned Enterprises Act* of 1986 and *State Sector Act* of 1988. Similar motives appear in the reform of the Netherlands' bureaucracy in the 1980s, including budget cuts, the use of performance incentives and the decoupling of ministerial bureaucracies from service delivery organisations.

Corporate governance emerged from this period as an attempt to subordinate the whole of public administration to the specific strategic and policy targets of a greatly empowered executive arm. The definition and clarification of goals and 'missions' became the unifying principle or rationality, replacing law and statute as the decision-making base of the public organisation. The key to this process was the enhanced role of management that was extracted from the routinised bureaucratic hierarchy and given its own autonomy and identity (Considine & Painter, 1997).

Not surprisingly, the corporate model also had its limitations. In Australia, for example, three years after the introduction of FMIP, every surveyed department had a plan, a mission statement and formal planning procedures in place, but most did not have an operational link between decision making, resource allocation and these formal planning processes (Considine, 1990; Zifcak, 1994, p. 106). In Britain the planners also fell foul of the complexity of bureaucratic systems. Planning processes often failed to take account of the rapid shifts in priorities which individual ministers wished to make. Nor was it always politically prudent to publish targets or evaluations of their achievement. Even small deviations from ambitious targets led organisations and ministers into political controversy (Pollitt, 1990).

A more sophisticated round of reforms which proposed the advantages of a stronger management system, but with fewer planning costs, took root in the Gore Report's (1993) 'reinvention laboratories', and the Thatcher and Major Governments' Next Steps program (Efficiency Unit, 1988, pp. 15–16). These initiatives released middle managers from many of the restraints imposed by tight program controls and standardised performance measures. There emerged instead a new climate of negotiation among central agencies and delivery agencies, but still within a system of public ownership and direct control. At the edge of the corporate type, and at the point of its near exhaustion in some early adopting countries, there also emerged a loose 'entrepreneurial' model which sought to combine the strengthening of management power with the use of certain, limited forms of competitive resource allocation. Osborne and Gaebler (1992, p. 309) saw 'market-oriented government' as such a case. More symbolic than strategic, they saw it as both establishing a stronger use of management prerogative and as gesturing towards an alternative world of private incentives, prices and contract-based decisions.

The Market Type

Market governance is the most radical ideal of public organisation yet implemented. As a theory of public organisation it seems to contradict standard texts on the nature of hierarchical governance by substituting private ownership, competition and market incentives for some of the traditional notions of regulation by statute and reward through the career service. It also mobilises the politician's political interest in using public resources to create privatised benefits for contractors (Becker & Mackelprang, 1990). Sometimes called 'entrepreneurial governance' and 'contractualism', the market type structures the internal elements of the public organisation and its environment through actual or quasi-markets, and real or hypothetical tests of consumer demand and variable pricing (Boston et al., 1996; Osborne & Gaebler, 1992).

Market governance strategies emerged in these systems when political élites opted to substitute competition for planning and contracts for formal hierarchies. This involved not only competition between bureaucracies, but also the adoption of market-style incentives and mechanisms inside public organisations. The theoretical foundations of this regime were built from the discipline of organisational economics (Barney & Ouchi, 1986; Niskanen, 1979). In the Australian and New Zealand cases, the emergence of market governance has taken the form of a rapid increase in the use of contracting in and between bureaucracies, together with the introduction of a variety of quasi-markets for such things as health, welfare and educational services. In the latter case an intermediate layer of contractors acted as a 'purchaser' of services from designated providers and did so according to judgements influenced by price (Alford & Considine, 1994).

Competition is seen as saving government decision makers some of the costs of rational-choice by allowing the market to determine the means to a defined end. Existing contractors are held to represent the feasible range of available strategies, combining considerations of both cost and quality. This reduces the decision makers' task to that of selecting public and private contractors. Typically the quasi-market approach to governance divides bureaucracy into a strategic core of senior managers responsible for policy and shielded from competition, and a series of separate operational units run as quasi-businesses (OECD, 1995). The latter develop their own business plans, devise quotes and decide work practices according to the real or potential threat they face from other contractors. This provides senior management with a means of restructuring their organisations without the costs of detailed negotiation and without previous forms of industrial dispute.

However, the declining use of internal rules and the increase in entrepreneurial behaviour by bureaucrats generates scope for increased distortion and goal displacement (Lane, 1991; Fox, 1974). It also raises the prospect of the corruption of central policy goals by contractors seeking to maximise short-term profits and other immediate material payoffs. This value system may also encourage officials to consider subsequent job prospects with outside contractors, while involved in regulating their behaviours. Weaker levels of public accountability also characterise this framework. Services put out to tender become subject to claims of commercial confidentiality which act as a restriction on the public's right to know how public funds are being dispersed (Craig, 1996).

The Network Type

An emerging idealisation of public organisation emanates from the image of network governance in recent accounts of interest group behaviour (Rhodes & Marsh, 1995; Streeck & Schmitter, 1995), in treatments of the impact of new technology upon the labour market (Castells, 1996; Amin, 1994), and in empirical descriptions of emergent structures in policy fields such as AIDS, pollution control and city management (Golembiewski & Gabris, 1995). Williamson's (1975; 1979) seminal work on relational contracting also gives credence to this notion that organisations might do best by entering longer-term relationships with those upon whom they are dependent for the supply of valued services, and suggests that more competitive allocations could undermine trust and long-term investment.

At the level of public administration, O'Toole (1997, p. 45) rightly points out that confusion still remains in the literature on networks, but interestingly he sees a positive future for this emerging framework, advising that 'practitioners need to begin to incorporate the network concept into their administrative efforts'.

Network governance has two distinct intellectual histories. One is provided by the policy studies literature where observers show that effective policy making, including implementation, is increasingly shaped by the nature of collaboration between officials and certain organised interests (Sabatier & Jenkins-Smith, 1993; Rhodes, 1990). The risks of capture by interest groups remains significant according to this view, and not all citizens find themselves included as part of a well articulated network. In this school the network ideal is part of a larger tradition of relationship building and privileged access to government by firms, unions and professional monopolies. And while interest mediation may offer governments opportunities to achieve valued political stability, observers caution against the tendency for such arrangements to create forms of exclusion and inefficient allocation of resources.

However, a second tradition emerges from the organisational studies literature and from contemporary political economy where forms of flexible specialisation are found to depend upon various non-hierarchical systems of control and exchange (Sabel, 1994, p. 103). In this sense the network is built around programs rather than interests, and upon co-production as much as overt political exchange. These networks imply a deeper and more stable organisational field than is evident in simple interest group accommodations and captures. Joint investment, shared research, common development ventures and flexible methods for linking financiers, regulators and a host of public and private service providers is promised by those advocating the 'social capital' road to reform (Putnam, 1993; Rhodes, 1998; Streeck, 1992).

While the market form of organisation was thought by its proponents to excel at certain types of cost containment, and is a favoured means for terminating old programs, it is less certain that it is able to build new systems of quality service delivery or to create effective institutional linkages within policy sectors. Network governance advocates using terms like 'strategic partnership' and 'joined-up governance' have thus begun to suggest that market governance may not be all that effective in mobilising commitment, sharing information, investing in new technologies, creating common service standards, or in focusing attention upon the real needs of suppliers and clients. Furthermore, it is suggested, markets may undervalue the rights of individual clients whenever the cost of difficult clients is higher than the benefit to be gained from 'creaming' off the better-priced customers (Le Grand & Bartlett, 1993; Allen, 1992).

Network governance attempts to avoid this potentially predatory environment and proposes interdependence as a binding characteristic. Powell (1991, p. 268) frames this distinction as a question: 'When the items exchanged between buyers and sellers possess qualities that are not easily measured, and the relations are so long-term and recurrent that it is difficult to speak of the parties as separate entities, can we still regard this as a market exchange?'

In place of a standard product, organisations that are enrolled in service networks are pressed to fashion sets of variable services that are mixed and deployed according to the particular characteristics of their customers, including perhaps their capacity to pay. Increasingly, the service system may also be defined by a culture of tastes and life-styles, rather than a regime of standardised needs or wants. In place of previous attention to notions of transaction efficiency, cost reduction and planning, this emergent framework concentrates its attention upon the repeated processes through which elaborate services are coproduced. This involves detailing the organisational processes through which services are 'tailored' to individual or small batch clients and costs are shared across an inter-organisational web of public and private agencies.

This new attention to 'process analysis' (Oakland, 1989) claims that the older definitions of public service as a form of industrial production tended to obscure the links between issues of supply, investment, distribution and consumption. The production metaphor cuts the public organisation off, conceptually and practically, from its field of operations. As Barzeley (1992, p. 123) argues, many services are actually produced, delivered, and consumed in the same process, often with customers participating as producers. Consequently new techniques such as case management in health and welfare have sought to apply a network logic to the process for assembling complex services.

In this governance system the network 'agents' are the local officials who take direct responsibility for establishing effective links between suppliers, producers and customers. They are thought to move up and down the hierarchy and freely between divisions and organisations. They also traverse the information systems of suppliers and distributors. This generates, at least in theory, a much more flexible hierarchy that develops certain matrix qualities. In other words, local 'process owners' have authority over supplier-customer chains, and act to eliminate regulatory friction and maximise the changes of a 'first-time fix' for complex problems.

Of course it is one thing to imagine a world of trusting, flexible agents acting as the client's 'relationship manager' or 'consultant', it is another to devise a complex web of public and private organisations capable and willing to use such methods efficiently. As suggested earlier the network type is the most hypothetical of the four strategies and devising a research method to describe and estimate its significance is no small feat. In undertaking this the book identifies two aspects of networking. The first concerns new levels of flexibility, case management and discretion inside the organisations under discussion. The second concerns the forms of interaction and relationships between officials in different agencies. The first seems to be a condition for the second but a complete account of the way the two interact has yet to be developed. Nevertheless, the study's empirical results are very promising.

Research Design

To investigate the extent to which these governance models actually explain the ordinary work of local officials in these different systems is a complex undertaking. While interviews with senior managers help define the nature of relationships between bureaucrats and politicians, these actors have good reasons to exaggerate the success of strategies they have designed. They are often also quite remote from the actual deployment of the techniques they have mandated and those who report to them might also have reasons to give biased feedback in official reports and reviews.

In seeking to understand the revolution in both the normative and empirical practices of public organisations within these four systems the study therefore used three strategies. First, there were interviews with senior governmental policy makers responsible for these services and reviews of the various documents and histories of these programs. These sources provide the bases for the country chapters dealing with the institutional dynamics of each country's Welfare-to-Work system.

After interviewing senior actors in central agencies and the head offices of the employment services, I then focused upon programs, codes, rules and other day-to-day practices at the service delivery end of these systems. The motive here was to look closely at the way forms of public service were actually constructed and connected to their intended recipients, to staff at the front line and to other interests and organisations clustered around each particular institution.

We visited several offices in each country. In each case[1] we interviewed local managers and a selection of front-line staff using a standard schedule of questions about the work process, policies and methods for dealing with problems. The interviews were tape recorded and a number transcribed. The names of respondents have been deleted to protect their anonymity, but all the other details reported below are factual. These interviews were conducted between 1996 and 1998.

In Australia and the Netherlands these visits were also spread between government offices and those of the private firms contracted to provide job seekers with services on the government's behalf. Observation visits also provided an invaluable means of experiencing the atmosphere of the workplace and of observing interactions between different staff groups, managers and job seekers. Although no job seekers were interviewed during the many hours spent in local offices there were many opportunities to observe them being interviewed by staff, discussing their experiences with one another and occasionally making use of information and training resources provided for them on site.

Following the interview stage, a questionnaire was developed to elicit a wider range of views on front-line work in these institutions and to map the impact of the changes observed in the selected sites. In each country this was distributed to a representative sample of front-line staff. In each country a slightly different method was used to locate and invite the participation of respondents, according to differences in the structure of the service in each case. The response rate for the survey as a whole was 56 per cent. No differences were observed between respondents and non-respondents based on type of organisation, sex, seniority or region.

The study's original plan was to complete matched studies in each country, beginning with the Australian case. A large survey of public, non-profit and for-profit employment agencies was conducted in Aus-

Table 2.2 Survey details

	Year	Number	Sampling method
Australia	1996, 1997, 1999	585	Individuals sampled from national list of contracted agencies
Netherlands	1998–9	274	Individuals randomly sampled from list of two large regions
New Zealand	1997	134	Individuals randomly sampled from NZES employee list
United Kingdom	1997	155	Individuals sampled as groups from offices in six regions

tralia in June 1996 (n=365). While work was under way on the interview stage of the UK study, the newly elected Howard Government in Australia undertook further radical reforms. These occasioned two further surveys in Australia, one of public service officials in July 1997 (n=70) and one a repeat sample of the whole competitive sector (public, non-profit and for-profit) undertaken in December 1998 and January 1999 (n=150). The complexity of the Australian part of the study was due to that country's experiment with using private firms, arranged in a competitive market, to deliver the main forms of job search assistance for disadvantaged people. With some three hundred organisations suddenly contracted to provide public services this case seemed to justify extra research on the impact of reform.

In each of the other countries there was just one survey. New Zealand uses a single public service organisation to deliver its core service to job seekers and a random sample of employment advisers was completed there in December 1997 (n=134). The United Kingdom is organised in a similar way and this single survey took place at the same time (n=155). The Netherlands has a core public service aided by two private firms (Start and Vedior) and in November 1998 an equal number of public service and private sector officials were surveyed using a version of the questionnaire which had been translated into Dutch (n=274). Small changes to the questionnaire were made to accommodate differences in terminology and regulatory practices. In both Australia and the Netherlands officials were only surveyed if their work included providing services to public clients of the employment service system.

The staff surveyed in the four countries were all involved in providing direct service to job seekers who were receiving income support from their public welfare system. This service typically involved officials meeting them when they came to inquire about registering for work, to seek information about job vacancies and in order to satisfy social security obligations associated with the 'active search' requirements which

Table 2.3   Statements used to define types of governance

1   Proceduralists were defined as having a strong orientation to rules.
    Statements such as 'I have rules and procedures to guide me in the work I
    do' were used to test commitment to this idea. This scale also contained
    variables testing 'knowledgeable supervision', 'standardised service to
    clients', and low interest in the role of output measurements.
2   Corporate management adherents were defined as less interested in rules
    and more clearly motivated by targets and plans for specified client groups.
    Major interest was seen to reside in the need for officials to service target
    groups who were valued in policy and program plans. Approaches to the use
    of sanctions and special treatments were presumed to follow recognition of
    such priorities.
3   Marketers were defined by items which measured responsiveness to the costs
    and prices for different services and different clients. A high consciousness
    of the need to beat one's competitors was also included. Objectives were
    viewed as less a matter of goals and plans, and more clearly defined by
    'payable outcomes'.
4   Networkers were defined as those who saw their work as based upon the co-
    production of results using brokerage and negotiation. A high value was
    presumed to be placed on trust and maintaining good contacts with clients
    and other service providers, including competitors. Adherents to this
    approach were presumed to be most likely to say 'when you get good results
    with clients it's usually a joint effort by yourself, the training person, the
    employer, etc'.

applied in all four countries. Although each country differs in its methods for serving job seekers, and often in its laws and regulations, the
basic task of the employment service is remarkably consistent. Whether
called 'advisers', 'job coaches', 'case managers', 'mediators' or 'consultants', these officials all have the same primary duty – to prepare people
on social assistance for finding work and to oblige them to undertake
any activity deemed helpful to this end.

The survey respondents in each country were first asked about their
general orientation to their work including attitudes to unemployment,
job satisfaction, the role of the public service and the government's
approach to unemployment. Then, in order to gauge the extent of identification with the four different governance models, the interview
material was used to develop forty 'governance' statements for inclusion
in the surveys. This allowed, for each type, ten statements which
reflected actual and probable sentiments on the role of goals, targets,
supervision, discretion, co-operation inside the workplace, co-operation
outside the workplace, competition, sanctions and technology.

As indicated earlier, the four countries were chosen for their reputations as energetic reformers of their public sectors and in particular of
their employment assistance systems. Of particular importance was the

fact that two countries (Australia and the Netherlands) had experimented with using private firms to provide services directly to welfare clients. While many countries have used private sector suppliers of technology and training, here the core service was being contracted or part-contracted.

The fact that the other two countries (New Zealand and the United Kingdom) had developed an energetic reform agenda which was based squarely on the dominant role of the public service offered a means of comparing the effect of this fundamental public/private or state/market difference. The role of the not-for-profit sector in the Australian case also allows us to consider how alternative forms of privatisation stimulate different governance strategies among officials and agency types.

The Analysis

In order to show how reform shapes these governance strategies and how these in turn influence the conduct of the four Welfare-to-Work systems, the book proceeds as follows. Each country is profiled and compared using interviews, information about institutions and published material concerning the reforms enacted. Then, using the survey data, I identify the key differences between each country and between the government, for-profit and non-profit services. All tables used in the text which follows (and all percentages and proportions) meet the minimum requirement of statistically significant differences at the .05 level.

Descriptive discriminant analysis was used to determine the issues and characteristics that best explain the separateness or distinctiveness of the four countries and three ownership groups. Details are provided in the Statistical Appendix. A core of twenty variables make up the discriminant model. These involve aspects of front-line work such as the amount of time advisers spend on key tasks, their relationships with other service providers, and a number of important background issues such as age, job experience and unionisation.

Following the discussion of the four countries and different ownership groups, I return to the larger issue of the nature of the governance and the value of each model in defining actual work. Factor analysis is employed as a means to test the strength of the four normative structures outlined above. This too is detailed in the Statistical Appendix. The factor analysis leads us to some important changes in the definition of dominant forms of governance in these systems: rather than four, there are only three realised types. We will then examine the practical application of these three to Welfare-to-Work institutions in the four countries to see which sort of agency adopts each strategy, and why.

Of particular importance is the emergence of 'network governance' as a new normative structure in these systems. This approach to governance is composed of three practical strategies – 'basic networking', 'public networking' and 'civic networking'. Each involves officials in developing relations with a different range of groups and agencies.

These results, as the following chapters indicate, confirm the book's central claims regarding the nature of Enterprising States. But there were also surprises, particularly in the way the four countries employed these new strategies. Nor were all of the expected differences between for-profit, non-profit and government agencies realised. Certainly it is clear that many of these organisations have already abandoned the traditional bureaucratic approach and that this is far more than a mere rhetorical accomplishment. Differences between the four countries, including those based on whether they use nongovernment contractors, provide a strong basis for defining the new enterprising state and for showing how its adaptation to local conditions raises major issues – both in theory and practice.

The break-up of the more certain world of bureaucratic entitlement and regulation therefore creates space for a new paradox: governance now seems to involve a more single-minded effort by agencies and officials of all sorts to engineer a particular form of flexibility and discretion. This generates a wider range of possible program interventions and sanctions, but all are directed towards a much more unified ideal of individualisation, which Beck (2000, p. 164) has recently described as 'living your own life in a runaway world'. Seen in this light, the working life of the job adviser actually resembles that of the job seeker, with both being asked to construct and invent their own engagements with the local world of institutions. This is a dramatic change in the way officials are required to organise their work. A greater range of strategies is now possible, while at the same time the objective of the work effort is ever more narrowly scripted. And exactly how these issues are settled and how national traditions filter these general imperatives are questions that can only be answered at the front line.

Note

1 In two cases this work was completed with the help of my research associate Jane Lakey.

CHAPTER 3

The United Kingdom:
Managing by Numbers

The quintessential civil servant has no stronger, simpler identity than the twentieth century English bureaucrat. As Peters (1989, p. 31) notes, Whitehall before Thatcher is the 'non-partisan', 'neutral' type grounded upon one of the oldest forms of organisational orthodoxy. The general élan of Oxbridge leadership at the top, coupled with a dispassionate commitment to inherited protocols at the base, describes the virtuous world of the generalist. Then, in the maelstrom of Thatcherism, these cool commitments rapidly submitted to the heavy blade-strokes of a political regime bent upon remaking the public sphere in a new image.

Yet no single country better demonstrates the paradox of the enterprising dynamic and of 'new governance' in general than the United Kingdom. Here we find one of the most traditional political and bureaucratic systems apparently engaging in the most radical reform program. This provides a paradigm case of the traditional, procedural form of governance seeking ways to reinvent itself. With the arrival of the new Conservative agenda in the early 1980s many of these classical civil service nostrums are challenged by increased policy control at the centre, and new forms of service delivery at the front line of public programs (Hood, 1991; Foster and Plowden, 1996).

Nowhere was this missionary zeal for neo-liberal strategies and market forms of organisation more open and vigorous than in regard to labour market change. With four Employment Acts between 1980 and 1989, and the *Trade Union and Labour Relations (Consolidation) Act* of 1992, the UK sought a new definition of the government role (Peck, 1996, p. 20).

These changes aimed to reduce the role of unions, weaken awards and other wage protections and create greater 'flexibility' in the use of unskilled work.[1] The new model was understood as 'downward pressure on the wages of the less-skilled' and an increase in part-time work and work at non-standard hours (Anderton, 1997, p. 21).[2] To achieve this the government sought to mobilise a variety of public agencies to limit access to the already minimal levels of welfare support, to make public assistance to recipients of benefits more conditional upon non-standard forms of work and training, and to bring the interests of employers to the apex of decision making.

Yet the privatisation agenda and the urge to deploy 'quasi-market' devices in the allocation of public programs proved far more limited than the reform rhetoric implied. Public institutions like social security and the employment assistance system remained in public hands. Indeed, to achieve the new focus upon work flexibility and benefit selectivity the Conservatives strengthened certain forms of central control and regulation. Interventions by the state were both more exacting and more carefully scripted than before. Far from being eclipsed by a new set of private institutions, the regular bureaucracy became more deeply involved in carrying through the reform agenda.

I will argue that the UK's new governance model of the 1990s used clearer separations of policy and service delivery inside the civil service, and more detailed forms of contracting and coordination of training and placement services in order to clear away older commitments to citizen entitlement and welfare benefits. The move to the enterprise model was therefore strongly represented in political efforts to reorganise the various interests involved, and to clear a path for important cultural changes in the way managers, officials and clients interacted. As a result the UK offers a view of a reinvented form of the centralised, rule-driven public sector.

This appeared to put the UK closest of the four cases to the procedural type (see Chapter 2), but with significant concessions to the new corporate strategy. How 'radical' or even 'revolutionary' this amended proceduralism would prove to be, and how significant as a model of new governance, depended first on the degree of 'fit', or accommodation between the government's policy commitments and those of the senior program managers. I will touch upon this realignment in examining the overall dynamics of the new institutional order. How would the new directives and commitments by government impact upon the work of local staff and their clients? Would it simply demonstrate the efficiency of a new path to old desires for effectiveness in delivering programs, or would the service itself look qualitatively different, expressing new ideals of governance?

By the beginning of the 1990s governmental institutions for assisting the unemployed differed from their antecedents in two important ways. First, the public agencies supplying benefits and employment assistance were separated from the regular civil service under the rubric of the

'Next Steps' model of policy direction and service delivery. Second, the training system formerly organised through the 'weak corporatist' structures of the Manpower Services Commission (MSC) were transformed into a network of Training and Enterprise Councils (TECs) managed by local business leaders and funded directly by government. I will focus on the social security and employment assistance changes, since their role in structuring the state's role is larger, but it is worth noting that the TECs closely reflected the UK's experiment with more overt privatisation in this field. Yet they were also rather ineffective in carrying this agenda beyond a commitment to involving business leaders in carving up public assets (King, 1995; Peck, 1996). Even in this obvious example of a shift towards forms of market governance, private endeavours and priorities were in fact secondary to the imperatives of an enhanced bureaucratic system.

The new forms of benefit delivery and job search assistance, on the other hand, were profoundly different from their antecedents, and they succeeded in implanting themselves as durable forms of reinvention. This was demonstrated by their success in meeting new government expectations and in the popularity they enjoyed among both successive conservative ministers in the Thatcher and Major administrations and those of the new Blair Government elected at the end of the period under study.

These Next Steps arrangements might best be described as a system of separated institutions sharing more detailed responsibilities. The service delivery divisions of the social security and employment ministries were taken out of the core civil service and given an autonomous charter under new legislation. This plainly had considerable potential to create fragmentation. It is therefore the mechanisms which were used to define and regulate these agencies which help explain the new forms of coherence which this governance system soon achieved.

This reinvention involved a complex set of formal contracts, agency agreements, performance targets and uniform, measured treatments: they were used to bind a federation of tightly structured public agencies in order to establish much stronger forms of central, public control. This highly regulated system contrasted sharply with the forms of flexibility, wage reduction and transformation being engineered in the private labour market. Governance at the level of the ordinary citizen in the UK thus reflected both this characteristic interplay of contracts and agreement and also combined new elements of 'self enterprise' which released the state from its previous commitments to universal assistance and entitlement through awards and welfare benefits. Old guarantees were set aside; new demands that citizens search for their own individualised pathways took their place.

For some observers this change was no more than the triumph of 'New Right ideas' flowing freely across the Atlantic (King, 1995, p. 169; Dolowitz, 1997). Yet the 'market-based values' which were said to drive this administrative framework often proved to have less to say about competition and privatisation in the UK case than was evident in other apparently more social democratic systems. This raises important questions about the variable character of the neo-liberal agenda at ground level.

The maintenance of a strong hierarchical employment service held in public hands, and the desire for greater deregulation of the labour market, may actually be more consistent than at first appears. In this case, the governance of unemployment appeared to benefit directly from having the unemployed create downward pressures on wages and conditions in the open workforce in the period after 1986. To help achieve this the UK Employment Service intervened using extensive, repeated interviews and other new programs to 'activate' the low-skilled unemployed.

Employment Conditions

Throughout the 1980s and 1990s the UK experienced significant rises in unemployment, reaching double figures and creating a rise in levels of long-term unemployment. In 1988 UK unemployment was 8.7 per cent. By 1992 this had jumped to 10.1 per cent. Both were in marked contrast to the 1970s when unemployment averaged 4.3 per cent (OECD, 1999, p. 17). The recognition that the UK had passed from being a system of strong employment participation to one marked by high structural unemployment probably came in the mid-1980s when the official rate of unemployment doubled and public concern, even among conservatives, intensified (Dolowitz, 1997, p. 25).

At first government policy was concerned with the liberalising of employment objectives and with fiscal objectives. The first Thatcher Government abolished earnings related unemployment benefit (the insurance based program) in 1980 and the Rayner efficiency scrutiny reviews also initiated cuts in the staff and budgets of the employment service. But in 1986 the first regime of regular interviews – known as the Restart Interviews – were introduced as a means for creating a more active program for job seekers. This signalled a break from the period of cuts and service reductions. Yet even then these were comparatively modest assaults upon the established rights and roles of welfare recipients; it would take a further six years of piecemeal experimentation and stop–start reform before a complete transformation of the governance system affecting unemployed people was completed. These were not changes directed at cutting the level of benefits, since they had always been low in the UK even before the Conservatives began trimming and reducing. Instead, the reform agenda was directed at the overall management of entry and exit from the benefit rolls. This 'tighter benefits regime' began in 1992 and was brought to fruition with the creation of the Job Seeker's Allowance (JSA).

In July 1995 a new Job Seeker's Allowance (JSA) replaced a dual insurance and tax-funded system and Britain became the only European system without an unemployment benefit linked directly to previous earnings. Because this occurred at a time of related labour market policies such as privatisation and de-industrialisation, British employees also suffered higher than average vulnerability to poverty expressed as 'catastrophic loss of income' – when unemployment occurred.[3]

This chapter examines the main institutional changes underpinning the new governmental strategy. These may be summarised as follows. During the 1980s and early 1990s the UK simultaneously embraced deregulation of the labour market, the creation of a new benefit system based on fixed payments and new, more stringent tests of eligibility. These were implemented through major reforms to the governance system used to deliver both benefits and employment assistance programs to the unemployed. These reforms lowered wage protection, reduced wage increases for low skilled jobs, facilitated easier retrenchment of workers, and increased fiscal stress within social assistance programs.

To deal with these pressures the Conservatives enacted a series of welfare reforms aimed at encouraging exits from the benefit rolls. These changes were aimed both at social security entitlement and at the administrative treatments used to manage the unemployed. While making the relevant government organisations more independent of direct ministerial control and more focused upon a system of targets and other performance measures, the new policies also aimed to replicate a number of US strategies for shifting resources from income support towards improved job search and greater compliance with more demanding administrative requirements.

Typical of the strategy was the last Conservative budget in May 1997. This emphasised the Government's continued interest in measures to 'ensure that benefits are paid only to those who are entitled to them'. The new 'spend to save' package included new efforts to reduce social security fraud (£800 million to be spent to recoup an expected £16.7 billion). Waiting times for receipt of JSA were lengthened from three to seven days, leaving more people to rely upon their 'week in hand' payment from former employers. The Government also announced a pilot scheme called 'Contract for Work' which involved private contractors paid to assist the unemployed find work. This was partly inspired by interest among Tory ministers in US initiatives by private companies such as America Works which involved clients from the public welfare roll being managed by private recruitment agencies. Importantly, these small but significant experiments indicated important differences between Conservative politicians and senior bureaucrats who had so far resisted privatisation within the core services for the unemployed.[4]

Next Steps and the Employment Service

Since 1988 government policy and administration in the employment field had been implemented via four civil service institutions. The two ministries responsible for assisting the unemployed were the Department for Education and Employment (DfEE) and the Department of Social Security (DSS). Each reported through its own cabinet minister. Following the Thatcher Government's introduction in 1988 of the Next Steps reforms, service delivery divisions within these ministries were devolved and established as Executive Agencies with their own Chief Executive Officers (CEOs) and their own staff. The Employment Service (ES) was established as an executive agency in April 1990 and the Benefits Agency (BA) in April 1991 as a central part of the first wave of such changes. Senior officials in the ES reported in interview that they now had more control than when they were a division of the employment ministry. As particular evidence of this, they cited the new authority they exercised over the pay and recruitment functions.[5]

While these de-coupled agency officials remained civil servants and Crown employees, changes to the definition of their duties made it easier for them to adopt their own specific employment policies. This included, for example, the implementation of performance pay for agency CEOs and for agency staff. These payment systems were linked directly to the achievement of stipulated performance targets.[6] According to the Government, the main virtue of the Agency arrangement was 'the principle of devolution to decision-takers nearest the action', and thus 'better service for people who rely on their services and better value for money for the taxpayer'.[7]

A series of mandated contracts regulated the relationship between the Minister, senior bureaucrats in the DfEE and the operational staff of the ES. A Framework Document set out the terms of the relationship, including the duties of Agency CEOs; an Annual Performance Agreement (APA) established the numbers of services to be delivered, the major programs to be conducted, the classifications of clients to receive programs, and the outcomes or targets for each year. Finally an Agency Annual Report included actual performance measures for each stipulated category of work undertaken by the ES. As a gesture to 'contestability' a Prior Options Review was also mandated for each three-year period to see if any public services could be better delivered by other, private means.[8]

In interview, senior officials from the ES said that they enjoyed greater influence under the new agency arrangements than under their previous status as a division of the department. They believed they had greater authority to control programs, free of direct intervention by departmental executives. On the other hand, Ministry officials agreed that they could no longer assert direct control over program decisions, including staffing, but pointed out that they had soon developed various indirect devices for setting precise requirements which forced the agency to follow central guidelines (Considine, 2000).

As part of the implementation of the new Job Seeker's Allowance (JSA) the Major Government had combined two previously separate departments to form the Department for Education and Employment under the leadership of a new Secretary of State.[9] Until then the UK system had two different forms of assistance for the unemployed: an insurance component which was funded by workers' own contributions which was not means tested, and an unemployment benefit paid by Social Security for those who had no insurance, or insufficient insurance to live on.[10] The rules for receipt of the new JSA established a stricter requirement concerning the claimant's availability for work. For example claimants had to show that they were now available for the full working week. They could not stipulate days or hours of the day when they would not work because of home duties or their spouse's commitments. Clients were also under far greater pressure to substantiate their status as job seekers 'actively seeking work'. This required employment advisers to use their own knowledge of the local labour market to assess whether job seekers were searching hard enough, since search activity had now to be linked to known patterns in vacancies.[11]

The new JSA rules also allowed the ES to pilot test variations in benefits and obligations, but importantly the legislation still privileged the public agency as the only means through which services could be provided.[12] The JSA also imposed a new level of regulation over the work of both the Employment Service and Benefits Agency. Many of their core programs had been standardised by the new legislation, limiting the discretion of ES staff to shape services to suit local and individual needs. For central ministry and political advisers, on the other hand, this was essential to their management of purchasing relations with the ES and the Benefits Agency. In other words, the separated authority imposed by the Next Steps formula reduced ES discretion over client programs.

The JSA changed the relationship between the ES and the payment of benefits. The Benefits Agency paid the JSA to claimants but had its own performance contract and was run by a separate organisation. To encourage co-ordinated effort, the local BA officers were usually located in the ES Job Centres. Senior officials at the ES indicated that this caused problems. The arrangements had evolved as a political compromise enforced by Prime Minister John Major after both ministers of state had insisted upon a more hierarchical mandate in which their own agency took control. Both agencies typically described the arrangement as 'too costly and too messy'. Both preferred a clear line of authority giving their own department in Whitehall control. Despite formal independence, the Department of Social Security was ceded greater influence in the implementation and ongoing monitoring of the JSA than was the Department for Education and Employment. This reflected the Government's priority in lowering the rising cost of benefit payments. Cabinet evidently believed that the ES was too ready to take the client's side.[13]

However the ES continued to have its 'finger on the benefit button' because any failure by the client to complete a fortnightly signing or other requirements required ES staff to make the all-important decision to stop benefits. So while the new system clearly signalled a priority for the goals of the social security system, this could not be pursued without the willing help of a formally autonomous Employment Service. This increased pressure to bind the ES through contractual obligations negotiated at ministerial level. As a result the Annual Performance Agreement dominated the relationship between the central bureaucrats, their ministers and the two agencies. In particular the 'annual process of target setting and agreeing business plans . . . (became) the main focus of the relationship'.[14]

Targets were set for all major functions within the ES. For example, there were targets for the numbers of clients to be placed into work, for the percentage of these who had to be long-term claimants, for the numbers to receive the 24-month interview, and for the numbers to be referred for the search training instrument, such as the Training for Work program. Targets also included requirements that the ES turn away a percentage of inquiries as inappropriate, submit a fixed number to adjudication, and meet specified targets for completion of successful applications. Not all targets were numerical. For example the 1996–97 agreement included the requirement that the ES offer all claimants 'a Job Seeker's Agreement at the first available opportunity'.[15] A footnote to the agreement specified fixed times for signing agreements with new claimants at the point of registration and for existing clients at the 13-week stage. Targets were also provided for annual 'efficiency' savings that were to be achieved within the total budget 'assuming there are no changes to workloads' caused by government policy change.

The target system was therefore mandated both through the annual agreement and through a variety of information gathering provisions. In essence, the department was able to demand regular operational reports from the ES in order to monitor its path towards annual performance targets. This also drew a much closer operational link between the two organisations than might be understood from the de-coupling objectives of the Next Steps formula. For instance, the 1997 agreement required the ES to provide thirty-four separate types of report on its own activities. These ranged from details of unit costs for each program, flows of various types of client through programs, speed of despatch of new JSA claims, and progress in achieving efficiency savings.

Specific work targets for local Job Centres were also included in the agreement in the form of stipulations for the minimum time to be spent with clients, including such things as answering client telephone calls within thirty seconds and answering letters within five days. These targets were also included in the Job Seeker's Charter. Local Job Centres were also required to display their own performance data, together with that of neighbouring centres. The ES facilitated the achievement of targets by appointing a 'tracking officer' in most local Job Centres.[16]

The ES soon felt the tight grip of the targets regime. Senior officials argued that the over-reliance on targets meant that Job Centre staff ignored any issue which was not currently being counted. They described the ES as a 'remarkably consistent machine', but pointed out that it was not necessarily desirable to have every program run in the same way in every office, a fact made necessary by targeting. One regional manager reported that he knew what every Job Club would be doing with its clients every Monday morning because this was the level of standardisation brought about by the 'target mentality'.[17] There were also inevitable conflicts between numerical output targets and those that required quality throughputs. For example, there were measures that enforced very high speed in the processing of claims at the local level, and others which required low error rates for the completion of those same files.

ES staff, including senior staff, pointed out in interview that this target regime soon became very restrictive. It was now more difficult to fashion individual programs for each client, or for groups of clients. Instead the ES quickly learned to organise its entire effort around meeting the quantitative targets set for it. And success became defined not just as meeting targets but as exceeding them whenever possible. For instance, the efficiency savings set for 1994–95 were £25.1 million. The ES actually delivered £29.1 million.[18] Evidently the reform logic, established by both political and bureaucratic leaders, was to meet any new challenges with revised strategies to strengthen central control and standardisation at the expense of local discretion, at least when that discretion might involve a relaxation of mandated activities such as interviews and referrals to standard programs. The whip hand in this process was that of the ministry and not the ES leadership.

In addition to using the Annual Agreement, the DfEE also achieved its own implementation agenda by 'inviting' the ES to participate in pilot programs which it funded and which helped shape new government priorities. These were jointly managed and gave the department the chance to plan the procedures and resource commitments that might later be needed for full implementation. ES managers sometimes resented the degree of direct surveillance that these pilots permitted, but acknowledged that access to policy debates in Whitehall made it virtually impossible to decline.

Work with Job Seekers

Three elements explained the characteristic relationships between policy makers, managers, staff, clients and contractors. These were mandated treatments, standardised information technology and centrally driven targets. All clients were required to follow a standard route through the ES in order to qualify to claim the JSA and then to remain on benefits. Job Centre Managers and local Advisers had little discretion over these processes. What was mandatory for the client was also mandatory for the employment adviser. By regulating the one, government effectively controlled the other.

At 'registration' UK job seekers were required to attend in person at the local Job Centre to register for work before they could claim income support. Registration did two things: it provided an assessment process in which job seekers could be matched to current vacancies, and it also allowed assessment of eligibility for income support. Here further details of job interests and skills were recorded and the Job Seeker Agreement (J-SAG) was completed and signed. This formal agreement had been in place since the amendment to the *Social Security Act* of 1989. Failure to sign and failure to adhere to the agreement was a primary means for sanctioning clients and cutting their income support. These rules were strengthened under JSA.

After this each client was required to attend the Job Centre on the two-week anniversary of their registration to sign on for continued receipt of their JSA. The JSA promoted what was called 'active signing'. This was a system through which clients were asked repeatedly to read leaflets about their obligations and were questioned about their recent job search activities. This signing and questioning was very tightly scripted by the ES, being allocated four and a half minutes for clients up to the 13-week period. After that each signing was allocated seven minutes. Although advisers were instructed to promote the two-week signing to clients as a form of 'ongoing support for the job seeker',[19] it was clear that this was primarily a compliance requirement aimed to place obstacles in the way of potential malingerers, fraudulent claimants or those able to support themselves by other means.

Following this, each job seeker who remained on benefit was required to attend interviews and undergo a review of their agreement every six months. This interviewing work was the main task of the Employment Adviser, the cornerstone of the JSA regime. The Job Seeker's Agreement (J-SAG) was reviewed and revised at each stage and clients had to sign and follow this new agreement or be sanctioned. The instruction manual provided to advisers encouraged staff to use this intervention to widen the job seeker's work goals and 'accept responsibility for broader job search if necessary'.[20] At six months the adviser might also recommend the client attend a job search seminar to improve interview skills and prepare a new curriculum vitae.

These programs underwent considerable refinement under JSA. The new focus was upon improving the search behaviour of clients rather than sending them to skill development programs. The latter remained an option but became secondary. For example, the Job Plan course was available for claimants after they received benefits for twelve months. It followed the same pattern as the other key training programs provided by the TECs. The focus was upon search behaviours and strategies, including preparation of the job seeker to meet the expectations of employers in matters such as dress, interviewing technique and demeanour.

The only really intensive assistance program provided during this period was called One-to-One. It required those in the 18- to 24-year-old range who had been unemployed for twelve months to be selected for a series of repeated interviews every two weeks for three months. At each interview the adviser followed a set menu which required them to review the search tasks set and to attempt to elicit more active job search preparation such as attendance at Job Clubs. Some other adults might be selected for One-to-One if the local office had space and believed them to require more active assistance.

Clients who failed to meet their obligations, including failure to attend a search seminar, or to attend this course every day, were subjected to sanctions. Clients might also be sanctioned for misbehaviour while at a course or while on a job placement program. Advisers reported that it was now more difficult to avoid sanctioning clients under the JSA because obligations and rules were included on the central database and could not easily be ignored. Each Job Centre also had targets for the numbers of clients to be sanctioned each month. Senior ES managers reported that they had lifted these targets three times in 1997 and ES staff had met their quotas each time. Sanctioning had therefore increased significantly as an organisational priority and an objective within each of the other steps in the client processing system.

Sanctioning involved referral of the problem case by an adviser to an Adjudication Officer. Under JSA there were two types of adjudication officer. Local adjudication officers dealt with administrative matters such as failure to attend on the two-week signing date.

To protect local adjudication officers from pressure and abuse by clients these local procedures were kept confidential. Clients were often told that their case was being referred to an officer in another office when in fact the matter was being handled locally. Moreover, staff frequently referred to the local adjudication officer as 'the secret person' in order to reinforce the office culture of confidentiality. More serious sanctions for not being available for work or not actively seeking work were generally referred to section or regional level for decision.

This arrangement of public agencies and local rules mirrors some key aspects of the procedural form of governance. Control was centralised in ministry agreements and legislative mandates. The ES remained large, layered and hierarchical. Its primary staff were clerks who learned on the job and depended entirely on this organisation for their ability to pursue their career. The organisational environment of the ES also resembled the typical bureaucracy in that each service was clearly delineated and relations with other agencies appeared to be carefully structured, even rigid. Alongside this rather traditional picture were other characteristics, however. These indicated a stronger corporate focus. The separation of executive department and agency under the Next Steps formula granted the ES, and the Benefits Agency, an identity of their own. It simplified the tasks and the purposes of each organisation as well as formalising its boundaries.

Broader notions of public service and the need to 'own' or defend policy objectives were less important than meeting targets at the program level. There were stronger and more direct pressures on performance, specifically on all those things measured through quotas and plans. Traditional bureaucratic norms of 'due process' and 'equal treatment' remained but were subordinated to scripted performance objectives. Local Job Centres resembled 'bulk handling terminals' for JSA clients.

The ES appeared not so much to be a point of access for labour market programs as a labour market program itself. The ES system of interviews was its main intervention and within that, motivational courses and sanctions were often the primary instruments. Other specialist activities such as Job Clubs played a much smaller role, as did referrals to substantive skills training programs or subsidised work in industry. The organisation was primarily equipped for interviewing on a massive scale and it must be assumed that it was this form of intervention which system designers believed would maximise outcomes for the organisation.

In other words, by retaining some of the traditional forms of supervision and routine which characterise the procedural bureaucracy, but reforming them through the use of a de-coupled Employment Service, an output-driven management system and a service delivery process which emphasised compliance, the UK appeared to have created an extremely consistent form of corporate governance.

This corporate logic was expressed as the continuous, nation-wide mobilisation of clients to become more active and flexible in their search for work. In practice, the range of possible enterprising interventions available to advisers working with these clients were few. What's more their deployment was too tightly scripted to allow the advisers themselves to engage in an enterprising strategy beyond a certain amount of threatening or cajoling, and the greater use of sanctions. In fact the stronger elements of the enterprise ideal were most evident in the negative. The penalties were increased for failing to actively search, rules changed to force clients to accept a wider and lower range of job possibilities, and sanctions were stiffened for any shunning of compulsory training programs. The enterprise elements were directed at governing staff and programs in response to central directives.

Comparing the UK Strategy

The stronger controls over front-line staff were a characteristic of the UK system as were some other important organisational differences. The average size of Job Centres was about thirty-five staff, making the UK offices the largest in the study and well above the average of around twenty-five. While hardly large offices by other standards, this number of staff provided the UK with a more distinct and formal division of labour at the local level. Within the Job Centre there also appeared to be more defined roles and ranks than elsewhere. Staff responsible for reception desk work and for conducting the fortnightly signing with job seekers were typically of a more junior status than those interviewing and deciding sanctions.

The UK offices mostly employed women who made up 70 per cent of staff, higher than for the other countries in the study. This contrasted with the client population who were mostly men and this required careful planning in situations where job seekers became angry and violent. The ES had the highest seniority rate of all four countries, 86 per cent of staff having five or more years of service. Interestingly they were not the oldest in our four country sample, with the mean age in the UK remaining in the twenty-five to thirty-four bracket rather than in the thirty-five to forty-four years range typical elsewhere. This combination of long service and comparative youth suggests that staff joined the employment service while quite young but did not move in and out of the service as their careers developed. Elsewhere such advisers were likely to be recruited at an older age, often having done some other job. Only 43 per cent in the UK had held other jobs. This of course was the typical profile of the traditional public service organisation. Supporting this pattern of the traditional civil service workplace was a high level of unionisation, at 61 per cent.[21]

Not all staff were involved with a defined caseload and as a result the average load in the UK was low, at only fifty-five per official. These caseloads varied with office size as did the number of clients interviewed each day.[22] The larger the office the higher the load. This appeared to derive from very high levels of specialisation and routinisation of work. Each member of staff was interviewing more than ten job seekers per day. The other case with high loads was New Zealand.

The work in the ES was highly structured and advisers rarely moved outside the doors of the Job Centre to conduct meetings elsewhere or to visit job seekers in training placements or new jobs. A constant flow of job seekers coming into the office to satisfy social security obligations kept officials to a fixed schedule. Nor did these officials join networks of other practitioners, or participate in meetings of this type outside work hours. In two of the other countries these outside affiliations caught the attention of staff and indicated an important form of 'connectedness', as Chapter 7 will explain.

The UK advisers were also the most likely to agree that their work was routine and the least likely to say that they had some say in how their job was done. They saw themselves as lacking influence over the sequence of work, its speed and over changes that might improve the work. The image of a well-drilled, highly scripted workforce was everywhere strongly evident. This came at a cost. When asked to what extent they were satisfied with 'present conditions of work' the UK advisers registered the lowest rates. Fifty-eight per cent reported that they were not satisfied, almost twice the rate for the study as a whole.

Job Centre staff also reported that local conditions had deteriorated since the shift to the new Job Seeker's Allowance (JSA), which they saw as having increased the workload without providing new resources to assist them to cope:

Table 3.1 Country and levels of job satisfaction (%)

	High	Medium	Low
Australia	62	15	23
Netherlands	59	15	26
New Zealand	49	21	30
United Kingdom	23	19	58

The amount of staff has just dwindled and dwindled, but there's more emphasis on advisory interviews and more work to do, and the staff's just getting less and less.

This negative sentiment flowed through to levels of commitment to the work. The UK advisers were the least likely of all to say they were 'willing to exert considerable extra effort' for the organisation. In the other systems most expressed a willingness to do more but in the UK most clearly felt that they were already doing enough, or even too much.

Of those interviewing job seekers, most said they regularly used standard classification or profiling tools to determine what needed to happen next for the client. For the most part these assessments were based on the duration of unemployment and were used to signal eligibility status rather than needs for special assistance or training:

. . . we decide whether we can take the claim basically . . . There's a range of questions we ask them, like, what they've been doing in the last twelve months, if they live in this area, what kind of work they're looking for, if there is anything stopping them from actively seeking work.

Compared to other systems the UK was the more likely to select activities for job seekers based on answers to these set questions, with 77 per cent rating these as important to their decision making.

All advisers agreed that they were dependent upon their computers to access job seeker files and to enter new information (Table 3.2). Rules committed the adviser to download and enter information in a standard way. There was little scope or discretion for holding a certain amount of information in one's own head or in handwritten files.

This pattern of predefined and routine work processes was highly client-driven without being client-oriented. Almost all the work done by UK local advisers was devoted to job seekers. In the study as a whole the average amount of time that advisers spent with job seekers was about half their total work, the rest being split between employers

Table 3.2 Country and percentage responses to 'Are you normally logged-on to your computer when talking with job seekers?'

	Always/Most of the time	Sometimes/Never
Australia	69	31
Netherlands	90	10
New Zealand	94	6
United Kingdom	99	1

and administrative duties. In the UK however the staff averaged three-quarters of their time with job seekers and the least time of all on contacts with employers. The UK also had the lowest level of intensive job seeker contact and the highest rate of what the Australian advisers called 'parking', a very low intensity service based on an occasional phone call or interview to check that the job seeker still deserved to be on the benefit roll.

As mentioned, the UK officials spent three-quarters of their day with job seekers. Not surprisingly, these advisers had comparatively weak external networks. When rates of interaction with other organisations such as municipal government, welfare agencies and local schools were compared across the four systems the UK had the lowest level of outside interaction of any sort. Chapter 7 reveals the 'network governance' scores for the UK were the lowest in the study for those items involving 'civic' connectedness with agencies and individuals outside the formal governmental process.

When clients were obliged to present for more intensive interactions they received counselling and standard programs directed at self esteem, interview skills and preparation of letters of introduction and a curriculum vitae. In other words the skills being imparted were modest in nature and mostly concerned with self-testing and behaviour management. Little effort could be devoted to tailoring interventions to individuals, except where this involved engineering opportunities to shift them off benefits:

> So it's much easier to dip into the system and pick out almost at random and say 'How's this one?' You know, 'what do you think of this one?'.
> You're looking for the client to feel that there's tedium that they can do without as well, and hopefully they'll say, 'Well I've had enough of this, I shall sign off and claim another benefit.'

The standard 'Restart' interviews were seen by advisers and their managers as an intervention to 'shake out' or 'clean the files'. Willingness to play by the rules and produce evidence of active search was at a premium:

> By checking what they're doing to look for work, to see whether or not they are applying for jobs (to see) if they are available for work, so they're not sick. There's a variety of things really that we look at and if there are any problems then it might be referred to an adjudication officer, and they may lose benefit in some cases.
> So you really need to just test people out, just to see where the . . . what the effort they've made to try and find work.

The emphasis from the adviser's point of view was on motivating clients and sanctioning them, with staff regularly being called upon to select clients for each reason. The advisers recognised that a key part of this role was to create a regime of heightened 'activity' and 'mobility'. Those with few obvious prospects for gaining work were nonetheless urged to continually approach employers, apply for otherwise unpopular jobs, and to work on any personal 'presentation' issues which otherwise might draw attention to their unsuitability in the minds of employers.

Communication between advisers and trainers was largely confined to filling places quickly and after that the priority was compliance. Advisers focused upon the problem cases that might require sanctioning:

> We don't get feedback individually about what a person did or didn't do on the course, but we do get lists every week that tell us whether somebody started or not, and then if they don't go then we, well we tend to follow that all up anyway to see what the outcome was. Really it is down to us to find out.

The staff recognised that these mandatory programs were often used to 'work' the client so that they had 'earned' their benefit. 'People have got to realise that they have got to do something to get the benefit, they've got to earn it.' More substantive issues to do with skills and retraining were not well treated, even though advisers saw this as an important issue in returning job seekers to the work force:

> I think some people are penalised . . . unless you're six months plus . . . they wouldn't be able to train for anything. And really they're the ones who need help, and they can't train for additional qualifications or anything . . . There used to be training courses, like long distance lorry driving, the government stopped funding the programs.

Most often the advisers linked training to a process of creating activity and flexibility, getting them to meet perceived obligations and responsibilities, and constantly re-establishing that they were still available for work. These behavioural functions often overwhelmed any instrumental employment purpose:

> The client needs to do something to earn the benefit, you don't get anything for nothing, you've got to earn it.

When speaking about training opportunities the advisers were uniformly critical. The TECs were regarded as being too focused on local business interests which advisers said manifested itself as both an unwillingness to modify courses to local needs, and a preference for training those who were already reasonably well off:

> It's not quite tiered enough to the community. (The TEC) is supposed to look at the local area, suss out the needs, and provide training for it. But I think they look more at the business point of view . . . I've got a guy here who can't speak English, he would really like to do this course. There's no course here for this kind of need. And like this area's got a high (non-English speaking) population.

Contact with employers was the lowest in the study, with advisers spending almost all of their time processing job seekers. Nor did these officials seem to be integrated into any outside meetings or networks in their field. Work started and stopped at the Job Centre door.

Sanctions

Given the strong emphasis upon checking eligibility and upon maintaining regular, routine contact with job seekers, it is not surprising that the UK also had a high rate of reported sanctions. Advisers saw themselves as having to take a tough line with clients. At more than three sanctions per staff member per fortnight, the UK rate is significantly higher than the Australian and New Zealand rate and approaching that of the Netherlands. Unlike the Netherlands, the UK also had a high estimate of the number of people who were not complying with their obligations. This is also reflected in questions about the numbers they believe would 'rather stay on benefits' than get a job. At 31 per cent of job seekers, the reported rate of inactivity or malingering was highest in the UK. So these advisers perceived their clients as breaking the rules more frequently than did other advisers in the study.

The UK advisers were also much more likely to sanction their clients for leaving a job than were others. Some 86 per cent said this was a reason for sanctioning while the average for the other countries was 30 per cent. Failure to adhere to the terms of the job seeker agreement was also a more important reason for sanctioning than in the other systems. UK

Table 3.3   Country and percentage responses to 'I often remind clients of the sanctioning power to get them to pay attention'

	Disagree	Neither agree/disagree	Agree
Australia	43	19	38
Netherlands	64	19	17
New Zealand	33	20	47
United Kingdom	25	21	54

advisers were also more severe about failure to attend training sessions or interviews, indicating that administrative sanctions played a much larger role than elsewhere. Their willingness to be tough was also reflected in the reasons they gave for not sanctioning when their own perception was that the job seeker deserved it. They would not make such a recommendation if they felt the formal agreement with the job seeker was not specific enough and they were the most attentive of all the advisers to this concern with accurate paperwork. In interview they explained this in quasi-legal terms and also said that they could not expect the backing of the organisation if the paperwork was not exact.

In taking this strict line the advisers clearly felt they were following the policy of the organisation and 86 per cent said that their office actively encouraged this approach to sanctioning clients. This confidence was also reflected in the fact that of those interviewed and surveyed, the UK advisers were most committed to the idea that sanctioning clients was a good way to gain their compliance. Sanctioning therefore occupied a far more central role in the day-to-day work of advisers here than elsewhere. The strong emphasis on compliance was also reflected in the fact that UK advisers were significantly more likely to use reminders about their own sanctioning powers as a part of normal interactions with clients (Table 3.3).

However this tougher approach also had its costs for advisers. Among the reasons they gave for not sanctioning those they felt were misbehaving, 40 per cent of the UK advisers listed 'fear for personal safety'. As Chapter 2 stated, the JSA protocols required continuous 'active signing' which meant that front-line staff had to ask each client if they had actively searched in the past fortnight and if so, what evidence they had. Most Job Centres supplied clients with a record book to enter details of all the inquiries they had made and all the interviews they had had. Clients could be asked to produce this at any time or face penalties. Staff allocated only four or five minutes to each client but were expected to adopt a tough, investigative approach and to refer doubtful cases immediately for possible sanctioning. This was the most

Table 3.4   Country and percentage responses to 'fear for personal safety' as a reason for withholding sanctions

	No Fear	Fear
Australia	76	23
Netherlands	87	13
New Zealand	66	36
United Kingdom	56	44

stressful task in the office and was often the occasion for outbursts of anger and violence from clients. Assaults and the throwing of furniture were common.

Violence was thus a frequent part of the service delivery environment. As most Job Centre staff were women and most clients men, the potential for harm was high. Moreover changed office layouts occasioned by the need to get closer to clients and to create a more personal form of contact put clients and advisers in 'open' plan settings. Staff did not use interview rooms and even when doing intensive counselling with long-term clients ('case loading') they said they preferred to share clients to avoid getting too closely implicated.

In order to manage this threat staff commonly carried out acts of careful deception. For example, in one office advisers used fake entries on client computer files to warn one another of problem cases. Because civil service rules and data protection legislation required that clients have access to any information about them recorded on file, it was difficult to enter perceptions and concerns over a job seeker's mental health, disposition or capacity for violence unless these were fully verified by superiors and specialists. Instead staff used local office signals to record such details in ways which clients, managers and outsiders could not recognise. For example, they added their own office telephone number in the box reserved for the client's phone details if they believed he or she was likely to react violently to submissions to jobs or threats of sanctions. In the unlikely event that this would later attract attention it could easily be viewed as a misprint. In another case advisers described using the 'conversations box' on their computer files to add irrelevant detail such as 'might be suited to hospital work if available' to indicate undiagnosed mental health problems.

Adjudication Officers and staff bringing forward a possible case for sanctioning adopted a policing role. They spoke of 'doing' the client, 'shopping' him, and 'shutting him down'. There was certainly room for the exercise of some discretion, although the rising targets for sanctions meant that if an adviser 'let this one get away she would have to catch

Table 3.5 Country and percentage responses to the extent 'Decisions about clients are determined by central rules and regulations'

	To a lesser extent	Neither	To a greater extent
Australia	38	19	43
Netherlands	25	20	56
New Zealand	10	13	77
United Kingdom	7	12	82

another'. It was clear that in both its attention to detail and degree of effort the UK system was highly tuned to matters of eligibility and well armed with formal and informal strategies to implement a strict sanctions regime. This placed advisers in a policing role quite unlike that found elsewhere. The extensive use of corporate and office-level targets as a means for regulating work enabled government policy to be driven energetically down through the organisation, even when this involved serious risks for advisers.

Governance Norms at the Front Line

These various forms of local organisation and service repertoires suggest the larger patterns of governance which help in assessing the UK case vis-à-vis the core argument concerning enterprising states and transition strategies. First, it's necessary to put aside the discussion of objective conditions and legislative requirements and seek an understanding of the adviser's normative orientation to work, clients and policy requirements. This means examining the findings from interviews and the data from qualitative, evaluative sections of the survey. Again the definition of the UK example becomes clearer by comparing it to typical responses from the other three countries.

Given the structure of this system it is not surprising to learn that the UK advisers described the fewest points of discretion where they might elect to do things differently and specifically for individual clients. They were also the most dependent advisers in the study. For instance, they were easily the most likely to agree that decisions made about clients were 'determined by the central departmental programs rules and regulations': Table 3.5 indicates that rule-dependence was typical of 84 per cent of the UK respondents, with the average for other systems being approximately 58 per cent. A similar pattern emerged when they were asked about the extent to which their work was determined by 'goals set elsewhere'. A significantly higher proportion of the UK advisers agreed that their work was structured by others.

However, the most telling difference between UK officials and others concerned targets. More than in any other system, these officials believed that their work was governed by targets, including 'targets for formal and informal priority groups'. Rather than a universal service, the UK system therefore resembled a corporate type in which strategic decisions about who deserved which treatment were inscribed within centrally determined benchmarks and quotas.

When it came to their evaluations of the system as a whole the UK advisers expressed similar views to others, saying they regarded their own system as effective at getting clients off benefits. They differed most on the selectivity of services. The UK advisers disagreed with the idea that they should pick the best clients and just give them the best service. Instead some 87 per cent said they strove to give all clients 'a similar service', the comparable figure for the other systems being significantly lower at 69 per cent.

Where UK advisers stood out was in their commitment to the idea that the 'objective in this job is to shift the maximum number of clients off benefits', a view held by 80 per cent in the UK system and 64 per cent in the other systems. They were less likely to be worried about competitors and said they would be happy to help another adviser sort out a problem with a client, although not with a problem concerning the computer system, this latter reluctance due no doubt to security concerns and rules which the ES and the parliament have enacted to protect client information and performance data.

They agreed that they had set methods for performing most tasks and it was clear that they had the highest sensitivity to targets. They also recognised that these were a means to justify their jobs to a wider audience outside the Employment Service:

> I think you've got to have targets. I think it's pretty stupid how things used to be in the civil service where you like had this pot of money and you went and asked for something and got it. I think you've got to show that you're delivering a quality service. And I think people respond better to that . . . Also it gives us something to justify to ministers, that we're doing our job.

Those who had experience of targets which were directly linked to individual performance figures reported that this had caused competition between staff and a suspicion that others were holding back opportunities to use for their own clients rather than open them to others in the office:

> I've worked in an office where we had individual targets and it put you under a hell of a lot of pressure . . . you can get a situation where someone's saying, you know, 'why haven't you suspended so many people a month?' and you say

Table 3.6   System evaluations by UK and other advisers (%)

Adviser Norms	UK mean	Mean for all others
In your judgement how effective is the current employment service in helping clients find a job? (Number who say effective or very effective)	58	54
In your judgement how effective is the current employment service in getting clients off benefits? (Number who say effective or very effective)	55	47
The practice in my agency is to pick out the most capable welfare recipients and give them the best service. (Number who agree)	12	25
Based on the practices in your office today, what would you say is the more important goal of your agency: to help clients get jobs as quickly as possible or to raise education or skill levels of clients so they can get the job they want in the future? (Number favouring getting a job quickly)	84	54
How much does your agency emphasise giving clients a choice about the services they receive? (Number who say choice is important)	44	58
In your opinion, which is more often to blame if a person is on benefits: lack of effort on their part, or circumstances beyond their control? (Number who blame clients)	41	34
How much leeway do you have in deciding which program or activity the client should be assigned to? (Number who indicate they have leeway)	51	65

'well, because they were available for work.' . . . Whereas these team targets, it tends to even itself out.

Using a series of scales developed in US studies (Handler & Hasenfeld, 1997) which test the trade-offs that advisers make between competing service objectives, the study compared each set of advisers and their perceptions and values regarding the operation of their own system. The scales measured the degree to which staff adopted strategies promoting job search rather than skill development, allowed clients greater or lesser flexibility in their choice of jobs, permitted clients to stay on benefits until a good job was found, or pressured them to take low skill and low paid work.

Such statements provide an approximation of the overall severity, client-focus and willingness to invest in training, as well as pointing out differences in the favoured strategies of advisers and of their superiors.

The UK emerged as a universal and prescriptive system. The virtue in this approach was that it does not simply 'cream' the best clients and leave the rest. The weakness was that the treatment it provided for everyone remained shallow and often punitive.

The UK officials were among the least likely to say that they were aware of the financial implications of their own efforts or to view their own work as linked to any form of 'price' or 'cost' to the organisation. This indicated that although target driven, these objectives were not primarily budgetary in nature, at least at the front line. The UK approach also supports the notion that the stronger the organisational emphasis on compliance, the more likely it is that advisers will see their clients as failing in their obligations, particularly on administrative tests and other conditions associated with participation in routine programs.

The comparative insulation of the UK advisers from outside pressures and opportunities was evident in their statements regarding negotiations for resources to help their clients. Only 36 per cent said this was a factor, while the average for other systems was almost 70 per cent. This did not appear to indicate that such resources were more plentiful in the UK, but rather that such decisions and negotiations were taken out of the hands of local staff dealing directly with clients.

Conclusions

In summary, the UK case suggests a form of reinvention in which primary attention is given to mastery of a limited set of interventions applied consistently by relatively simple means. Little is left to chance and individual treatments might well be aimed at activating clients but only in order to get them to perform rather superficial tasks. In other words expectations of both advisers and job seekers were very modest, even if the rhetoric of greater responsibility was loudly proclaimed. Can we really regard this as the fruit of an enterprising spirit?

On first reading it seems not to employ many of the more embracing elements of this dynamic. Discretion is low, case management of clients is the exception not the rule, and when advisers are more actively engaged it is most often around questions of compliance and sanctioning. This might be viewed as the negative side of the enterprise model. Its intentions are plainly to break down the previous regime of entitlements, expectations of secure, full-time work, and freedom to stay on benefits until a favourable opportunity arises. But the mere fact that most of the strategies were devoted to removing the certainties of the old order should not diminish appreciation of the power of this reinvention motive. In de-coupling the ES from the regular bureaucracy, then imposing a more regulatory set of JSA requirements, policy makers succeeded in denying local offices the scope to adjust their efforts to values other than those mandated by government. In other words the corporate mission of the ES became a more overt extension of Conservative party doctrine than would otherwise have been possible in a 'neutral', generalist civil service. What was being enterprised was the management of the ES, and decision makers plainly preferred this to a strategy which allowed more attention to the reconsideration of the role and needs of clients.

The UK case was therefore a governance system in which more traditional bureaucratic norms of equal treatment and universal entitlement had been mobilised and then reformed as a new process of corporate enforcement and compliance. Clients were carefully managed by a process that also managed staff and public resources. This depended less upon individualised service or the mobilisation of career commitment, than upon applying strong and systematic pressure on both clients and advisers.

The clear, organisational separation of training, employment assistance, policy making and social security did not create new opportunities for the development of either markets or networks. Chapter 7 returns to this topic and compares the four governance types using factor analysis. This shows the UK to be a system of very strong corporate governance attributes in which neo-liberal aspects of self-enterprise remained remarkably weak and highly regulatory commitments predominated. Yet by proving that the ES could be effectively reformed in this way, policy makers opened the door to other departures from traditional, non-partisan treatments and thus made it possible to imagine a time when a single corporate approach might be modified through further reinventions. Senior policy makers were aware of this advantage and in interviews stated openly that one of their conclusions from the JSA experiment was that 'any significant change' or 'repeated shifting of the goal posts' could now be used to force local officials to look upwards continually for signals regarding the forms of performance which should guide their actions.

Notes

1 There were also important revisions and repeals of other Acts dealing with trade union governance, including the repeal of the *Employment Protection Act, 1975*. See W. Brown and S. Wadhwani (1990) 'The economic effects of industrial relations legislation since 1979', *National Institute Economic Review*, No. 131, pp. 57–70.

2 He concludes this detailed empirical study with the comment that 'the less-skilled and low-paid seem to be responsible for the bulk of any wage flexibility evident at the macro-level'.

3 *New Statesman and Society*, (1995) 8 (377), p. 8.

4 Department for Education and Employment officials confirmed in interview that these measures came directly from Tory leaders such as Michael Heseltine, rather than from policy advisers within the bureaucracy.

5 In 1993 the Government published its fourth Next Steps review (Cm.2430) which identified changes in a further ninety-two agencies. This review added further requirements and procedures for the clarification of ministerial and CEO responsibilities, detailed new flexibilities for pay and grading systems within agencies, and outlined the application of market testing policies.

6 The Hon. Mr Portillo, House of Commons, 29 November 1993, p. 340.

7 ibid.

8 The only major ES review resulted in the retention of all major client services and relatively minor alterations in some outsourced training services.

9 Implementation took until October the following year to come into full effect because policy makers underestimated the administrative change needed to give force to the new measures.

10 Employment advisers and local ES managers reported in interview that job seekers would come to the Job Centre to register for work and would indicate that 'they had paid their insurance premiums over a number of years and were now ready to collect'.

11 In the early stages of implementation officials indicated that this authority was not being widely used but it was expected to increase as the new system became familiar to local staff and their confidence in dealing with clients grew stronger. Interviews with the author, Sheffield, December 1996.

12 Officials interviewed during the implementation of JSA indicated that they believed it would be difficult to use JSA as the basis for private provision of core services. The obligations under the new legislation indicated that clients would have first to sign a special agreement 'waiver' before their JSA could be administered through a private agency.

13 That evaluation had to be completed after two years of operation, or by October 1998. It was contracted to Stephen McKay at the Centre for Research in Social Policy, Loughborough University. The JSA Project Team contained 100 staff from both agencies and worked out of its own office in Sheffield.

14 Treasury and Civil Service Committee, House of Commons, *Fifth Report*, Vol. 1, p. liii, HMSO, London, 1 November 1994.

15 Department for Education and Employment, Employment Service Annual Performance Agreement 1996–1997, p. 2.

16 According to the Government, in 1992–93 agencies met approximately 77% of their targets, representing a 'small improvement over the proportion of targets met last year', and indicating a need for 'further improvement' in the coming years.

17 Interview with the author, Sheffield, September 1998.

18 DfEE Departmental report, 1996, p. 15.

19 Employment Service, *A Quality Assurance Framework for Business Managers, Back to Work Team Leaders, District Managers*, ES, Sheffield, 1996, p. 65.

20 ibid., p. 68.

21 It is also worth noting that this represents a fall in the pre-Thatcher level of unionisation which averaged 80% of public servants.
22 r=.205, p=.06 for caseload and office size; r=.175. p=.03 for office size and number interviewed each day.

CHAPTER 4

New Zealand:
Two Steps Forward

That a small country at the periphery of OECD policy debates could quickly become the centre of worldwide speculation concerning the right path to governance reform was testimony both to New Zealand's 'radical' approach, and perhaps also to the 'suitable conditions' for experimentation which for a time prevailed there (Shand, 1996; Kelsey, 1995, p. 19).

Between 1984 and 1994 the Labour and National Governments of New Zealand set out to transform almost every key public institution. Tariffs, labour market policies, public enterprises, hospitals, tax, electoral laws and welfare all underwent fundamental change. This was a revolution waged at changing the relationship between state and society. The underlying reform model used by parties of both the left and the right derived explicitly from neo-liberal institutional economics (Boston et al., 1991). Its purpose was to deregulate economic activity and remove the state from as many areas of social life as possible.

The imperatives for change were certainly substantial and it might be argued that New Zealand had fewer choices than any of the other three systems. Fundamental doubts about the viability of the protected economy of the postwar years had led to the belief that the only hope for a return to prosperity lay in some form of thoroughgoing restructure (Castles et al., 1996). There had been signs of decay in the inherited model before 1984, most notably in the fact that New Zealand had run a current account deficit for virtually every year since the mid-1960s. An orgy of misdirected public spending by the conservative Muldoon Government in the late 1970s was widely understood to have radically overcommitted the state, pushing the budget towards insolvency. Leading politicians spoke of the reform task as 'transforming the New Zealand economy from an object of national shame to a source of national pride' (Richardson, 1995, p. 81).

The chosen model was the neo-liberal ideal of a diminished public sphere dominated by market and quasi-market instruments. This, it was said, would enable government to cut costs and raise efficiency. This in turn would release resources for greater private initiative and self-responsibility. Cradle-to-grave social assistance was lampooned as a cause of organisational malaise and social inflexibility. And by stimulating individuals to respond to market signals the new bi-partisan ethos promised to re-enterprise a society which had once been the envy of other advanced countries. Here then was the paradigm case of the 'market governance' type. Or was it?

Employment Conditions

The shift which took place in the structure of the New Zealand economy involved a comprehensive dismantling of most forms of regulation and public investment. Instruments previously used to protect industry and to guarantee jobs were discarded in favour of a national policy of deregulation. Most forms of industry assistance were removed between 1984 and 1990. Although the most zealous reformers in both parties agreed upon the model, implementation differed in speed and emphasis.

Not surprisingly given its constituency, Labour took industrial reforms at a slower speed than the Nationals would later do, but insisted that agriculture move more rapidly. It was also less willing to cut social benefits and wage levels, which meant that when deregulation caused unemployment to increase, it also forced public expenditure and budget deficits to rise. New Zealand had a system of universal entitlement to unemployment benefit in which all job seekers could draw a basic form of income support for as long as it took for them to find work. Benefit levels remained relatively generous under Labour and so did eligibility. But attitudes among policy makers were nonetheless changing (Castles and Shirley, 1996). A massive electoral victory by the conservative National Party in 1990 resulted in an extension of the deregulationist agenda to labour markets and social benefits for the rest of the 1990s.

The Nationals introduced the *Employment Contracts Act* in 1991 which abolished the system of national wage settlements, awards and forms of union bargaining. Individual contracts replaced collective bargaining institutions. Union rights to represent employees were withdrawn and various forms of workplace protection were reduced. The purpose of the new system was to 'put downward pressure on real wages for some workers', while offering hope of higher productivity and participation in the medium term (Treasury, 1990, p. 157). Although the advocates of reform failed to get cabinet agreement to abolish minimum wages and to disband the Labour Court, a new concept of voluntary unionism shifted power away from unions and towards employers.

The effects were soon felt. During 1992 the average weekly earnings (AWE) index fell by NZ$15 and the loss of allowances and overtime cut some semi-skilled salaries by as much as NZ$7000 per annum (Walsh, 1992, p. 71). Union membership declined rapidly in most sectors, falling by as much as two-thirds in some industries (Kelsey, 1995, p. 185). Social welfare spending was cut by $1 billion per year. Beginning in the financial year 1990–91 this was achieved by 10 per cent cuts to unemployment benefits for couples and in income support for supporting parents. The Nationals complained that benefit rates had become too close to the ever lower wages being paid in the new deregulated economy, thereby reducing work incentives.[1] Eligibility requirements were increased for unemployment benefit, requiring a wait of twenty-six weeks for those who left their job voluntarily, were dismissed for misconduct or who refused a suitable offer of work or training. Rates for young people were also cut severely.

Between 1990 and 1992 the New Zealand unemployment rate escalated from 7.3 per cent to 11 per cent. By the mid-1990s the Nationals could boast an increase of 150 000 new jobs in the period after the passing of the *Employment Contracts Act* of 1991, but were forced to acknowledge that the unemployment rate overall was no lower than when the government took office. Moreover the unemployment rates for disadvantaged workers such as Maori and Pacific Island peoples were stuck at very high levels (20 per cent or more) and New Zealand was 'increasingly becoming two societies' (Richardson, 1995, pp. 197–8).

Corporate Management and the Employment Service

Inside the state the first wave of public sector reforms came in 1988 and 1989 and took the form of legislation designed to empower senior public managers to restructure their organisations in response to clearer policy mandates. The *State Sector Act* of 1988 and the *Public Finance Act* of 1989 were the keystones in this framework. The primary purpose of this first set of initiatives appears to have been to make government organisations more 'businesslike' through the adoption of corporate structures and private management methods of performance measurement. Departments which had previously had responsibility for economic activities were corporatised, put in the charge of boards and new Chief Executive Officers with enlarged powers, and were listed as private companies 'owned' by their portfolio minister and the Minister of Finance.

Inside the remaining public service, tasks were made more explicit and organisations were required to view their minister as their main 'customer'. Contracts based on increased salaries and performance pay were introduced for senior staff, annual reporting rules required bureaucratic activities to have measured outputs, and agencies were encouraged to write contracts with one another as a means for making more explicit the basis of all resource sharing and co-operation.

A second wave of public service changes between 1992 and 1994 reshaped the corporate agenda to make the actions of empowered senior managers more accountable to government. There is some difference of opinion among commentators as to whether these second round reforms were simply a natural extension of the first or involved a correction of some of its excesses (Mulgan, 1997; Schick, 1996). Certainly there is evidence of disquiet in the Logan Report commissioned to review the state sector reforms of the first period (Logan, 1991). The two major initiatives which followed this review both emphasised the need for greater accountability by public service organisations and their managers.

In 1993 the National Party Government strengthened its control over the bureaucracy by instituting a system of Key Result Areas (KRAs) for every department. These took the form of annual objectives and targets which each department and chief executive were required to meet. When placed within longer term Strategic Result Areas (SRAs) the annual targets were regarded as a means by which a 'whole of government' view might be imposed upon individual agencies. The earlier strategy of CEOs to promote the objectives which they regarded as best for their organisations and its key clients did not endear all CEOs to their ministers or to the minister's cabinet colleagues (Richardson, 1995).

The *Fiscal Responsibility Act* of 1994 required governments to explain the fiscal impacts of all economic policy decisions and to report to parliament on their progress in meeting debt reduction targets, a balance in operating expenses and revenues and the prudent management of risks. This acted as a further source of authority for Treasury which could now do even more to curb expenditure proposals from line departments on the grounds that they threatened these larger targets.

Along with its other progressive welfare state initiatives early in the twentieth century, New Zealand had also developed a national public employment service which provided training, subsidised employment and job brokerage services. As in other countries, the mix of these interventions changed with each government and became more elaborate and complex over time.

Following a review in 1988 the Department of Labour was split into five separate services each with their own organisations. The employment assistance section of the Labour ministry became the New

Zealand Employment Service (NZES) with its own General Manager. Like the other four, it achieved decentralised or de-coupled responsibility for its own programs and budget. The restructure also created a 'flat' hierarchy with only four levels of staff: the General Manager, four Regional Managers, Employment Centre Managers and the Employment Adviser-Project Officer class who now made up 82 per cent of the total.

The key agent in this change process was the new general manager of the Employment Service, George Hickton. His career biography neatly expressed the business character of the corporate management reform process. He came to the NZES from his post as General Manager, Sales and Marketing at Honda New Zealand. Hickton was an advocate of the then-fashionable Management by Walking Around which downplayed rules and procedure in favour of problem-solving and the building of corporate culture. Hickton favoured a strategy he called 'imaging' the organisation, by which he meant creating a strong, unified corporate identity, complete with vision, mission and professional pride among the staff (McDonald & Sharma, 1994).

Hickton constructed an employment service mission that focused attention upon achieving improved outputs through a reorganisation of internal work systems. Typical of this approach was the creation of a set of standard outputs which identified one key performance measure for each activity within the organisation. Each local office or Employment Centre was then measured according to the number of clients it placed into each major program as well as according to the numbers who left the register in order to take jobs.

These monthly statistics were published inside and outside the organisation to promote a sense of progress towards agreed targets and to engender competition for status. This also became a key tool for managing the new relationship with the Secretary of Labour, the bureaucrat with overarching responsibility for each of the five services within this portfolio. Through the agreed target system the Employment Service could stabilise its relations with the rest of the Labour portfolio, with the Minister and with the rest of the government.

Secured as a source of external legitimation, the corporate management targets were then skilfully and remorselessly deployed as a means of focusing internal effort. In addition to the more detailed monthly statistics provided for senior management and regional managers, Hickton created a daily output schedule for controlling the work of advisers and local managers. In a table called The Nine O'Clock News, he identified the outputs he regarded as critical to performance. Each column listed the program, activity or output regarded as important. Each day his head office auditors tallied the efforts of every local office across the country. This included the updated figures for successful referral of priority clients into jobs and approved programs.

The table listed each Employment Centre, its progress against a set annual target, its actual performance for the month and movements for the previous day's activity. The audit office then faxed these results to every office around the country at nine o'clock each morning, showing them where they stood against one another and against their required objectives. The effect of this ruthless combination of measurement, comparison and publicity was to focus the efforts of managers on improving their measured performance and that of their section. Local offices became completely governed by their targets. Local resources were marshalled to make sure the best results were achieved. Only activities which produced movements in the defined activities were given priority.

From 1988 the NZ Government also began a process of instituting performance agreements with the Chief Executives (CEs) of all its agencies. This was a necessary step occasioned by the shift towards greater managerial responsibility and a sharper separation of ministerial and managerial powers. Boston et al. (1996, p. 110) argue that Chief Executive performance agreements soon became 'an accepted, important, and increasingly sophisticated accountability device within the public sector in New Zealand'. In the employment case 'the purchaser' was the Minister for Employment and 'the supplier' was the Chief Executive of the Department of Labour. The agreement stipulated that the purpose of the agreement was for the Minister to determine the outputs to be purchased, the measures to be used to check such outputs, comparisons to be made with other services, to provide assessments of risks and obligations in the supply of the outputs, and to hold the supplier accountable for the delivery of the outputs specified.

However, this system of contracts and targets could not achieve a more flexible method for achieving outcomes. While activities within the organisation certainly became more results-oriented, the definition of what constituted a good result was largely based on throughput. A client going onto a training program and then returning to the unemployment roll counted as a positive placement. Job Centres responded by filling quotas as fast as they could, regardless of the ultimate outcome for the client. Output categories had to fit on one page and be easily tabulated each day. Qualitative judgments were reduced and levels of client disadvantage could not be well expressed in the 'body count' methods required.

During the latter 1980s and early 1990s the effect of rising unemployment and new demands for 'working' the unemployed to get them back to work resulted in an expansion of programs. In 1988 when the first reforms were enacted the tasks and functions of the organisation could be grouped into eight program areas. By 1995 there were twenty-three such programs and the complexity of the role of the Employment Adviser had grown beyond the grasp of even the most able and well qualified staff. Nor did managers have a good grip on the more complex environment.

As one senior official put it:

> We really could not tell why programs seemed to be popular and crowded in one area and almost empty in another similar locality. It just seemed to be a matter of what the local office was pushing at the time . . . that in turn seemed to be largely a matter of luck, ignorance and ease of administration.

Employment Advisers reported the same patterns, preferring a standard repertoire of programs and being reluctant to take up new options if the criteria were too complicated:

> You don't want to be getting yourself and the client tangled up in administrative problems and maybe not getting accepted or getting someone further up telling you (that) you didn't read the guidelines.

Nor did the corporate orientation do much for inter-agency co-operation. The Income Support Service (NZISS) had its own targets for rapid processing of claims and these had little to do with checking employment service records. In fact both local agencies had strong incentives to minimise downtime caused by negotiation with the other.

The other key agencies with whom clients interacted included training agencies and the Community Employment Group, both of which were directly responsible to the employment service but both of whom had their own organisational structure and distinctive cultures. Although these programs underwent budget review, particularly under Richardson's stewardship as Finance Minister, and although the target setting process instituted for the NZES and NZISS resulted in stronger pressure on senior management, the ordinary work of the employment system was not greatly altered. The list of programs expanded and contracted with changes of government but the primary focus remained upon giving each job seeker a standard service. Advisers were left to make critical judgements regarding referrals to job vacancies and did so with the employers' preferences in mind. The introduction of local targets made it rational for those doing referrals to prefer the least disadvantaged clients for they were obviously more likely to win places on programs or find jobs.

Task Force and Re-engineering

The reductions in benefits, the new contract employment laws, the greater use of user-pays and the further privatisations introduced by the Nationals after they won office in 1990 widened a gap in New Zealand public opinion which had already become evident under Labour. The unemployment rate rose sharply after 1990 and by the end of 1991 it had reached 11 per cent. When the Nationals faced the electorate again in 1993 their leadership was searching for a means to allay widespread concern about social exclusion and deep divisions between those prospering from the new deregulated economy and the large numbers who were losing ground. Under pressure to create a more unified political process which might bind these wounds the Government agreed to put forward proposals to reform the electoral system. The proposal approved by voters at the 1993 poll gave support to a system of mixed representation which would make coalition government the likely norm for future governments.

Undoubtedly influenced by this new mood to restore some form of social cohesion, the Nationals then announced the formation of a Prime Ministerial Task Force on Employment to be convened in early 1994. In the new spirit of 'social healing' the terms of reference were set through negotiation between the Government and both the Labour and Alliance parties. The Department of Labour, and through it the NZES, were asked to provide administrative support. The NZES was by now in the hands of acting General Manager Tony Gavin whose preference for involving staff directly in the reform process reflected his own experience within the ranks.

Following an extensive process of consultation which revealed 'anger, frustration . . . hopes and aspirations . . . (and) suspicions that this was yet another consultation leading to more talk but no action', the Task Force reported in May 1994. At the centre of the proposals was a recommendation that by the year 2000 the long-term unemployed be guaranteed work, training or education. This was deemed to apply to all those registered as unemployed for more than twenty-six weeks.

It was also proposed that all the long-term unemployed should be involved in 'individualised assistance', and there were also particular programs suggested for Maoris, Pacific Islanders and for youth. Among many criticisms of existing programs the Task Force singled out the futility of sending people to programs which did not work well and which were unmonitored.

The Task Force proposed a new approach and this was also supported by senior NZES and Department of Labour staff, although they were less happy with the strident critique being popularised by the Task Force:

Many unemployed people say they feel like pinballs being ricocheted around an inhuman machine. Their individual needs aren't recognized, their strengths are left untapped (Prime Ministerial Task Force, 1994, p. 6).

The alternative to this universal processing model was viewed as one in which the specific attributes of clients would serve to trigger different levels of service and forms of intervention which would activate clients through intensive contact:

> The most successful way of breaking out of unemployment, particularly for youth and long-term unemployed, may be intensive individual assistance from initial interview through to completion of a job action plan and post-placement support. More personalised service will require giving greater discretionary power to front-line service providers – the people who are closest to the individuals being targeted (Prime Ministerial Task Force, 1994, p. 6).

Priority assistance would depend upon the development of mechanisms for the early identification of job seekers at risk of becoming long-term unemployed. Formal Activity Agreements with these clients would be developed and these would include sending clients to appropriate training and work experience programs and in the case of young people, making continued access to income support dependent on taking part in 'agreed activities' (Prime Ministerial Task Force, 1994, p. 19).

Central to the new approach was a recognition by policy makers and critics that long-term cases were becoming a major problem. Between January 1990 and January 1994 the number of claimants who were receiving benefits for two years or more increased from 9208 to 39 270 and this group grew from being 6 per cent of the roll to 19 per cent. The new methodology proposed to treat this group was termed the 'structured stair-case approach', or 'stair-casing' (Prime Ministerial Task Force, 1994, p. 23). The model drew explicitly on Business Process Re-engineering methods brought into the organisation in late 1995 by consultants from Deloittes, New Zealand. This was far more than simply a repackaging of existing programs. The two aims of the Re-engineering strategy were to reconfigure the process by which clients were selected and enrolled into the organisation's services, and at the same time to develop new systems for managing the opportunities available to job seekers. Employers, training agencies, consultant psychologists and other service deliverers were redefined as 'opportunity providers' who needed to be effectively incorporated into the NZES work process. Critical to the restructure was the development of new information technologies which were designed to facilitate client-based tracking of resources and outcomes.

In the previous system a mainframe computer system stored data on clients, programs and other interventions in different files. Small differences in filing methods meant loss of cross-referencing. The process was very time consuming and often inaccurate, leading local advisers to limit their search to only the most recent data. The new model was to honour Business Process Re-engineering theory by using the client file as the basis of all information storage and by ordering a network of PCs with flexible windows-style software to replace the mainframe system.

Better IT was the platform for a different organisational role. This aimed to give the NZES more latitude in selecting its priority clients. This new selectivity met the political need to remove a threat to the new labour market but, importantly it could also be justified as a means to help the most needy. If large numbers of workers became discouraged and were to choose welfare rather than low paid work, there would be insufficient pressure upon the rest of the unskilled workforce.

Work with Job Seekers

In order to mobilise resources in a more tailored, selective way, the NZES now required far more elaborate assessment procedures. These were based upon statistically verified knowledge about the levels of risk experienced by each client and the impact of particular barriers to employment upon their re-employment prospects. This information was then matched against a better understanding of employer needs and the structure of local labour markets.

Employment Advisers were defined in this system as the key linkage or 'node' in a dual track which created both a planning role and a marketing role. The former included the development of a work plan with the client and steps to overcome employment barriers. This contract with the client was premised on the offer that the NZES would fulfil its side of the bargain by providing intensive support to the client. This was primarily expressed as a willingness to provide personal support through interviews, but it also included access to some programs to facilitate the return to work.

The marketing role was defined as a method for targeting opportunities, establishing the needs of these opportunity providers and then 'selling' the available placement to the client. It emphasised the role of the adviser as broker of deals between these two processes. Both client and employer needed to be convinced, supported and given resources to achieve a satisfactory result. Advisers were defined as the 'process managers' who linked these two tracks to a common purpose.[2]

The main feature of the new system was the Job Action initiative. It was first introduced as a conscious adaptation of the UK model of

Restart interviews and the widely publicised OECD preference for 'work focus interviews' (Department of Labour, 1995, p. 1). The target group were all those who had reached two years on benefit. Job Action was to be a program based upon administrative treatments. This consisted of a compulsory interview to be conducted on a one-to-one basis. Those not attending were to be 'lapsed', the New Zealand term for having one's benefit suspended.

All those attending interviews were asked about their barriers to employment, had new data recorded regarding the work they now wished to find and any training needs they might have. They were also informed of their obligation to attend a five-day workshop run by local contractors. The purpose here was to motivate job seekers to search for work and to assist them in developing a signed search contract called the Job Action Plan.

The providers of workshops were appointed after a tender process conducted by NZES. Interestingly, unlike the UK model it copied, the NZES did not specify the actual content of the workshop and those tendering were required to nominate their preferred methodology. There was thus a good deal of variation among workshops. This increased the role of the local NZES managers and advisers who were called upon to assess and co-ordinate these agents.

Integration of the training and interviewing processes was provided through a shared responsibility to produce a signed contract using a standard form. It contained three pages on each of which the client was to nominate a job preference. Under each preference they were to list 'what I need to do', 'how I'm going to do it' and 'when I'll do it by'. These could include applications clients proposed to make for training courses, efforts to update résumés and numbers of 'cold canvass' inquiries to local employers.

Once signed the agreement formed the basis of future interviews at the local Employment Office with an adviser from one of the teams. The contact to be expected of clients and advisers was then left open, although internal documents did indicate that a minimum would be 'once every eight weeks' (Department of Labour, 1995, p. 5). The performance agreement between the government (Minister of Labour) and the NZES specified the exact number of outcomes to be achieved under each program heading. Targets were set for follow up interviews.

Further modifications enacted after 1996 were called 'Operation Future' and these used the Business Process Re-engineering design provided by Deloittes. It sought to improve the methods for streaming 'at risk' clients. Clients were assessed using a standard instrument which codified their likely degree of difficulty in finding work. This profiling system was the first major experiment in incorporating details of client demography and personal barriers into a systematic streaming process. This was also incorporated into new software and staff training systems. Those not in the 'at risk' categories would continue to attend the registration desk and avail themselves of vacancy listings pinned to Employment Office notice boards. However they would generally not receive active attention and continuous interviewing until they had claimed benefits for six months.

To perform the new roles of intensive interviewing of long-term and disadvantaged clients, and to broker new opportunities for assistance programs, the NZES elected to empower teams of advisers within the local offices rather than create a case manager relationship with a designated staff member. This was seen as a way of guaranteeing management flexibility at the local level as well as avoiding the perceived traps of case management which New Zealand bureaucrats viewed as 'welfarist' and prone to increase continuing claims for program assistance.

The pressure to implement the first stages of Operation Future meant that intensive assistance began before the new computer system was in place and before staff had been fully trained in the new disciplines of interviewing and client accountability. Implementation also proceeded ahead of plans to link the new local office roles to a system of performance payment for staff and a revised classification scale for advisers.

The chief effect of the Operation Future reform was to shift attention from routine processing tasks and the referral of 'best available' clients to vacancies towards work with a sub-population of priority clients. These 'at risk' groups were defined by their duration or predicted duration on benefits and to manage these groups the new regime used intensive interviewing and some motivational courses. Other clients were assigned to self-assistance and regular attendance to satisfy benefit requirements.

This system placed greater pressures on advisers to act as a personal advocate and counsellor, even though few had any formal training in these fields. Their task was to prevent long-term claimants becoming discouraged or lethargic, to get them interested in part-time or lower paid work that they might previously not have accepted, and to encourage them to alter any personal habits or attributes which might be unattractive to employers. This strategy was similar to the UK model. Some payments were also available for employers. But for the most part the exits from unemployment benefit by longer-term clients had to be achieved by finding open employment.

Despite the pressures, the NZ staff maintained a more optimistic outlook than did many of the advisers elsewhere, as Table 4.1 shows.

Table 4.1 System evaluations by New Zealand and other advisers (%)

Adviser Norms	NZ mean	Mean for all others
In your judgement how effective is the current employment service in helping clients find a job? (Number who say effective or very effective)	71	59
In your judgement how effective is the current employment service in getting clients off benefits? (Number who say effective or very effective)	56	35
The practice in my agency is to pick out the most capable welfare recipients and give them the best service. (Number who agree)	10	20
Based on the practices in your office today, what would you say is the more important goal of your agency: to help clients get jobs as quickly as possible or to raise education or skill levels of clients so they can get the job they want in the future? (Number favouring getting a job quickly)	31	55
How much does your agency emphasise giving clients a choice about the services they receive? (Number who say choice is important)	68	53
In your opinion, which is more often to blame if a person is on benefits: lack of effort on their part, or circumstances beyond their control? (Number who blame clients)	12	15
How much leeway do you have in deciding which program or activity the client should be assigned to? (Number who indicate they have leeway)	80	68

The regime was therefore designed to be intensive but informal at the interpersonal level. Claimants were 'trained' to reply promptly to interview requests from the Employment Office, to co-operate effectively in interviews and in the writing of new contracts or plans. To support this work-like environment for job seekers efforts were made at the local office level to avoid having clients stand in queues, miss appointments or fill out unnecessary forms, all of which were viewed as parts of the older attributes of client demotivation and bureaucratic dependency.

Comparing the New Zealand Strategy

If economic theory explains any part of the New Zealand reforms we can see that the NZES approach was more indebted to the 'theory of the firm' than to market theory. The re-engineering model (BPR) sought to enhance the role of the public employment service, not to break it up into a quasi-market. These institutional transitional changes departed from a more traditional form of bureaucratic service. But where were they heading? Apparently towards a hybrid form of corporate management which was to replace a previous infatuation with programs and targets with more elaborate and flexible relationship-building with employers and job seekers.

Terms like 'intensive assistance' and 'process management' were the outward signs of an experiment designed to rescue social programs from the onslaught of the neo-liberals. These neo-liberal critics at home and abroad saw benefits and training programs as impediments to creating a new kind of labour force motivated only by price signals and low wage incentives. They also regarded the NZES as an agency already captured by its job seeker clients.

The core of the strategy was the idea that those with the greatest barriers to employment could be 'walked' back into the mainstream of the labour market with an organisational process that gave priority to maintaining continuous contact with, and attachment to, the labour market and almost ceaseless activity. Next, the strategy aimed to systematically clear a path through the maze of entitlements and obligations using local advisers empowered by a better, simpler list of interventions. The creation of a climate or culture with activity and forward movement as the hallmark of both ultimate success and immediate performance gave the NZES a powerful framework for defining its new approach. The 'stair-case' metaphor provided advisers and managers with a new language for personal initiative and enterprise.

The NZES's efforts to develop this re-engineered model of service indicated a strong internal ethic in favour of job outcomes and program completions rather than sanctioning or shifting clients off the rolls. Virtually every signal to staff included the idea that the system was to be 'client centred' and every effort made to assist the most disadvantaged to overcome the obstacles created by a weak labour market.

Being a relatively small organisation the NZES could establish these stronger links between head office service philosophies and goals and local office protocols. The earlier attempts to use targets and 'The Nine O'Clock News' to tighten the head office grip on the local outlook enhanced the later impact of the BPR approach. A mix of senior and more junior officials worked energetically to model local office practices and then incorporate knowledge of these processes into the new system:

> there is an enormous front-end to this . . . you just disappear for the first months, trying to map what is really going on, it's quite rigorous in fact.
> They have been in and out of here quite a bit, particularly with the new computer system that drives all this (Futures) system . . . teaching us the steps

Table 4.2   Country and percentage responses to 'Have you always worked in this organisation?'

	Yes	No
Australia	38	60
Netherlands	29	70
New Zealand	22	77
United Kingdom	57	43

and also we have been sort of an experiment site to see how it works in practice . . . I was also quite a bit involved in earlier stages when they were, you
know, trying to really understand how clients move through the system.

The stronger and more individualising role of front-line staff was supported by recruitment practices which saw the NZES achieve an older
than average cohort of advisers and a career profile which was significantly more likely to have included work in some other agency or in
some other job (Table 4.2). As in the other three countries most advisers
were women (64 per cent). The fact that the NZ advisers had the highest
level of unionisation also suggests that many of these recruits came from
other public sector jobs such as teaching, welfare work and training.

The NZES offices were significantly smaller than all but the Australian private sector agencies, averaging twenty staff, almost all of whom
were involved in direct service to job seekers. Even more telling in the
New Zealand case is that most offices were small to medium sized, even
in the larger cities. In other countries the distribution of large and small
was more even. All of this tells us that, in the NZES strategy, the small
teams of advisers working in these settings had a multi-function role with
few levels or distinctions separating them:

> there are six of us doing interviews and two who mostly do registrations,
> induction . . . that sort of thing. I do a bit of that too if needed but it's just
> those two sort of roles . . . except for (the manager) of course.

The caseloads in the New Zealand system were high. The average of
138 was achieved by more staff carrying loads over 200 than in any other
system (Table 4.3). They reported an average of thirteen per day and
thus had three more appointments each day than the average across the
study. In other words this system processed by far the highest numbers
through its client contact regime. This high contact rate was also confirmed in the numbers of job seekers these advisers said were being
'followed closely', which at 47 per cent was the highest for the study.
High caseloads were also negatively correlated with the numbers of job

Table 4.3   Country and case loads (%)

	Up to 100	101 to 200	Over 200
Australia	36	40	25
Netherlands	53	9	38
New Zealand	22	18	60
United Kingdom	48	2	50

seekers being followed closely, indicating that there was a trade-off between the objective of contacting clients regularly and the degree of intensity that advisers brought to this relationship.[3]

To process these large numbers advisers used discretion and some flexibility. Despite the official commitment to profiling, the use of standard classification systems to define job seeker needs was not as popular as in the other systems. This was not a form of local governance that placed great store on detailed diagnostic work, nor on targets which required careful distinctions between hard and easy cases.

Instead the processes were driven by local availability of jobs and programs. The New Zealanders were the most likely to say that the availability of space within labour market programs and access to funds for special assistance determined the activities they recommended for each job seeker. This confirms the image of a re-engineering regime in which clients were moved energetically through steps which the adviser chose from a small defined list of options. Unlike the UK, however, neither targets nor time-triggers mandated these decisions. Advisers could decide the timing and in many cases the choice about whether clients went to a given activity. This both released them from some of the lock-step routine of the UK approach and also allowed the organisation to shift program resources around the system more easily. This also meant that advisers had to deal with the consequences of rationing from above by deciding for themselves who should have first call on scarce program places, further increasing the negative aspects of flexibility for them.

The level of knowledge and confidence which advisers expressed about these processes was high. They felt well informed about what was to be done in their job and rated highest in how well informed they felt about their own organisation's policies. Most interesting was their above average level of confidence in the use of technical knowledge and equipment. The BPR model relied very heavily on the central role of flexible information technology. While in interview these advisers expressed reservations about how well the system performed and cast some doubt on its flexibility at the local level, it is clear that they nevertheless felt involved and informed.

Table 4.4   New Zealand and other advisers' use of economic signals at work (%)

	New Zealand	Average for all others
I am well informed about the dollar value of interactions with each client (agree)	14	42
More and more the objective in this job is to maximise the organisation's financial outcomes (agree)	32	59
I do tend to take note of those actions with clients that will generate a payable outcome for the office (agree)	40	47

Of course information about the nature of their role and tasks, such as the best way to use the IT system, was not the same as knowledge about the adviser's actual performance. These advisers said that they did not feel as well informed about how well they were doing their jobs, perhaps because the process objectives involved high levels of personal effort but only rather general, global outcomes over which they lacked any real control:

> You put a lot into getting them going again . . . too much some times! You like get into all aspects of their lives, help them with everything . . . You ring them out of work hours to see how they went and you worry about them if you think (a job) rejection will send them back into depression or drugs or something . . . But we are not welfare . . . in the end you have other people to deal with too so you have to just keep going.

In systems that have a precise economic criterion for judging effectiveness, the ability of advisers to deliver value to the organisation is often measured in dollars. This is certainly the case in 'mixed economy' models such as those in Australia and the Netherlands. No such measures in New Zealand existed and advisers gave the lowest rating to this factor when describing the way they selected different forms of intervention for their job seeker clients. They were also least likely to say that they 'take note of the actions with clients that will generate a payable outcome for the office'. Similarly, the BPR approach holds targets to be a weak measure of real performance and one likely to create distortions, with advisers working to satisfy targets rather than to achieve real benefits for clients.

As well as being the least concerned with dollar outcomes the New Zealanders were also less likely to say that targets determined their work. The one place where such objectives did impact was in their work with special populations such as Maori, Pacific Island and the disabled for whom there were defined targets which almost all the advisers recognised. They rated these kinds of targets and their dollar outcomes more highly than any other country except the UK. But having targets for some types of client is not the same as having a target-based work system in which different interventions, such as referring to training or sanctioning, attract points on an output performance register.

Given the high work loads and the pressures they undoubtedly placed on local offices, it is not surprising that advisers defined their work as rather routine and said that they had little say in how their job was to be done, the sequence of tasks to be completed or the speed of work. They were above average in their tendency to be logged-on while interviewing job seekers – a good measure of the pressures they were under to manage large numbers using standard steps. The strong emphasis upon process objectives had its cost in far lower flexibility for staff to develop local approaches to their client population. These staff gave the lowest rating in the study to factors measuring adviser influence over changes to their work system; their level of job satisfaction was also low, although not as low as in the most tightly scripted system, that of the UK.

The paradox in this low level of satisfaction is that these advisers were nevertheless the most likely to say that they would be prepared to do even more to help their organisation. In other words they remained highly committed to their work even if the pressures sometimes pushed them harder than they wished, or provided worse pay and working conditions than they viewed as desirable and fair.

Front-line Networks

Measures of workloads tell us little about the interactive elements of the employment services system. Far more depends upon how their available time is spent on the range of possible interactions with those around them. Indeed it might be argued that in this case everything depends on the link between this high level of activity among advisers and the nature of the networks they created for themselves and their clients.

Following this logic, staff were asked to chart the way they divided 'an average week' and to map their frequency of contact with key actors involved in the return-to-work process. On the way they divided their time between different aspects of their job, the New Zealanders placed 'time spent with job seekers' at the top of their list, as did others. But the comparative measure showed them actually devoting less time overall to this task than others in this study. How can this be? If NZ staff have high loads and high numbers of daily contacts with job seekers, what time is there for other things? The analysis revealed that they spent more time contacting employers than others (21 per cent compared to the average of 14 per cent) and they did this more often:

Yes, it's just part of the approach we use now, to treat the employer as what we
call an opportunity provider and to just keep including them in the process.

It's quite a normal thing for me (to ring employers) and you know it's a
fine line, you don't want to hassle them but just follow-up 'How did it go?'
that sort of thing . . . I make a lot of those calls.

In New Zealand the front-line staff pursued a variety of employment-
oriented strategies. This brought advisers into direct contact with three
types of other agency. Daily interactions with welfare organisations were
far higher in this case than in any other system. For example some
45 per cent of New Zealand advisers reported that they spoke with
welfare agencies on a daily basis while the equivalent figure for advisers
in other systems was less than 4 per cent.[4]

High rates of interaction were also typical in the case of employers
and training agencies and in both instances the rate of contact was significantly higher than elsewhere. Also typical was higher than average
interaction with advisers in other agencies. In this case advisers said in
interview that they regularly discussed job seeker needs and barriers
with staff from rehabilitation organisations and the advisers in the
income support agency and social security department. But the highest
level of interaction was with other government agencies. Advisers regularly spoke with income support officials, health and housing office staff
and others who had some stake in the job seeker's future. Chapter 7
takes up this distinctive pattern of 'public networking' which involved
the officials doing far more than the basic task of directing job seekers to
available job vacancies. While it fell short of case management, this was
nevertheless a more elaborate service than that provided by the procedural governance type.

The higher levels of interaction with outside agencies helps explain
why these advisers spent less than half their time with job seekers even
though they still maintained regular contact with a larger number of job
seekers on their office case file. In other words, they used time during
interviews to sort out other problems as well as making many more calls
outside the formal interview process to follow up these issues. This kind
of networking was often done without paperwork and, together with the
greater reliance upon a more flexible PC-based computer interface with
programs and benefit issues, this also explains how the New Zealanders
came to have the lowest level of administrative downtime. Lower rates of
sanctioning also contributed to this reduced expenditure of effort on
paperwork for reasons discussed below.

Compared with advisers elsewhere, the New Zealanders showed high
confidence in the role of the newly acquired information technology
systems and few kept their own separate records on clients, preferring

Table 4.5 Country and percentage responses to 'I use the IT system to track priority clients'

	Disagree	Neither agree/disagree	Agree
Australia	36	23	41
Netherlands	24	33	43
New Zealand	6	16	76
United Kingdom	9	20	72

instead to use the computer files and interfaces with programs and procedures. Their high level of confidence in these new systems was evident in their willingness to use them to track the progress of priority clients (Table 4.5).[5]

The service these advisers provided to clients was based on frequent short, informal interviews and follow-up phone calls rather than highly scripted, standardised forms of case management or counselling. They frequently said in interview that they did not see their role as providing individual counselling and for this reason they often pointed out that theirs was not a welfare service or a form of case management. They distinguished their intensive employment assistance (IEA) service from case management on the basis that the latter was often person-centred and defined by deeper, quasi-professional efforts to understand and remedy health or psychological problems.

The advisers claimed that their role, skills and their high case loads did not permit this individualised commitment. Instead they acknowledged that their objective was actually to shift the maximum possible number of job seekers through the system and into work using the activation method. This shows through in the study's findings regarding client choice and the strong emphasis upon gaining trust where, in both cases, the New Zealand system rated significantly higher than the other comparable employment services. While all these systems place some priority on giving job seekers 'more choice about the services they receive', in the New Zealand case this was highest. They wished clients to 'take a positive step' towards the various activities on offer and saw their primary objective as being to find a way to tap the agency or volition of otherwise passive and disheartened clients:

> So many of them have really had enough of being pushed and pulled around . . . they have seen it all and done it all, some of them over five to ten years. You have to win them over, convince them and get them to choose to seize the opportunity.

The considerable effort expended in gaining trust, holding discussions about client progress, involving other agencies and developing an agreed, re-motivation plan for each selected client was established and then reinforced throughout the BPR plan. It was interesting then that these advisers placed the highest rating in the study on the need for everyone involved to reinforce the same message with the job seeker. This was not a matter of personal empowerment or marketing by the adviser working with her own job seekers but of structured organisational effort.

Sanctions

Nevertheless, advisers used pressure to activate clients. Disciplinary objectives were not ignored. While policy makers inside the NZES made a conscious effort to view the new model as largely a 'pro-client' methodology, so far as NZES was concerned, an important part of the new system was to be 'a change of role regarding work testing'. Work testing is the New Zealand term for the use of disciplinary powers to alter client behaviour and to remove wayward clients from benefits. Staff were now to be encouraged to be more vigilant in work testing clients who failed to undertake agreed activities.

In the corporate management system established in the late 1980s there had been increases in powers for staff at the front line to recommend a work test if they regarded the client as seriously remiss in their efforts to find work, or flagrant in their refusal to attend training programs. However the standard penalty then for failing a work test was loss of benefits for twenty-six weeks. This regime of very severe penalties was further reinforced by the restrictions to benefit enacted by the National Government after 1990.

However the corporate management system created after 1988 had given local managers very strong incentives to move clients through the system in a fast but friendly manner. This approach was replicated in the income support service. There were thus very few incentives for advisers to spend time and effort on individual cases or to engage in conflict with other agencies to prove their case in disputes over work testing.

The actual method for implementing the work test at that time was also purpose-built to allow clients maximum flexibility in avoiding sanctions. Employment advisers reported in interview that they seldom reached even the early stages of dispute resolution over sanctioning and even less often did they remove clients from benefits.

A variety of reasons were given. Many advisers viewed the long period without income as impossibly harsh and said they would only proceed where they were convinced the client had already taken some form of paid work and was thus cheating the benefit system. A deeper reluctance based upon commitment to the client and professional pride in being an advocate of the client's future prospects was also evident in interviews. Moreover, the numbers of clients subjected to work tests were not reported in the main output tables used to measure performance in the corporate management period, unlike the system adopted in the UK under the JSA.

Under the new 'intensive assistance' system implemented from the mid-1990s work testing became an integral and official part of the process for re-motivating priority clients to reach sustained outcomes. In place of the 26-week rule, benefits could now be withdrawn for set periods graduated according to the severity of the offence and often initially targeted at periods of six weeks. Senior management in NZES acknowledged that the lower threshold was set as a direct response to the fact that their advisers could not easily be made to enforce the stronger penalties that were likely to deprive families of food and rent. The new, graduated and case-sensitive set of penalties also allowed system designers to incorporate compliance objectives more easily into the defined steps outlined in the 'stair-case' process, thus removing some of the discretion from the sanctioning process.

Movement through these steps now became the organisational means to define compliance. This was reflected in the fact that the New Zealand advisers were those most likely to use referral to a program as a means to prepare a case for sanctioning. In other words, the compliance issues now rested on a series of micro-objectives rather than simply on major eligibility disputes.

While managers reported in interview that this process engineering had led to an increase in sanctioning, especially for 'administrative' matters, compared to the other three systems this was not a harsh regime. The sanction rate reported by advisers was the lowest in the study. Furthermore New Zealand advisers also gave the lowest estimates of the numbers of clients they believed would 'rather stay on benefits' than take work.

Where New Zealand differed from other systems was on penalties for being sacked or leaving a job. Here, two factors played a part in determining which issues would attract a sanction: the greater willingness to accept that job seekers have legitimate choices about their employment options and the pro-client stance implied in the reactivation strategy. Since these were the issues which required independent knowledge about who was at fault, the New Zealand case might also be regarded as the one in which advisers remained unwilling to pit their own judgements against what job seekers might say. Given that all such cases still had to be presented to an independent decision maker at the income support agency, these could also be regarded as the kinds of cases where hard facts were more difficult to establish and costly disputes more likely to consume scarce time at the front line.

While this system clearly remained highly regulated, it was also less procedural than the classic resort to rules would lead us to expect. Central policy directives, communicated uniformly and hierarchically, continued to motivate advisers. They did admit to regularly reminding clients about the sanctioning powers and they were the most likely of all the advisers to refer cases to a superior for advice. However the bureaucratic elements were focused in a particular way. There were few rules. Targets for such things as sanctioning were either absent or minimal. Uniformity and standardisation occurred through the transactions and processes mandated by the BPR method rather than by formal regulation and supervision.

This appeared to create an openly acknowledged trade-off between motivating and activating clients and punishing them. Issues that would occasion a sanction in other systems did not produce such actions here. For example, these advisers were significantly less likely to 'work test' their clients for failure to contact their office, a very common means for generating higher sanction rates in other systems. And the universal focus upon moving large numbers through the stair-case method sent a clear signal to advisers not to become waylaid by costly efforts to use sanctions as a way of diverting clients off the rolls and into welfare from where, sooner or later, they would return to the employment assistance system.

Conclusions

The New Zealand reforms drew their authority from a temporary bout of bi-partisanship occasioned by the changed electoral system and subsequent Task Force recommendations. This placed great emphasis on an informal, national social contract to give long-term job seekers priority for new services. In addition the institutional autonomy of the NZES gave it flexibility to define its own strategy for meeting the budget objectives set in the Chief Executive's contract. Of particular importance to this form of authority was the separation of employment objectives from wider social security concerns such as sanctioning and the cutting of benefits.

The New Zealand distinction between policy and administration was therefore expressed as a division between outputs and outcomes. The Minister was seen as responsible for outcomes (policy) while the contracted agency was in change of producing the outputs ordered by the government. This plainly gave the public servants employed in the NZES some short-term insulation from complaint if actual levels of employment and unemployment rose or fell. As senior staff saw it this output–outcome distinction preserved the important right for the Labour Minister to be allowed 'to find his own road to hell'.

Advisers moved from a target-driven bureaucracy to a process-driven service. They focused on the more difficult clients, they worked energetically to use direct personal contacts as a means to re-motivate these clients, and they employed a set of simplified programs to 'step them' towards the labour market and open employment. The adoption of the re-engineering model for reform was thus able to have a significant effect upon front-line work. Advisers became process managers but not case managers.

Training programs were cut back to a small list of search-related activities of short duration. Some courses designed to 'polish' skills in word processing or hospitality did play a part and there were a few special initiatives designed to help Maori and Pacific Islanders. But the path for most was defined by the selection by local advisers of a set of minimal interventions aimed at activating clients and bringing them into close and regular contact, first with the Job Centre and then with employers.

Provided they kept moving forward, clients were not subject to strong pressures to take jobs they did not want. The more limited list of programs was also a means of allowing advisers to move their high case loads efficiently and in large numbers and this they did using an integrated set of re-motivation steps. The exact sequence and selection of these steps was left to advisers at the local level, the main imperative being funding levels and program vacancies.

This then was the charm and the paradox of the New Zealand approach: an underlying system of treatments was clearly prescribed for advisers who worked with very large numbers and who had limited resources. Yet the heart of the strategy was to motivate both advisers and clients by encouraging them to view regular and sometimes superficial interactions as a means of jointly creating new opportunities. In place of rules, directives, incentives and targets it elevated a few standard, well accepted processes based on informal interactions. It also depended upon the recruitment of an experienced, older team of advisers capable of working with high numbers and selective, informal interventions.

The concerted movement of clients through the 'stair-case' method, supported by better IT systems, acted as both a structure for containing the discretion of front-line staff and for limiting the recourse to programs for programs' sake. Instead advisers evidently moved within a flexible environment where there were few rules, little recourse to classifications and measurements but many 'softer' day-to-day expectations for both job seekers and their advisers: softer in the sense that no one's payment schedule was immediately at stake. But the process-driven approach to re-engineering also remained very centralised from the budget point of view. Advisers had some access to funds for one-off expenses such as getting clothes for job applicants to wear to interview, or paying travel expenses to get to a new job, but these were in short supply. The dominant philosophy of the local office was to channel clients through the existing set of steps, using centrally funded programs.

This intensive assistance regime was thus a pool of interventions which was shallow at one end. The depth of the service was to be found at the management end where it was measured as a series of highly effective project team initiatives, system-wide processes, clever combinations of flexible technology and the sustained use of short programs. But at the client and adviser end this flexibility was more limited and the performance regime was shallow. Either the personal commitment levels and maturity of advisers would have to sustain it, or new reforms to link employment assistance to other public interventions would eventually be needed.

The clear emphasis of the service was to create a highly positive, informal interaction with clients, particularly the long-term claimants. The point of the contact, however, was to make clear to the job seeker that they were now on the road back to work and that every effort was now going to be used to see that they arrived. This would involve some sanctioning and threats of sanctions, but it did not depend on this. The social model implied in the strategy was integration through active brokering between the individual and key 'opportunity providers'. Working as a guide and coach, the adviser was viewed as the primary form of agency through which bureaucratic and institutional obstacles could be negotiated. This was less a matter of the expenditure of resources than a question of skill and recruitment.

That this strategy conforms with key attributes of the 'corporate governance' model is obvious. Keeping the service limited to a few core programs and objectives, and linking these directly to ministerial dictates and central budgets, speaks loudly of the centralising logic of the corporate type. But by releasing advisers from the prison of lock-step processes and targets the NZES approach also broke new ground. The 'process manager' attributes hinted of a network model yet to come. Interactions with other agencies increased. The emphasis on trust was strong. Employers became a structured part of the process. Only the rigidity of the divisions between the various government organisations in the field and the lack of any real resource flexibility at the local level stopped this from evolving into a stronger form of network governance.

Notes

1 Finance Minister Ruth Richardson argued that the lowest wage rates being paid at the time were NZ$363 per week and an unemployed person with three children was entitled to NZ$341 from unemployment benefits, supporting the claim that 'low-income workers should not be penalized compared with those on benefits' (1995, p. 84).

2 Implementation of the new IEA system did not wait for the Task Force Report but began in September 1994 with the introduction of the Job Action program for long term claimants. It was then refined and modified by a more systematic internal restructure in 1996–97 called 'Operation Future'. For present purposes these two internal reforms may be considered as part of a single regime directed at intensive, selective service delivery for the 'risk management' of the system's most costly clients, the long-term unemployed.

3 Caseload and numbers followed closely; r=.30 sig. at p=.03.

4 'How often would you have some form of contact (including telephone) with welfare agencies' By Country, significant at .0000.

5 Since these systems had only been in place for approximately twelve months at the time of the study it may be that their confidence in them could be discounted as an artifact of their novelty. Repeat visits to the Wellington Central office nine months apart gave no indication of such effects, however.

CHAPTER 5

The Netherlands:
The Part-Time Miracle

In the summer of 1983 the Netherlands unemployment rate jumped to an alarming 14 per cent, forcing the political élite to contemplate its first radical revision to its postwar welfare state. This shock was a particular insult to a system in which, by its own account, 'the government "takes care" of its citizens from the cradle to the grave' (Sociale Zaken en Werlagelegenheid, 1997, p. 10). Yet by 1999 the unemployment rate had fallen to 4 per cent, while neighbouring countries continued to battle with double digit levels. This change, and the government strategies underpinning it, led to widespread debate about the vices and virtues of the 'Dutch Disease' and 'Dutch Miracle' (Visser & Hemerijck, 1997; van der Veen & Trommel, 1999).

By the mid-1990s so widespread was the acclaim for the Dutch approach that *Die Ziet*, *Le Monde* and *The Economist* held it up as a model for others in the OECD to follow. However, under sustained attack, especially from the Germans, where no less an authority than the Wissenschaftzentrum in Berlin condemned the Dutch reforms as 'nothing more than a shell game' (Cox, 1998, p. 210), *The Economist* promptly withdrew its endorsement and it became equally fashionable to dismiss all the Dutch achievements as a mirage. For present purposes it only needs acknowledging that the Netherlands during this period became one of Europe's leading exponents of public management reform and that the enterprising spirit seen in the other cases was clearly evident here. Moreover the Dutch strategy appeared to employ a form of co-operation and institutionalised bargaining that seemed to qualify it as a strong case of 'network governance'. For instance, it had an elaborate system for involving employers and unions directly in the running of employment services. It also structured these interests into a complex system of training and supported employment. And to complete the picture of elaborate inter-dependency, in the two years prior to study the Dutch had been experimenting with service delivery partnerships between the public employment service and two private recruitment agencies. To what extent could the Dutch miracle be associated with successful co-production and networking? And what would the Netherlands experience tell us about the durability of network theories and concepts for the wider debate about new governance strategies?

Like the other countries in this study, the Netherlands reforms to employment assistance were born in the early 1980s when the costs of social assistance seemed to rise without relief. As elsewhere, changes in the state's own institutional arrangements were occasioned by strong economic and budgetary pressures, although the path chosen was unique. Between 1970 and 1985 the number of Dutch citizens receiving benefits doubled. Unemployment had grown rapidly during the recession of the early 1980s, had then recovered in the second half of that decade, only to jump again in the early 1990s.

After 1979 the Dutch government began experimenting with financial incentives to encourage firms to develop part-time work. Although later seen as a failure because of its cost to government and its overly complex goals, the experiment helped set new expectations for employers, unions and other interests. Most important to this new framework of expectations was a joint agreement in 1982 between unions, employers and government to achieve wage moderation, known as the Agreement of Wassenaar. This was the first step towards a complex set of agreements over workplace change which are often referred to as the 'Delta Model' (Becker, 1999). This resulted in statutory wage increases staying below the level of economic growth in almost every year from this point onwards.

However this was not simply a process leading to neo-liberal orthodoxy. The unions along with their parliamentary allies on the left had now largely accepted the economic doctrine that reduced wage claims result in higher profits, higher investment and better job growth. With collective wage agreements covering approximately 80 per cent of the Dutch workforce, unions were in a position to deliver restraint. Employers and governments had to take union interests seriously. Moreover the Dutch political system had for most of the century produced three large and powerful party groups – Labour, Liberal and Christian Democrat – with none commanding sufficient votes to enforce a majority view. So when efforts initiated by the Christian Democrats in the early 1980s to couple wage restraint with curbs on social security benefits resulted in rising unemployment, coalition politics quickly demanded a different bargain: 'Hence, instead of welfare for work, the shared or parallel need became jobs for welfare' (Kemen, 1999, p. 264; see also Hemerijck & van Kersbergen, 1997).

Employment Conditions

Part of this strategy involved creating more flexible employment opportunities and included a government initiative to reduce impediments to part-time work which were created by aspects of the social security system. Already comparatively sympathetic to part-time work, these social security laws governed such things as access to full health insurance. In January 1993 the government removed the working hours threshold, making access to minimum wages and holidays available to part-timers. Access to attractive pension schemes was also made compulsory, forcing employers to grant new security to those in part-time work.

These policies made a virtue out of necessity. Part-time work was already a major element in the Dutch economy and it got there by dint of social change rather than political engineering. Women entering the workforce often started with part-time jobs. Dutch policy makers admit that part-time work did not originate with them, nor was it the preference of unions and employers; 'It just came our way', one senior public servant is quoted as saying (Schmitter & Grohe, 1997, p. 539).

The growth of part-time work in the Netherlands meant that average annual working hours were lower than anywhere else in Europe. The rate also fell relative to earlier Dutch levels.[1] Most importantly part-time work became the more likely destination for unemployed people. Three-quarters of unemployed women entered the workforce through a part-time job as did 40 per cent of men. The comparable rate for men in other European countries was 10 per cent (Becker, 1999, p. 4).

In December 1994 a moderate Liberal-Social Democrat Coalition again brought together the employers and unions to strike a new deal for jobs, social assistance and government spending. This 'packet' involved a trade-off between future wage rises and reductions in working hours, these reductions to be felt either in weekly hours or in annual leave. For example, five collective agreements saw annual leave increase to 5 weeks in many industries. 'In many sectors (public as well as private) the number of working hours has been reduced to a maximum of 32, 36 or 38 per week by collective agreement.'[2]

This also encouraged employers to look for more part-time and temporary workers to fill the empty spaces thus created, rather than rely upon overtime or full-time replacements. The government reduced the social insurance contributions which employers and employees made, the health insurance contributions made by employers and the income tax paid by low wage workers. These things all made part-time work more attractive and helped create the Dutch model of the 'one and a half job household'.[3] While the basic 'floor' of social benefits was maintained, after 1994 the administration of benefits began to follow a 'logic of incentives' rather than a 'logic of entitlements'. This meant that more was expected from recipients in their efforts to gain work, social security staff were required to enforce stricter rules of eligibility, and municipalities and other providers of services were given budgets which rewarded them for being tougher in their allocation of funds to recipients (van der Veen & Trommel, 1999).

Further changes to the unemployment benefit system were made in 1995 when the entitlement period for 'monitoring and training subsidies was reduced'. The new *Social Assistance Act* of 1996 required claimants to give more information about assets, earnings and their personal living arrangements. Job search activity was made more stringent and penalties for failure were increased substantially. Those required to search for work now included parents with children over five and certain categories of disabled workers. The range of administrative sanctions available to social security staff was increased. Van der Veen and Trommel (1999, p. 305) show that sanctions increased from around 7 per cent of claimants in 1987 to 17 per cent in 1994.

The Employment Service

The policy of all Dutch governments since 1950 had been to use a tripartite structure to manage the welfare state. The selection of the 'social partners' – labour and business – showed the central importance of the wage earner as the object of social assistance. Attention to the needs of families and women outside the work place had been less central. At ground level a mix of social insurance and public welfare determined access to income support among unemployed citizens. The government provided a basic welfare benefit but also obliged employers and workers to take out insurance against unemployment. Benefit entitlements and rights had dominated this system. However after the shocks of the early 1980s the development of an active labour market policy had been far more energetic, resulting in a transformation of the public employment service.

Until just before this study a single public employment service had managed all Welfare-to-Work activities for job seekers. This service – the Arbeids Voorziening (AV) – had become a stand-alone public organisation during the 1980s when many service delivery organisations were separated from the mainstream public service. As a statutory agency it was managed by a National Board composed of employers, unions and representatives of the Ministry of Social Affairs and Employment.

According to the Ministry a 'large part of (its) policy was implemented by autonomous organisations'[4] such as the employment service.

The employment service (AV) negotiated partnership agreements with other organisations involved in providing social assistance or return to work services. It wrote contracts with the Dutch social insurance companies which managed income support for those paying unemployment insurance. It also formed strategic partnerships with two recruitment firms, Start and Vedior. Each of the eighteen regions had the same structure composed of a tripartite board (RBA) and local agreements with other agencies.

The AV registered job seekers and provided job matching, counselling and vocational training. Those seeking income support had first to register as job seekers and any failure to comply with AV requirements could result in a report being sent to the social insurance company responsible for that person's income support payment. During the late 1980s and 1990s the AV took the view that it should provide employers with a comprehensive service and not simply submit unemployed job seekers to whatever vacancies were available. This was a model of flexible co-production; 'the basic premise here is not to provide the full service ourselves but to enter into cooperation with a view to achieving a win–win situation'.[5]

The Netherlands also had a sophisticated internal system for vocational training, responsibility for which was shared between central government, employers and employees. At each regional level employment councils took responsibility for implementing training policy through their own network of training services. These 'social partners', as they were called in the Netherlands, were actively involved in defining the national qualification structure and through collective agreements they negotiated such things as training leave, employment of apprentices and local programs for in-work subsidies. Attention by government was focused on 'second chance education and training' for disadvantaged social groups including the long-term unemployed. Grants were provided for unemployed people to undergo training.

The central philosophy of the employment service was that the key problem for unemployed job seekers was their lack of 'a good competitive position'. This position included a 'discrepancy' between worker and employer with regard to 'social and personal skills and attitude . . . (client and service orientation, flexibility, entrepreneurship, motivation etc.)'.[6] Using a structured and systematic approach, the AV during the 1990s divided their service into four types. A basic ('phase one') service was provided to all job seekers and this included the standard forms of registration, assessment, vacancy information, some career information and submissions to available vacancies. There was also a workshop available for those needing help with making job applications. The assessment was based on answers to set questions: age, country of birth, hours of work wanted, ability to specify an appropriate job, work experience, length of unemployment, willingness to travel up to three hours per day, strategy in mind to find work, home care responsibilities, and physical and mental health status.

In Phases Two and Three the employment service used some government funds and some funds raised from the insurance boards and the municipalities to provide certain extra services for 'distant from the labour market' clients. This mainly involved work experience programs, retraining or refresher training. In Phase Four the service sought to 'keep active those employment seekers who are too far removed from the labour market to be competitive in order to be able to approach the labour market at a later date'.[7] In essence these workers were transferred to special programs run by the municipalities or community sector organisations where they had quasi-jobs, or jobs which attracted a full subsidy.

Underwriting the phased-service model was an elaborate vocational training strategy based on what they termed a 'flexible modular system' in which clients received just enough training to get them a job with a known employer or in a known industry. This might mean two days, one half-day per week, or several weeks. Training was said to be 'custom made for the individual student and the future employer'.[8] Officials claimed an 80 per cent employment outcome for graduates of training, and this included graduation into part-time work.[9]

Private Partnerships

Undoubtedly the most interesting feature of the Dutch case from the governance perspective was the partnership developed between the AV and two private recruitment firms, Start and Vedior. These two companies specialised in the temporary work market. In order to capitalise upon the opportunities provided within this sector, in the late 1970s the Dutch Ministry of Social Affairs and Employment began to experiment with placing unemployed workers in temporary positions. Until this point this had been forbidden because their insurance and social security rights had stipulated that only full-time, regular work was to be considered an appropriate outcome.

Using a tripartite board and a non-profit company structure, Start was created in 1978. The Ministry began offering employers job seekers chosen from the unemployment rolls of local labour offices. At first the senior management of Start was drawn from the public service, but by the late 1980s the organisation had evolved into a private agency, much like its competitors. In the mid 1990s when unemployment pressures again made public sector job creation a difficult option, policy makers sought to strengthen the role of private agencies. Start was made independent of the Ministry, its constitution as a foundation (non-profit organisation) was removed and it was reformed as a private company.

In addition another major temporary work agency, Vedior, was contracted as a supplier of opportunities for unemployed job seekers. Vedior/ASB is a subsidiary of one of Europe's larger employment agencies, Vedior International N.V. From 1996 these two private agencies were established as the preferred providers of temporary work opportunities in the Netherlands. A key to understanding the partnership strategy was the December 1994 agreement which followed a critical evaluation of the AV. Budget cuts and reductions of staff were implemented at this time.[10] Co-operation between public and private agencies was also mandated, but 'not based exclusively on market forces but on statutory regulation'.[11]

In 1997 the three organisations entered a further stage of innovative partnership in the establishment of a new special projects foundation or company, ASV. This was a private company owned equally by the three organisations. Its purpose was to offer combined services to social security and insurance firms, large employers, and special new developments. In practice it meant that there need be little adverse competition and far less secrecy between the three. They agreed that current clients remained with their existing employment agency, and new services would be split equally via ASV, a vehicle for sharing out new opportunities.

The success of the private firms was based on their ability to supply employers with temporary workers. The temporary work companies had two types of contract with employers and they used these to find jobs for some job seekers from the AV rolls. The first type was called 'Uitzenden' and involved placing a job seeker in a job of one day to six months. The employer took the job seeker as a regular employee and met all costs, wages and so on. A second type of contract, called 'Detacheren' involved the temporary work company acting as employer for one or more employees who were then outsourced to a firm under a labour supply contract. In this case the firm owed no direct obligation to the employee and all wages, insurance and the like were paid by the temporary work company.

The contract between the AV and these private firms was open-ended and evolutionary. For example the actual agreement was not tied to a fixed period. In 1998 it involved a commitment 'for a number of years, that will be evaluated periodically'. In contrast, contracts with vocational training centres were based on annual block purchases of places, but were later required to 'realise a business-like purchasing relationship'.[12] This was viewed by advisers and managers as a key development that would indicate the future structure of the whole sector.

In practice these partnership relationships with Start and Vedior were somewhat complex. While there was no direct competition for job seekers, there was evident rivalry between the two private agencies, and sometimes within the AV itself. Each might seek to refer a job seeker to a job and in theory the individual job seeker might be contacted by each of the three offices. In practice the private firms only used the public office list when they could find no other client on their own list or when the use of a public office client attracted a subsidy for an employer. Middle range public clients, that is, those ready for work but not yet placed, were less a problem for the public office than were more difficult, or in the Dutch idiom, more 'distant' clients. These were also less attractive to the private offices, reducing the effect of overt competition. However this dampening effect was far from uniform. In some regions and sectors the Netherlands had labour shortages and in these cases there was pressure to take even the more difficult cases out of training and place them in temporary work.

The employment service staff said they had emulated many aspects of what they saw in the private sector. They reported these changes with enthusiasm and no sense of loss of their previous work methods:

> We learned a lot from them, in the time we worked together, in a way to approach a company for instance, to work very fast when you needed that, and to think in a commercial way. I think that's good, because companies do that also. We have to talk the same language.

In other words the private employment agency provided another bridge into the world of the private employer and into new ways to organise the delivery of services.

The view which private agencies took of themselves confirmed a difference in emphasis. Managers of private agencies stressed that they sought new staff who 'are used to earning their own living', and 'practical people' who 'cannot possibly come from a social organisation'. The term 'social' in this context referred to 'welfare' or 'philanthropic' organisations who were seen to be too soft on clients and too relaxed in their work habits.[13]

Relations between the AV and the two private agencies underwent some strain during 1998 and 1999 as the government put greater pressure on the employment service to place larger numbers of longer-term job seekers. Start and Vedior had no such commitment and therefore did not necessarily do anything explicit to help meet this target.

So our first task is to bring people who are long-term unemployed to the market. And Start is not equipped to do the same. They want to have a fast contact with an employer and make the deal and earn the money.

In summary, the reform of the Dutch system had involved three macro-level components. The demand for labour was conditioned by a social and governmental preference for part-time work that had become a key element in rising employment levels and declining unemployment. This was coupled with strong growth in the economy as a whole, and with clever strategies for introducing job seekers to temporary work opportunities. The second element of the reforms involved changes to social security rules and entitlements that saw greater pressure being applied to restrict access, punish poor performance by recipients and accelerate exits from benefits. The third component was the institutional change within the employment services system that saw a more devolved form of neo-corporatism being drawn back under tighter central control. This included cuts to the AV annual budgets, targets for improved outcomes, and pressures to involve private providers of services in a more incentive-based system.

Comparing the Netherlands Strategy

By the mid-1990s many of the same pressures seen elsewhere were evident in the Dutch system. Managers and policy makers were questioning the 'entitlement mentality' of the social security system. The authority of unions and employers sitting on government boards was being eroded in favour of stronger forms of political management. And the governance arrangements more generally were evolving towards a 'mixed-economy' of public and private agencies working in partnership but under conditions of increasing pressure over levels of performance.

While there was less political heat in Dutch debates over privatisation, as one central agency bureaucrat put it in interview, that might have been because 'we are already privatised . . . the unions and the employers share ownership of these businesses and have done for many years'. This was also acknowledged by the advisers:

Ownership? This is a point. It used to be government owned and now there are three parties, like government, employers, representatives from employer's organisations and unions.

How this might affect services and how a de-coupled, 'autonomous' public employment service would interact with its clients and customers could certainly be expected to differ from elsewhere. In particular the Dutch model appeared from its design characteristics to embody a 'networked' structure. This was supported by other studies which identify the Netherlands as part of a 'Rhenish' model of collectivist, consensus-seeking democracies (Rhodes & van Apeldoorn, 1998). In fact the findings of the research point not to elaborate and flexible networks so much as a more structured form of partnership in which a strong public sector was used as the hub of a co-ordinated system of universal, relatively non-coercive services. These included some more selective activities for job seekers and some defined, carefully managed forms of private sector participation. The partnership was enterprising in the sense that the public and private participants sought to increase business and to create new products to sell to employers. But a strong public service mission to assist the unemployed also continued.

So the public office remained central to the new system. Dutch job seekers who received income support had to register with the public employment service and after that were required to follow a plan devised by a public employment adviser. This process brought everyone to the door of the local Arbeids Bureau (Labour Office) where a diagnostic assessment process then determined which mix of training, counselling and job search was to be provided. The Dutch public advisers were the most likely in the study to use formal assessment tools to decide activities for their clients, closely followed by their private sector colleagues. At this stage the private firms were then empowered to select job seekers they believed might be suitable for a private placement. This was done with the co-operation of the local employment service office and the resulting placement benefited both organisations. The public office claimed one more successful placement and the private temporary work company satisfied its employer client who would then pay for this service.

This public sector work was done in comparatively large offices where unionisation was surprisingly low. In the 1997 sample only 37 per cent of public officials reported union membership and only 12 per cent of private advisers were members.[14] Given the neo-corporatist history of the Dutch institutions, this low level of unionisation was unexpected. Looked at across the four countries the AV was just above average for its rate of union membership, while the private advisers were well below the mean.

The Dutch staff were also considerably younger than their colleagues in the other countries with the Dutch average being in the twenty-five to thirty-four age group. Two-thirds of these were women, a pattern replicated in the other countries. These advisers were also much more likely to have recently started work in their current job and to have had other job experiences in addition to their work as an employment adviser. This latter characteristic was despite their comparative youth. So while performing what are usually held to be traditional administrative tasks they were less like the standard image of the long-serving, single-employer type which we expect in public programs. Only 37 per cent had worked with their current employer for more than five years, easily the lowest rate in the study as a whole. Youth and mobility were therefore the distinctive characteristics of the staff.

The nature of the working environment was typified in the very high case loads carried by Dutch advisers. The loads were the highest of all four countries. At more than 140 job seekers for every adviser employed, this ratio seemed well outside the norm for any recognised intensive service approach. Interviews and the observation visits suggest that job seekers were being managed in a highly standardised manner, at least for the purposes of registration and initial service provision. Advisers in the local office sought to follow up their own contacts with their own clients but they also shared files with other advisers using the common IT platform. In contrast to systems which use customer or client-focused methods for dealing with underlying health and welfare problems, the Dutch advisers did not normally have an exclusive list of their 'own' job seekers for whom they were responsible. This did not mean they lacked any intensive engagement with those they served. Rather this closer checking and support was reserved for a smaller number and tended to be shared with others in their office and perhaps with temporary work agencies where they saw an opportunity to refer individuals to Start or Vedior.

Importantly, then, these high case loads did not translate directly into high levels of time spent in contact with job seekers. For example, the Dutch advisers reported quite low numbers of job seekers interviewed each day. More than half of public sector advisers saw five job seekers per day or fewer. Approximately one quarter saw more than eleven each day. In the private sector just over 40 per cent saw eleven or more.[15] In other words the Dutch staff combined high intensity with a minority of job seekers with a high overall responsibility for managing a larger pool of job seekers.

This mix of high case loads and low rates of daily contacts by public advisers indicated that many of the ongoing relationships with clients were of quite low intensity. Either everyone received a limited amount of contact through interviews, or the total population of job seekers registered at any given office were divided into those who would receive greater attention and those who would be left to search under their own steam. In interviews advisers reported that the intensity of contact with the client varied considerably, depending on which of the four defined categories of need, or 'phases', the client fell into. In other words this change in intensity was a direct result of standardised forms of assessment and streaming in the public office.

Public officials saw significantly fewer clients than their private colleagues and spent more time assessing their needs and evaluating their barriers to employment. They also devoted more effort to considering training opportunities and in-work activities than did private advisers, the latter being primarily concerned with immediate placements. Advisers at Start agreed that they had some training services to offer job seekers, but these were limited and included only such things as helping administrative-clerical job seekers learn new versions of the necessary software, or polish their skills in using new telephone systems. Job seekers who needed more than this level of assistance would either be sent back to the public office or, in a small percentage of cases, allocated to the Start Foundation, a philanthropic arm of the organisation devised to assist disadvantaged groups such as the disabled. However, this was not considered normal business for advisers who mostly placed their emphasis upon meeting the employer's need for staff, not the job seeker's need for assistance.

As noted above, almost all public officials used a classification instrument and approximately three-quarters of the private advisers reported doing so. However when asked whether 'answers to set questions' were used to determine what activities were to be recommended for job seekers, less than half said that such instruments were important. The figure was significantly lower for private advisers. Here the use of set questions and common data gathering was regulated through a quality management process based on ISO protocols. This set the objectives for the induction of job seekers into the organisation's processes and for recording decisions and outcomes ('it's a method of work and we follow that method'). Public and private advisers had in common the need to follow set processes for gathering information, but it appears that actual decision making about clients was not then determined by these processes. This suggested that classification was mostly used to stream clients after which the advisers were empowered to use more discretionary strategies.

The greater reliance on the use of set questions by the public adviser therefore had two likely explanations. No doubt the compliance aspects of the public system required a higher level of certainty, if not uniformity, in the way actions were selected for each client. The wider range of job seekers served at the public office might also explain why they resorted to more standardisation in order to manage the consequent complexity. Private advisers started with a narrower base of applicants and could always decide not to register someone if they did not believe they would find a job quickly. Public advisers could not. They had to be better prepared for problems or challenges. Nevertheless when asked about the extent to which they were able to use their 'own judgement' in deciding what to do with clients, the public advisers reported higher levels of discretion. In other words the paradox of higher standardisation coupled with high discretion is explained by differences in the range of job seekers and therefore in the level of risk faced by the advisers. Higher risk required both more standardisation and higher discretion.

Public advisers who worked with higher risk job seekers, who were termed 'further distant from the labour market', also had more complex choices and strategies available to them than in the other countries under study. When job seekers reached six months' unemployment or were deemed by advisers to be in an 'at risk' category, they were said to be involved in a re-entry 'process'. Both local advisers and those at the regional office participated in diagnosing which kind of process would suit the client and in the selection of activities:

> when somebody comes in, we do an intake, we call it . . . we always have a diagnosis . . . And then we decide what to do. And we have different products, let's call it, very simply. One of the products, it is a very big one, in this region, is work experience with Philips.

The complexity of these actual strategies, perhaps involving negotiations with training institutes, sympathetic employers and staff from the social insurance office, meant that the level of routine was quite low, in fact the lowest of any group in the study, including their private sector colleagues. It also helped explain why the Dutch advisers actually spent less time with job seekers than did almost all others in the study. Instead their amount of time with employers was the highest of all, with the private advisers even higher than those from the Dutch public office.

The amount of time devoted to administrative work was also high, perhaps because the Dutch system involved more formal relationships with other service providers such as training institutes and Regional Employment Boards. The transactions for these various processes, special agencies, local deals with employers and unique projects generated a variety of reports, meetings and extra forms of accountability. As discussed below, their increased involvement in sanctioning clients was also a reason for increased administration.

Although flexible, discretionary and complex, this work was done within a largely bureaucratic order where layers of staff were specialised in quite different activities. In describing her local office one adviser attempted to put a figure on exactly how many people were employed and what their roles were:

> It's hard to say because desks are so mixed with people from Start, but I think about ten (who are advisers), there's a secretary, everything has a team

Table 5.1 Country and percentage responses to 'To what extent are the activities which make up your job routine?'

	routine	neither	not routine
Australia	49	20	31
Netherlands	34	23	43
New Zealand	56	23	21
United Kingdom	67	18	15

leader, above the team leader there is of course another manager, and there is another manager. There is two people who work with foreigners, special minorities.

That this complex set of roles also required a significant amount of technical control was confirmed by the fact that Dutch advisers were more likely than any others to conduct interviews with clients while logged-on to the IT system, indicating a programmed and supervised approach to implementing the organisation's goals. It also suggested an IT system which had a flexible set of options and a fast data recovery capability. While in other systems computers were used to load information on clients, to find vacancies and to enter compliance data, in the AV there was also a range of adviser-friendly information.

So if I want, at the moment, what is the newest development . . . let's click for example to this one. Here is the news. For example in newspapers was the news that our organisation has very big financial problems at the moment, and this is the latest news about it. There was a meeting of the Board, Wednesday evening, and you can read about what they discussed about.

The high workloads and the obvious bureaucratic elements of this system were also reflected in the fact that these advisers reported the lowest likelihood of ever working outside their own office. Few conduct outside meetings with clients and of those who did, the private sector advisers were the ones significantly more likely to leave their offices from time to time, with 30 per cent doing so at least once in a typical week.

But while limited and controlled in the overall structure of the organisation, they were not bound by lock-step procedure. Within this system the low level of routine in the work of officials was matched by a high degree of involvement in the decisions influencing their roles. The Dutch advisers were the most likely to say they were consulted about how their work was to be performed, about the sequence and speed of work and about possible changes to the work process. Consequently job satisfaction was very high. Only 10 per cent of public advisers and 13 per cent of their private colleagues reported low satisfaction. Private staff were significantly less likely to say they were highly satisfied, presumably due in part to the fact that they had higher case loads and a much narrower commitment to filling job vacancies than their public colleagues.

The private advisers also worked in a more centralised environment in which head office targets and decisions were more likely to shape local actions. For example, at Vedior the task of using the employment service database to find public clients to refer to employers was done by a specialist centre in Amsterdam. They processed the employment service database for their whole organisation and local advisers then had to seek specific help in regard to a particular vacancy:

> So we can put the demands, we can give them and say, 'well we need such and such' and they look into the database and give answers to us . . . It's not like Start where everybody has access to the database. Or direct access.

These forms of centralisation caused the kinds of complaint which are typical of bureaucratic organisations. In the above case, for instance, the advisers interviewed said that they had asked for a computer link in their own office to do the matching of employment service clients to local job vacancies.

> We do it so often that we'd like to do it ourselves. It doesn't take that long. Because you can imagine if you get all the calls from the whole country then it takes a little more time to answer them. We've asked for it, but it takes a lot of time before you get it and that's all well . . . politics. It's also mostly financial.

The private companies also had a high level of internal standardisation, with advisers reporting that across the country their 'structures and levels and procedures are all the same', and indicating that the individual performance of staff was highly likely to be recorded and discussed on a regular basis. Even so the performance regime was positive rather than punitive. For instance, at Vedior, the most assertively profit-oriented of the temporary work companies:

> each person who has worked with us a certain time has to make three targets. And it's, you make them yourself. Well of course you meet with your manager and ask if that's OK. And for each target you get 2 per cent of your year's salary.

Front-line Networks

In interview the advisers said that greater flexibility had recently been allowed in what had previously been a very bureaucratic service. Public advisers said that they now had much more freedom to construct a program for their clients using their own regional training centres, outside training agencies and in-work programs. They also enjoyed more choice in deciding to tackle the client's problems themselves:

> Then also I can decide to do something myself. I think well, maybe, if we talk then I can do something. And that's up to me. I can tell about that . . . the tradition is not that we are supposed to do that, but we get more and more the freedom to start.

The character of the Dutch system was also reflected in patterns of contact with job seekers. Advisers said they gave close attention to about 40 per cent of their clients and left some 28 per cent on a low contact diet. This was broadly similar to the pattern evident elsewhere and confirmed the view that intensity of involvement now often varies quite considerably across the client pool. In an average week the private staff spent about one-third of their time with job seekers while the average for public advisers was just over 50 per cent.

Asked if they attended 'any regular meetings outside your own organisation of employment program providers, case managers or trainers from other organisations', the private officials were the least likely in the study to say yes. Those from the public office were also below the mean. Far from creating a social network involving many potential partners, the networks used by Dutch advisers were most likely to be their own organisations and this was a significantly stronger attribute than seen in the other systems. The advisers were all asked to estimate their frequency of contact with anyone outside their own local office.[16] They were given a list of offices typically involved in employment support, and a measure of frequency ranging from 'daily through to quarterly or less'. The Dutch advisers were most likely to select another office of their own organisation as their most frequent form of contact. While this was also true of other systems, the paucity of other interactions stood out in the Dutch case.

Contrary to expectations that the Netherlands exemplified a broader form of inter-agency networking, Dutch advisers had low levels of involvement with other agencies with a potential interest in job seekers. Municipal institutions, welfare organisations and schools did not rate highly in the networks ordinary advisers used.

Interestingly the public advisers were less internally focused than their private sector colleagues, suggesting that this aspect of the enterprise motive may not be found in private agencies. Sixty per cent of them were in daily communication with other offices of their own organisation while the level for private advisers was 74 per cent. Public officials were also more likely to link their work with other government departments, while their private colleagues had far fewer engagements with this wider public system. The public offices were more likely to deal with social security issues or other entitlement problems such as child care.

On the other hand private advisers had higher levels of interaction with employers. Given that the question excluded contacts associated with helping clients to secure job interviews, this higher employer involvement suggested a quite different network character. Plainly the private advisers interacted with employers on a wider set of issues including prospective vacancies, information gathering associated with redundancies and new ventures, and issues concerning pay and leave entitlements. Asked to compare their networks to those of the public agency, the Start officers were quick to point to the profit motive involved in their desire to build close alliances:

> Our attitude to companies, I think, is much more close because the profit has to come from companies who are prepared to have our employees (the job seekers they wish to place). So we have more contacts.

Sanctions

The Welfare-to-Work systems which impose the strictest regime of obligations upon job seekers are thought to be those in the US and UK, where claimants are thought to be regularly forced off the rolls by aggressive use of sanctions. In the European countries where insurance has been more widely used it has been more common to see citizenship expressed as an obligation of the state to provide assistance, with individuals retaining rights to draw income support while they seek equivalent work to that lost through unemployment. In other words the weight of the system has rested upon the notion that the unemployed have 'earned' their income support through their own insurance payments and should not be coerced into low value jobs or unpopular programs.

Nevertheless the Dutch case shows that the new governance arrangements also result in more exacting demands in this insurance-based system. In interviews the advisers said that in the past this system had been too easy for job seekers to abuse. They indicated that the system had become much tighter, but that problems still existed. In particular they pointed to cases where job seekers claimed benefits while holding down jobs in the black economy:

Table 5.2   Fortnightly rates of sanctioning by country

	Survey N	Mean
Australia	513	1.73
Netherlands	267	4.27
New Zealand	109	1.37
United Kingdom	142	3.20

To what extent is that a problem here with people having jobs on the black market?
    Oh it's huge, it's really huge.
    So there'd be a lot of people claiming and working at the same time?
    Exactly.

When this outlook is combined with what we know of changes social security rules brought into play after 1996, it is perhaps not so surprising to find that in the Dutch case the rate of sanctioning was quite high, in fact the highest in the study (Table 5.2). Asked 'How many clients have you referred for possible sanctioning in the past two weeks?', the Dutch advisers averaged twice to three times the rate reported by New Zealand and Australian advisers and a quarter more than their reputedly more draconian UK colleagues.

Of course it might simply be that in the Dutch case there were more job seekers who were perceived by advisers to be failing in their obligations. This was the simplest explanation of higher sanction rates. Consequently they were asked to estimate 'approximately what percentage of people who apply for benefits would rather be on benefits than work to support themselves and their families?' As Table 5.3 indicates there were broadly comparable estimates across the four systems.

The structured nature of the 'phases' system and the streaming of clients into intensity groups evidently left fewer gaps and spaces in which non-compliant job seekers might become casualties of weaker forms of accountability. The advisers then used their discretionary powers to 'work' the troublesome job seeker. This in turn brought any sanctioning issues to light:

How do you deal with the situation if you suspect someone is doing that (working on the side)?
    I try and get them in front of my desk as often as possible, so I interrupt any action going on, or I suggest a very intensive program.
    And then, are there consequences if they don't show up for the meetings or programs?

Table 5.3   Proportion of advisers and their estimates of the percentage of job seekers who 'would rather stay on benefits than get a job', by country

	Advisers			
	Australia	Netherlands	New Zealand	UK
Job seekers				
up to 20	48	53	55	44
21–40	28	34	27	30
over 40	24	12	17	26
	100	100	99	100

Exactly. That's when it all falls apart. We just write it all down and send it to the social security office and they deal with it.[17]

The second part of the explanation of the higher sanctioning rate was that advisers had available to them a better list of interventions which they could use to place clients. The existence of sophisticated training institutes, temporary work placements, disability pensions and in-work subsidies for those unable to compete for open employment empowered advisers to come down harder on those who still failed to meet their requirements. When combined with the fact that jobs are more plentiful in the Dutch economy, this suggests that sanctioning reflected the adviser's sense of the opportunities available to job seekers and not simply their behaviours as clients of the employment service.

Interestingly, involvement of the private firms in sanctioning was very low, with almost 80 per cent of them reporting two sanctions or less per fortnight, while only half the public sample recorded this lower rate (Table 5.4). This was also a pattern among Australian private agencies, raising questions about the extent to which policies promoting tougher social security rules can be made consistent with privatisation.

Paradoxically, the higher Dutch sanctioning was achieved without turning the regular work of the employment office into a sanctioning system. For example, the Dutch advisers did not use formal agreements or 'mutual obligations' contracts with their clients as a primary tool for setting job seeker expectations. Arguments and conflicts with clients about their compliance obligations evidently played a smaller role in defining the work at the front line in the Netherlands.

Consequently what distinguished the Dutch case was the lower interest in what are often called 'administrative breaches', or sanctions associated with failure to obey internal employment service rules. In the other systems job seekers were sanctioned if they failed to attend an interview at the employment service after they had been duly notified to

Table 5.4   Fortnightly rates of sanctioning and type of organisation (%)

	Two or less	Three to five	Six or more
Public	50	29	22
For-Profit	79	13	8

Table 5.5   Netherlands advisers and use of sanctions when a job seeker refuses a suitable job offer (%)

	No sanction	Sanction	Neither
Public	19	77	3
For-Profit	52	34	14

attend. In the Netherlands this was not so likely to be a cause for sanctioning, particularly among private advisers. Forty-eight per cent of public advisers said they sanctioned job seekers for this reason and 62 per cent of private officials said they did not.[18]

In applying sanctions or making referrals for sanctions to a job seeker refusing a suitable job offer, private agencies again took a softer line. They were much more likely to allow job seekers to refuse such an offer, this being a cardinal sin in virtually every other system. Public policy objectives to do with 'mutual obligations' or 'social citizenship' received strong support when phrased as worthwhile general objectives, but they did not act as tangible incentives for profit-maximisation. Indeed such objectives may have attracted unwanted administrative loads and forced advisers into appeal and negotiation tasks for which they had little skill and few job satisfaction payoffs.

Moreover, only in the Dutch case were interviewees concerned with balancing the needs for sanctioning job seekers with sanctioning employers who paid wages below the legal minimum or who obliged employees to work more hours than was allowed. They could see that their efforts to enforce harsh compliance standards upon reluctant job seekers made it easier for employers to lower their standards:

> if you push people too hard, then employers are going to use that situation by not paying enough salary and things like that.

Governance Norms at the Front Line

Virtually all advisers, most managers and most policy makers accept that effective front-line work involves the exercise of considerable discretion.

Many, including Mead (1997, p. 61), claim that 'reform is primarily an administrative problem' which 'makes great demands on the bureaucracy' (Mead, 1997, p. 71). A great deal therefore depends upon the orientation and norms of staff in regard to discretionary work. Conversely we can learn a great deal about the architecture of these new governance regimes by seeing how officials construct the normative purpose and meaning of their work environment.

When viewed as a single group the Dutch advisers appeared largely positive about their job seeker clients and their own goals or mission. As stated, they worked in relatively large offices where routine was low and involvement in decision making was high. Their comparative youth may also account for an optimistic outlook. They said they had high discretion to use the set forms of intervention they were able to make and even though their administrative load was high in comparison to others, they did not report their work environment as excessively rule-driven. Even their administrative burden involved flexibility. Advisers controlled their own diary and reported in interview that they shifted their administrative tasks around, sometimes spreading them through each day, sometimes ruling out a whole day just to catch up on the paper work.

Interestingly the Dutch officials were less satisfied with their government's efforts to help unemployed people than were others, despite the fact that the Netherlands had both the lowest unemployment rate in the study and had been energetically involved in building new institutional arrangements such as temporary work and part-time employment. One in five wanted more assistance to be provided and only 40 per cent were satisfied compared to over 60 per cent in the other countries.[19]

When considering the plight of job seekers the Dutch front-line officials were more likely than many others to say that 'external circumstances' rather than 'lack of effort' was the reason for unemployment. Thirty per cent were prepared to blame external circumstances and this was higher than in the UK or New Zealand. Only the Australians rated the structural causes of unemployment more highly. But most importantly the private staff in the Netherlands were significantly less sympathetic than were public advisers. One in five thought job seekers were responsible compared to one in ten of the public bureaucrats. Similarly when asked to rate the goal of their own agency – 'help clients get jobs quickly or raise skills so they can get the job they want' – most private advisers (60 per cent) favoured jobs over skill development while a minority of public officials (33 per cent) took this tougher view.

This pattern was even more obvious when the advisers were asked about the selectivity of their service. That is, the willingness of officials to cream the best clients and leave others to accept an inferior treatment.

Table 5.6 Netherlands advisers: Percentages who say their organisation picks out the most capable clients and gives them the best service

	Agree	Neither agree/disagree	Disagree
Public	24	11	64
For-Profit	60	11	29

The two systems with private participation, the Netherlands and Australia, were significantly more likely to opt for the selective approach. A large majority of the New Zealand and UK advisers disagreed with 'creaming' the best clients for available vacancies or programs, while a minority of the Dutch and Australian staff found this undesirable. Most of the difference is explained by the orientation of private advisers as is evident in Table 5.6.

Public advisers retained a commitment to universal treatment and opportunity, while private staff viewed their organisations as openly committed to selecting out the best job seekers. Even so, viewed from the comparative perspective the Dutch public officials were actually less committed to universal service than many others. Only in Australia was support for the 'equal treatment' ideal more at risk among public servants, indicating that once in a 'mixed economy', public officials appeared to adopt more competitive orientations which brought them closer to the views of private advisers.

As noted, the paradox in this case was that while many public servants displayed orientations to their work which had an enterprising spirit, they did so from within a very different organisational culture. When asked about the extent to which 'decisions you make about your clients (are) determined by the central departmental program rules and regulations', public advisers answered quite differently to their colleagues in the private sector. Two-thirds of public servants agreed that rules still determined much of their work with clients, while the figure for private advisers was much lower at 42 per cent.

The differences expressed in these answers were also evident in the orientations of advisers to questions of competition. As above, Dutch advisers did not compete with one another in any structured or overt sense. When a temporary work organisation referred a public agency client to a job both organisations benefited. There was one less job seeker for the public official to serve and the private firm got a finder's fee from a satisfied employer. That at least was the theory. In practice of course there were small points of tension, particularly in labour markets for which there was an inadequate supply of qualified job seekers. Public officials sometimes indicated in interview that they preferred to place

Table 5.7   Netherlands advisers, public and for-profit, and percentage
responses to 'I don't show competitors how I go about getting my results'

	Disagree	Neither agree/disagree	Agree
Public	55	21	23
For-Profit	11	12	77

the 'cream' of their job seekers themselves, rather than have the private
firms take them.

When asked to respond to the statement 'I do not like my competitors to know how I go about getting my results' it was the private sector
advisers who were most likely to agree. As Table 5.7 indicates, most public advisers were untroubled by competitiveness but the reverse was true
of their private colleagues. Compared to those in the other countries,
the Dutch public advisers were also less competitive. However this does
not mean that they were uninterested in the business aspects of their
work. As in Australia, the fact that the institutional arrangements
included firms as part of the service delivery system created new
pressures for public officials to identify with, or even match the kinds of
financial objectives found in these corporations.

For example, in interviews conducted in Australia and the Netherlands the advisers were asked if they could normally tell if their
interventions led to a result which produced an economic benefit for
their agency. Most could identify results that were of value to their
clients, but only some had the information and incentive systems to
recognise when they were also helping their agency's bottom line. Using
testimony extracted from these interviews, they were then asked to
respond to the statement – 'I take note of those actions with clients that
will generate a payable outcome for the office'. The Dutch advisers were
strongest of all in their agreement. As Table 5.8 testifies, the public
officials were no less aware of the financial consequences of their
actions, but in fact were even more attuned to this issue. This premier
enterprise value was clearly central to their work.

At first sight it is perplexing that the private advisers were not more
aware of such economic considerations. One clue to the difference was
provided by the fact that their work was more pressured and contained
fewer activities likely to involve discretion. Enterprising activity is only
relevant where discretion is high. It may also be less necessary to enterprise an organisation which already has all its processes directed at the
bottom line than it is to develop enterprising strategies in one where a
mixture of motives is present. Similarly the Dutch showed high levels of
agreement with the statement, 'I am aware that my organisation pays

Table 5.8   Netherlands advisers, public and private, and percentage responses to 'I take note of financial outcomes'

	Disagree	Neither agree/disagree	Agree
Public	9	20	70
Private	13	35	51

attention to the funds I generate by placing clients', higher than for countries without private participation. Private officials were better informed and perhaps more motivated by economic objectives, but it was the public officials who had to devote more effort to thinking about the way such objectives should be used in day-to-day work because their transactions with clients were more complex.

Conclusions

Paradoxically perhaps, the Dutch employment system was both highly structured and also relatively discretionary. The enterprising or 'mixed economy' elements were less risky than they might have been because discretion was localised and contained. The assessment and 'phases' system provided one control, the inter-organisational partnerships with training institutes and temporary work agencies provided another. The more bureaucratic elements of the Dutch case were easy to distinguish and related to the high case loads and very systematic forms of treatment at the front line. The willingness to sanction clients not adhering to reasonable job search demands also reflected the stronger disciplinary aspects typical of corporate governance. Central goals did indeed get implemented at the base and they also seemed to lack partisan passions, bringing a cool discretion to bear on their work. For example, they did not report seeing themselves as 'advocates of the client's rights' and nor were they among the front-line staff most likely to say they viewed building trust with the job seeker as one of their most important tasks.[20]

Nor was the Dutch system 'networked' in the manner expected of an institutional structure in which public and private organisations shared responsibility for service delivery. Advisers at the front line did not negotiate their roles with those outside their offices, nor did they traverse different organisational structures in pursuit of optimum outcomes. They were not likely to agree that the important rules 'are those to do with relations with other organisations'. Their inter-organisational work was in fact quite structured and did not result in shared forms of authority or responsibility. They were the least likely of all to say that they had to answer to different bosses in different places. They knew their functions and they knew where the boundaries lay.

The networking they did undertake was not based on resolving ambiguity, but on bringing existing partners into structured co-operation. Of all those in the study they most strongly supported the idea that their work was concerned with finding 'the middle ground between clients, trainers, employers and the social security system'. Within this secure environment they nevertheless aimed for economic performance. This appears to have little to do with direct competition for clients and income. Public and private offices were not regulated by price or cost, at least not in any market-based method. Objectives for numbers of job seekers to be served and various target outcomes were stipulated in the appropriation process. These formed the basis of negotiations with regional boards and managers in the employment service who in turn rationed resources and defined targets for each of their own offices and programs.

Yet the Dutch advisers showed great awareness of the economic value of their work. In the public sector they counted the cost and potential financial outcome of different strategies they used with clients. In this regard it is perhaps more accurate to say that they adopted entrepreneurial orientations rather than competitive ones. The virtue in this approach was to be found in the fact that the system managed high case loads and adhered to high standards of compliance in treating job seekers. The weakness lay in the fact that the public system was still left to carry most of the burden of treating barriers to employment among very disadvantaged job seekers. The advent of private partners only served to increase services for the already well off.

The limited form of private participation allowed strong central management to be retained in the AV and the ministry. This also reduced the transition and transaction costs to vulnerable job seekers and unwilling employers of having to navigate a more complex set of competing agencies. Creaming by the private firms was also balanced by the AV's commitment to defining a service for every category of client, even if this also involved uneven opportunities.

In learning to deal with one another these organisations learned key methods for dealing with employers. This process of organisational emulation was matched by the methods identified in the Australian case for treating the job seeker. Interactions inside the agency acted as a script for certain relations with an employer. The need for different models of self-representation were sometimes put forward as a special problem for second (or third) generation unemployed youth who lacked practical networks and whose parents could not 'model' the appropriate work habits at home, leaving younger unemployed people without the practical skills of managing time and the discipline of work.

What then should we conclude about the Dutch model of governance? Clearly there is evidence of a decisive turn away from traditional notions of bureaucratic governance. Chapter 7 shows that the various forms of procedural governance discussed at the start of the book are certainly in decline. The surprise is just how weak the Netherlands appears to be compared to expectations that they would rate as an exemplar of network governance. Instead, its strongest characteristic is an amended form of corporate governance, different from both the UK and New Zealand in that various economic priorities are stronger, including among public officials. Despite a history which was more strongly identified with social democratic institutions and neo-corporatist structures, the Netherlands had used its de-coupled public agency and its new alignments with the two temporary work companies as a recipe to forge greater central control over key objectives and greater local flexibility in finding methods to achieve those goals. This, perhaps, was the hallmark of the enterprising method – to use hybrid forms of restructure, and new relationships and incentives to create the particular type of flexibility likely to deliver policy objectives.

Notes

1 Average Dutch hours in 1973 were 1724 per year and by 1996 this had fallen to 1372 hours. The equivalent annual rate in Australia was 1900 hours (OECD, 1996; Visser & Hemerijck, 1997, p. 30).

2 European Commission, *Employment Observatory*, Tableau de Bord 1996, Brussels, p. 51.

3 To achieve these gains employers have to keep the employee for a minimum of 12 weeks at a rate of no less than 15 hours per week.

4 Sociale Zaken en Werkgelegenheid (Ministry of Social Affairs and Employment) (1997) *The Whys and Wherefores of the Ministry of Social Affairs and Employment*, The Hague, January, p. 5.

5 Reimslag, Wynand M. A. (1997) 'Public and Private Employment Service in the Netherlands: From Coexistence to Public-Private partnership'. Paper delivered to the Conference of Public Employment Services, Geneva, 20 January, p. 2.

6 Arbeids Voorziening, *Employment Service Chooses the Future*, The Hague, 1996, p. 6.

7 ibid., p. 15.

8 Centrum Vakopleiding, *National Statistics*, May 1997, p. 4.

9 Lelystad, May 1997. Interview with the author.

10 Arbeids Voorzeining, op. cit., p. 20.

11 Reimslag, 1997, p. 1.

12 ibid., p. 17.

13 Interview with Manager, START, Gouda, 22 September 1998.

14 Staff were sampled from two major regions rather than from the entire national system. This was done in order to simplify the process of obtaining regional management agreement for the survey to be done in their area. Characteristics of the two regions were broadly similar to those found elsewhere in the national system.

15 This comparison and the others quoted in this study are significant at .05 level.

16 The question was, 'Excluding contacts associated with assisting a particular job seeker to obtain a job interview, how often would you have some form of contact (including telephone) with the following: Another office of your own organisation, an official from (other) government departments, local government, welfare agencies, employers, training providers, advisers in other agencies, local service clubs (Lions, Rotary etc.), schools and universities, local media?'

17 ibid.

18 When would you normally recommend a job seeker be sanctioned by having their benefits reduced or withdrawn? Job seeker fails to contact our office?

19 The item was, 'Governments should do more to help job seekers', Strongly Agree to Strongly Disagree. Five point Likert-type scale significant at .0000.

20 They do agree that trust is important but their mean score is lower than any of the other three systems. The item was, The main thing I have to do in this job is gain the trust of the client. In a scale from 1 = strongly disagree to 5 = strongly agree, the Dutch mean score was 3.2; Australia 3.8; New Zealand 4.1 and the UK 3.6. Results for country comparison of this item were significant at .0000.

CHAPTER 6

Australia:
Governance as Competition

In the previous three cases there was radical rhetoric and dramatic reform. Staid and steady governmental systems were de-coupled, realigned, reinvented and even re-engineered. If the results of these changes did not always fit the models being espoused by politicians or in management texts, they certainly lived up to the claim of being systematic and deep-rooted. It is therefore somewhat difficult to find yet another superlative to describe the radical credentials of this last Australian case. Suffice it to say that in just four years of reform endeavour the Australians succeeded in transforming every single aspect of their system, throwing out the public employment service and creating a market-like system based on more than 300 contractors.

Between 1994 and 1997 two different Australian governments set out to attack the country's high rate of long term unemployment by implementing the most experimental reform of any social program yet attempted. In place of the routine work of the public employment service the Commonwealth Employment Service (CES) with its standard suite of regulatory requirements, the unemployed now faced a different set of expectations. These included some very complex and demanding alterations in the way services were delivered, as well as new pressures on entitlement to income support. So radically different is the Australian case that it may well be regarded as the most important OECD initiative in social policy in the post-war period. Certainly Prime Minister Keating and others directing it felt that this was their aim in developing the 'Working Nation' initiative (Commonwealth of Australia, 1994; Robinson, 1995).

Employment Conditions

Like the other three countries, the Australians faced rising unemployment through the 1980s and into the early 1990s. Between 1988 and 1992 the rate rose steadily from 7.1 per cent to 10.8 per cent where it hovered for another two years (OECD, 1999, p. 17). If this was not bad enough, within this group was another with even more severe problems. Long-term unemployment increased significantly during this period. In fact between the start of 1990 and the end of 1993 the number of those searching for work for more than twelve months trebled and every indication suggested that this was a phenomenon which could 'be expanded quickly, but dissipated only slowly' (Chapman, 1993, p. 3).

While economists had long disagreed on the causes of unemployment in Australia, there could be little doubt but that long-term dislocation from the labour market had emerged as the single biggest threat to both economic policy and social cohesion. In budget terms the long-term recipients of income support were costing more than $1 billion a year (Hughes, 1993). The earlier doctrine of allowing each new upturn in activity to 'soak up' the excess supply of labour was plainly no longer tenable. Economists advising the Keating Labor Government began to argue that growth on its own would not be enough and some more elaborate form of job redistribution would be needed to draw the long-termers up from the bottom of the pool of the unemployed.

The problem for the Labor government was that many economists and business leaders were proposing labour market deregulation along the New Zealand lines as the way to generate greater demand for labour. But the government was neither impressed by the actual results of these experiments, nor willing to give up its positive relationship with the Australian union movement. Yet to sell the idea that it remained a government committed to opening the economy and removing restrictive forms of government intervention it would need more than another round of subsidised job creation programs.

The core element of the changes adopted first by Labor and then by the conservative Coalition Government involved a different version of the deregulationist agenda. Instead of a restructure of the labour market following one of the three paths as in the other countries under study, the government opted for a restructure of welfare and employment assistance. Delivery of core public services was put in the hands of hundreds of small and medium-sized contractors. A public agency, together with for-profit and non-profit agencies had to compete for the right to provide basic services to the unemployed. These were not the ancillary activities such as training which had long been subject to contracting. This was the core service of job counselling and job matching. These new agencies were then paid according to the outcomes they achieved with each client, thus making this the most outcome-focused system so far devised. And the unemployed too were enterprised through requirements that they choose which contractor they worked with and then negotiate a service contract with them to suit their individual needs.

Working Nation – The New Model

The first version of this competitive system was defined in the Labor Government's White Paper, *Working Nation*, as a part of a new client focus:

> The emphasis will move away from processing large numbers of job seekers through relatively rigid national programs. The key elements of the new strategy are an accurate assessment of the needs of job seekers and an intensive plan to assist disadvantaged people (Commonwealth of Australia, 1994, p. 127).

The key to the delivery of this new method was stipulated as the harnessing of the non-profit welfare and for-profit recruitment sectors – 'Healthy competition will lead to service improvement' (Commonwealth of Australia, 1994, p. 127). The new approach was also frequently contrasted with the weaknesses of the old welfare state with its 'universal provision of a highly standardised and centrally controlled group of services', said to result in a 'traditional one-size-fits-all approach to service delivery' (Robinson, 1995).

The first Working Nation reforms occurred between 1994 and 1996 and involved:

- individual case management for all long-term unemployed clients;
- referral of clients to both jobs and subsidised work and training;
- use of both a large public sector service provider (EAA) and many new private providers Contracted Case Managers;
- regulation of this quasi-market by an independent government regulator (ESRA);
- payment of private providers on a fee-for-success basis;
- competition between providers on quality not price;
- empowerment of unemployed clients to choose their preferred agency and negotiate a service contract.

Under the Labor Government's direction, one third of the public assistance effort for long-term unemployed people was moved out of the public service and contracted to both for-profit and non-profit agencies, subject to regulatory oversight by the Employment Services Regulatory Authority (ESRA). The central initiative in the reform was the government's Jobs Compact. This guaranteed that job seekers on benefits for eighteen months or more would be given access to either employment or training or both. Outcomes were defined as either jobs or placement into a new raft of training programs that Labor was funding with a billion dollar commitment to this new Working Nation program. Meanwhile the CES had opened a new service called Employment Assistance Australia (EAA) where its staff were dedicated to the new contracts for long-term clients.

The second set of changes began in March 1996 when the newly elected conservative Howard Government abolished the training programs which Labor had established and announced that Working Nation had been a failure because less than one third of those undertaking Labor's training programs had found real jobs afterwards. While there certainly had been problems with many of the training programs, the results overall were promising. The Howard Government, however, preferred partisan attack to incremental adjustment. It announced a desire to make labour market assistance both more limited and more clearly linked to the client's 'capacity to benefit'. The revised 'Vanstone'[1] scheme included:

- increase of private provider role from 30% to almost 50% of the market;
- closing of brokered training programs;
- delegation (cashing out) of remaining program funds to providers;
- payments driven only by exits to jobs;
- termination of the role of the independent regulator.[2]

Although both governments championed the market for employment services as a major experiment in public administration and both were totally committed to contracting as a means of achieving efficiency, this was not their only common objective. Contracting as a policy tool was to be underpinned by a new and different methodology for deciding treatments. Labor termed this 'case management' and the Coalition called theirs 'intensive assistance'. They meant much the same thing. In place of standardised treatments by staff in the CES, long-term unemployed people would now receive an individual or 'tailor-made' service in which an adviser or consultant would put together a package of measures to meet the client's needs. Under Labor this might include a greater range of interventions such as training programs and assistance with any personal impediments to employment such as drug dependence or health problems.

In the most developed of these models, in theory the case manager had authority for the procurement of the services deemed most useful for the individual client, combining the skills of 'counsellor, salesperson and accountant' (Hammond, 1997, p. 34). Where such a role included responsibility for the assessment of client needs, together with the purchase of services from supplier organisations, the potential for both improved service for the client and greater cost effectiveness were to be realised. In other words the new model promised an interesting new form of 'governance at ground level' in which clients were called upon to help produce their own program effects, rather than being consumers of pre-existing, or finished, services. As Hasenfeld and Weaver (1996, p. 236) have pointed out, this mix of both intensive support and increased obligation creates 'unique organisational pressures' on clients and staff in these programs and organisational factors therefore dominate evaluations of success and failure.

To establish a common system of service delivery the Labor Government established case management as the required methodology to be used by all providers. Each client would be classified by the CES when they reached twelve months unemployment, and according to their 'degree of difficulty' they would then attract a different payment for the contractor. All case managers were also authorised to recommend that the client have his or her social security payment suspended or terminated for any noncompliance with the case management process.

The contractors were to be paid a fee per client, composed of an up-front amount to begin the case management process and then half or more of the fee when the client obtained work, was approved for training, and had completed thirteen weeks of either.

The new system saw the percentage of business conducted by non-government case managers grow steadily under ESRA's careful cultivation of the new industry. However the new system was far from stable. The government provider, EAA, remained outside ESRA's purview, thanks to successful lobbying by the CES and its head office, the Department of Education, Employment, Training and Youth Affairs (DEETYA). Predictably this state of affairs left the new 'market' some distance short of achieving the departure from bureaucracy which advocates and ideologues desired.

On their own these pressures would almost certainly have forced the government to reform these arrangements further, either in the direction of bringing EAA under ESRA's purview or by removing ESRA and managing all the contractors on equal terms in a 'tender and supply' system. However these probable changes might have taken four or five years to become necessary had another problem not undermined the Labor scheme.

The key to Labor's Jobs Compact was a commitment that all those eighteen months or more out of work would receive case management and following this would have either a job or training. Labor funded the training part of this commitment with a major increase in the budget for employment. At first it appeared that a significant part of these funds would be used to finance a high quality case management relationship with each client. In fact most of the funds were devoted to short-term training programs and the funds spent on case management were so low that many clients received only a brief, routine interview and assessment. Instead the funds flowed to thousands of New Work Opportunities (NWOs) that included the 13-week programs which would serve as an outcome for contractors, and therefore as a payment trigger for DEETYA. While many of the actual programs were undoubtedly success-ful and valued by those who participated, the effect on the dynamics of the service delivery system was problematic.

In 1996 the newly elected conservative Coalition had ample ammuni-tion with which to attack Labor's reforms and they did not refrain. Their less sympathetic view of the unemployed neatly coincided with the desire to cut public expenditure. They removed more than three billion from the DEETYA appropriation and closed most of the training programs which had provided contractors with many of their outcomes. They would base all assistance on individual needs and upon the unemployed person's 'capacity to benefit'. After a new tender round ESRA would be closed and the government itself would become the 'purchaser' of services. That is, DEETYA would be separated from the public employment contractor and would act as supreme policy maker, regulator and banker for the new system. The public provider, now to be called Employment National, was established as a private corporation wholly owned by the government but answerable to the Minister for Finance. This was put forward as a commit-ment to 'competitive neutrality' (Vanstone, 1997, pp. 8–13).

The government cut contractors' ability to refer job seekers to train-ing programs, but did not allocate any extra resources for contractors to spend on intensive work with job seekers. The new role for contractors was to include finding and filling job vacancies. They were now required both to help job seekers prepare for work and also to convince employ-ers to lodge job vacancies with them. And in practice not all the long-term unemployed would be referred to a contractor. Instead DEETYA would set criteria to determine which clients had the capacity to benefit from extra attention.

The ongoing problem of setting payments for the most lucrative part of the new system – the intensive assistance work, called Flex Three – had been decided using a three-part classification and a three-stage payment regime (Table 6.1). The Department acknowledged that this fee structure left it entirely to the contractor to decide if any of these fees would be invested in either the job seeker or the employer. If contractors chose to pay employers a 'subsidy' or bribe to induce them

Table 6.1 Australian governmental payment schedules for intensive assistance

Client classification	Share of total places (%)	Maximum duration of activity (mths)	Payment at start ($)	Interim payment ($)	Payment at 26 weeks in a job ($)
1. Least Disadvantaged	67	12	1500	1500	1200
2. Medium Disadvantaged	26	12	2250	2250	2200
3. Most Disadvantaged	7	18	3000	3200	3000

Note: Australian dollars.

to accept a very disadvantaged person into a job for at least six months, that was their business. Or if the contractor simply chose to absorb the entire fee as profit to the firm, that too was up to them.

In addition to the rate of payment for each client, the other method by which government controlled contractors was by rationing the total number of clients flowing through the system. The key to this process and to the overall movement of clients around the 'network' was the creation of a new One-Stop-Shop for all social security clients, called CentreLink. Some former CES staff and many former Department of Social Security staff were brought together to manage all the benefit payment services for various government programs. In the employment sector not only would the employment ministry monitor assessments made by CentreLink, to ensure that not too many clients were classified into the expensive category, they would also be able to ration the flow of clients through the system by squeezing CentreLink resources, since the ministry (and several other government departments) sat on the CentreLink Board and decided its corporate strategy.[3]

Job Network – A Model of Competition

A new cast of more than 300 contractors was licensed and put to work in May 1998. Undoubtedly the most difficult part of the implementation of the new order concerned the contracting out of the 'labour exchange' function of the old CES. In the new system this was defined as the 'Flex One' service where contractors would gather and fill their own vacancies. Most began by copying the practices of the recruitment companies. They developed telephone 'call centres' and employed staff to contact prospective employers. This also led to the development of new minimal-cost services for job seekers who were only eligible for this service. Since the price for Flex One was variable, each agency had to guess the likely cost of finding and filling these vacancies. The Department had indicated that bids around A$250 per vacancy were expected. Most were awarded at rates between A$245 and A$400. At this price even minimal efforts using call centres were unlikely to produce high returns. Making the service profitable depended on the ability of the agency to win both this Flex One business and a good quota of higher value 'intensive assistance' work of the kind outlined in Table 6.1. In this case the job-matching functions would simply become an opportunity structure for placing the high-return clients. Some agencies received this mix of clients in their contracts and others did not.

Once the 'call centre' method was in place agencies had incentives to use it for managing job seekers as well as employers. This placed further pressure on job seekers to accept a new and more limited service. In place of attendance at the CES they now waited at home for a call from any one of the agencies with whom they had registered. Only in the intensive assistance cases would the relationship with a single contractor be binding. Contractors wanting to raise their profiles in the new job-matching business soon developed a variety of dubious tactics. For example, in occupations where there were known to be labour shortages, agencies would advertise positions that did not exist. Qualified applicants were then told the job was filled and were asked to supply their details so that they could be contacted when 'the next position becomes available'. Armed with a reserve of qualified applicants in a valued field, the agency would then begin approaching employers with offers to guarantee same-day filling of vacancies for employers willing to sign an agency agreement or place other vacancies with the contractor.

In order to pacify agitated job seekers, annoyed employers and anxious contractors the government made several changes to the new system. During 1998 the job-matching restrictions were relaxed a little to allow a larger number of job seekers to use this service. The restrictions on asking job seekers for payments for assistance were also relaxed to help contractors find new ways to earn income. Perhaps most indicative of the political vulnerability of the Job Network arrangements was the decision of Minister David Kemp to pay contractors an extra A$10 000 for each site they operated as a means to soften the criticisms about the job-matching part of the service and the imminent collapse of several contractors operating in the worst labour markets.

Against this negative picture of the job matching requirements imposed by the Coalition reforms, many interviewees believed this function had worked well and created a beneficial focus upon employers. Significantly, in the more than twenty interviews, conducted twelve months after the start of Job Network, of six managers who saw job matching as a good function to have devolved to contractors, five were from private sector firms and one from a larger non-profit organisation.

Those with the most negative experiences were leaders of church and smaller non-profit agencies.[4]

The intensive assistance function which had previously been termed 'case management' was now classified as the Flex Three service and as Table 6.1 shows, this was the lucrative part of the contract. Most agencies did their planning on the basis that only 20 to 40 per cent of this group would reach the job outcome stage, so their viability was very much built upon the commencement payments provided by the government. And herein lay the problem. With the government ideology moving away from the job seeker's employment barriers and towards self-motivated search, the signals being sent to front-line staff in the agencies seemed very different to those of the Labor Government period. Job seekers still had to sign an activity agreement and were still at risk of sanctioning if they failed to comply. But the notion that all of them should receive regular interviews or any other particular intervention was now widely criticised. It would be up to the agency to decide what it expected of job seekers. If some form of training appeared likely to result in a job, some funds from the commencement payments could be diverted. And if the job seeker was judged as unlikely to find work the agency could 'park' or warehouse their file at the back of the queue and have no further contact until the twelve months elapsed and they were reclassified as no longer having a 'capacity to benefit' from intensive assistance. This would take them off the contractor's list.

The formal part of the relationship between job seeker and agency was thus less structured than before. The signing of an activity agreement was no longer the trigger for the commencement payment, leaving the agency free to negotiate this at a later stage after the job seeker had agreed to be assigned to the agency. Advisers indicated that they did not rush to complete the agreement in the first session. Because job seekers retained some element of choice regarding their referral to a particular contractor this first meeting was considered as an important screening opportunity for many agencies. By indicating interest, hostility, sympathy or toughness the contractors could influence the job seeker's decision to register with them. Once past this stage a decision to withdraw would incur a sanction for the job seeker unless they could convince CentreLink that they had been severely mistreated.

In practice the choices exercised by job seekers were little different to those available under the Labor Government scheme. As the primary point of contact with benefit recipients, CentreLink was obliged to inform job seekers of all the employment agencies in the area able to offer intensive assistance. However, because of the unpredictable nature of the client flows through the CentreLink assessment and referral process, combined with uneven rates of exit by job seekers finding work, some contractors might have a full list while others had space for many more referrals. Job seekers were only permitted to maintain a particular preference for twenty-eight days, after which CentreLink had the power to compulsorily refer them to any available contractor. Perhaps more problematic even than these cumbersome referral arrangements was the fact that job seekers were to be given no information concerning the performance of the various contractors, the number of vacancies contractors had listed, or their success in finding job seekers a job. The Department said it hoped to resolve data verification problems and certain legal impediments in order to provide these data ultimately. However, since to do so would also grant the public direct information on the performance of the Job Network as a whole, it had common cause with contractors nervous about this kind of exposure. Job seeker empowerment therefore remained one of the weakest parts of the new order.

Here was the most serious weakness of the new scheme. What occurred inside the contractor's office was not only driven by the vastly unequal relationship between the job seeker and the contractor, it was also hidden from the Department's gaze under the commercial-in-confidence protocols accepted at the time of the tender. While the Department could view performance outcomes from every site and could monitor information it required contractors to lodge on the national information system, it could not require contractors to reveal the methods they used to obtain results. Known as the 'black box' among many agencies and described as the 'eleven different herbs and spices' by others, these methods had replaced the protocols of case management when that model fell into political disrepute. Understanding what was actually happening at the front line of the service was therefore both a more interesting and a more difficult task for the study, since this structure was more opaque than elsewhere.

Summarising the Core Strategy

Although there was no political consensus concerning the objectives that should guide the Australian approach to reform, there was de facto an accord on the means to be preferred. Both Labor and the Coalition were convinced that competition among a large industry of contractors would address key issues identified in each of their ideologies. For Labor this mostly concerned increasing the performance of the delivery system so that the long-term clients 'at the bottom of the pool' could be lifted into work and training opportunities without recourse to deregulation of the labour market. For the Coalition the competitive system was a means both to cut costs and to put greater pressure on job seekers to accept any available work. They had also proposed to create exactly the kind of contract labour system found in New Zealand, although legislative compromise produced a weaker effect. Perhaps if these political positions had been the only cards in play the Australians might never have attempted so large a reform but the senior bureaucracy added a further trump which would prove decisive.

Among neo-liberals the conventional wisdom about public agencies was that they sought their own expanded realm as a means to enhance the power of their élite. The budget-maximising-bureaucrat was the main protagonist in the popular account of bureaucracy put forward in organisational economics and by Public Choice exponents (Barney & Ouchi, 1986; Moe, 1984; Donaldson, 1995). In the Australian case there is little evidence to suggest that senior bureaucrats preferred large departments with big programs and in the case of employment services there is strong evidence to the contrary.

During the production of the Green Paper which Labor commissioned to investigate ways of managing the problem of long-term unemployment the senior bureaucracy adopted the more critical stance about the role of the public service (Carter, 1998). The economists and social policy experts brought together to define the shape of a better system produced the notion that case management and training would provide the best possible platform. The committee discussed the role of non-government agencies and saw them as an important means to add new training and work experience opportunities. But there was no interest in either privatising the CES or giving the bulk of the case management role to private contractors. Nor did the community consultations undertaken by this committee uncover a ground swell of public antagonism directed against the CES. Certainly job seekers disliked the queues and the obligation to attend each fortnight. Some found the officials difficult to deal with, especially when sanctions were threatened. But most advisers believed the problem lay in too few jobs and training opportunities and the need for new strategies to lift long-term clients out of their discouraged state.

Criticism of the CES did not come from any study conducted into the operation of the CES and considered by the committee (Carter, 1998). The only pertinent report available at the time was a Morgan Research study conducted for the then Department of Employment Education and Training (DEET) in early 1993. This study examined job seeker satisfaction with the service they received from the CES and found that 75 per cent were indeed satisfied. Half felt their employment prospects were improved as a result of their experience at the CES and most showed a high awareness of their rights and entitlements. The majority of complaints were in regard to benefits and sanctions, not in relation to job search or training. The Morgan study quoted one such complaint as typical, 'I thought they were subjecting me to undue scrutiny' (DEET, 1993, p. 16).

Between the Green and White Papers came a shift in emphasis that owed much to the preferences of senior bureaucrats in Canberra's central agencies. They inserted the idea that contractors ought to compete with the CES to obtain jobs and training for the long-term unemployed. In an interview twelve months later an official from the Department of Finance explained the problem and their preferred solution:

> We had been working on this problem, you know, for years. Since the mid-1980s with various programs run by the CES. We just came to the conclusion that something major had to be done about labour market inflexibility, you know, until that was managed we weren't going to get anywhere . . .
> Yes, I understand. Long-term unemployed people face major barriers to labour market participation . . .
> No! I'm not talking about the labour market for the long term unemployed!
> What then?
> We were interested in the labour market for public servants. Until they faced some real pressure to perform we couldn't expect much overall change.

So the unlikely consensus which made possible one of the most radical reforms of any large social assistance program in the OECD was less to do with the cure for unemployment than with the restructure of the public service in accord with the new enterprise ideal. On this the senior bureaucrats in central agencies such as Treasury, Finance and the Department of Prime Minister and Cabinet were agreed. Those in the organisation most affected, DEETYA, were less enthusiastic. They succeeded for a while in keeping ESRA from assuming authority over the public agency, but this was no more than a holding operation.

By the time the first contractors had begun work there were three agendas driving the reform process. The first was the stated commitment by the government to case manage long-term unemployed job seekers using personal attention and new training opportunities. The second was to exact greater effort from these recipients by increasing their obligations to attend interviews with case managers, participate in training and seek work. And the third was to completely refashion the delivery of this major public service by installing a regime of competitive comparisons, performance-based funding and other labour-saving incentives.

Working Nation – From Model to Actual Methods

The Labor initiatives were put in place between May and September of 1994. As noted earlier, in addition to empowering ESRA to contract services to new agencies, Working Nation involved a significant increase in training programs. In the first year, 1994–5, the growth in such programs was modest and the politicians driving the changes, Prime Minister Paul Keating and Labour and Industry Minister Simon Crean, complained that a greater effort was required. By the financial year 1995–6 the flow of program funds was much higher and the prospect for a drop in the number of long-term unemployed grew more promising. In that year 530 000 job seekers participated in either a Job Club, a 13-week training program or a job search preparation course (Stromback, Dockery & Ying, 1998, p. 3).

ESRA had come into existence in July 1994 and its first contracts were offered for a twelve-month period in the financial year 1994–95, with the aim of getting 20 per cent of long-term job seekers into services run by the private sector. In this first tender round which closed in January 1995, some 400 organisations submitted 964 tenders and ESRA let it be known that they could easily 'double the market share available to private and community sector case managers' if policy makers would only let them do so (1995, p. 28). Indeed ESRA was adopting a 'market development' role which, while necessary to ensure a smooth transition to the new system, left it vulnerable to the complaint that it was in fact an advocacy organisation for the private contractors. By mid-1995 ESRA was able to boast that the flow of clients into the system was increasing rapidly. Nevertheless it was also clear that control over the fate of the system was now awkwardly divided between ESRA and its contractors on one side and DEETYA and the Department of Social Security on the other.

At the front line the new caste of case managers were now empowered to treat their 'own' list of clients referred to them through the CES. They were armed with stronger disciplinary powers and with a list of training and work-subsidy programs. This balance of 'carrot and stick' was the government's regime of 'reciprocal obligations' and at its core was the work of the case manager. This role carried several expectations. The first, from economists, was to break the cycle of 'adverse job matching' in which long-term job seekers became demotivated and deskilled and prospective employers became less and less interested in choosing them even if they were qualified (Chapman, 1993). For the social policy experts case management was expected to address the job seeker's substantive barriers to employment by referral to professional assessment and treatment programs for such things as drug dependence or literacy and numeracy deficits. And finally, for the managerialists the objective was a faster and more efficient passage of clients around the service system and into unsubsidised employment.

The gap between what case management promised and what it delivered was so wide that both the unemployed and the case managers were

Table 6.2   Australian case loads, 1996

Case load	Frequency	Per cent	Cumulative per cent
Up to 50 job seekers	17	4.7	4.7
51 to 100	145	39.7	44.4
101 to 150	110	30.1	74.5
151 and above	93	25.5	100.0
Total	365	100.0	

soon disappointed. A basically sound idea which enjoyed wide, if contradictory, support among policy élites failed to satisfy some key objectives. Individualised service could not be provided because case loads were too high, contractors therefore resorted to 'parking' and 'creaming' strategies to manage their workloads and meet outcome requirements, and clients were often 'herded' in a manner quite contrary to the stated intentions of the reforms.

Although no benchmark was ever published, the ideal driving the scheme was that all those receiving case management would enjoy a close relationship with their own case manager. This relationship was to include regular contact through interviews and phone calls, as well as the individual planning of activities and programs. In practice this implied that a single case manager would have a case load of approximately ninety clients, up to half of whom would be on programs and half receiving intensive support from their case manager. However during 1996, as Table 6.2 indicates, most Australian case managers averaged case loads above 100, and more than a quarter were personally responsible for 150 long-term unemployed job seekers. In interviews they admitted that the only way they could manage this was to divide the long-term unemployed into two informal groups, one to receive active support and one to be 'parked' in a low-maintenance regime which consisted of an occasional phone call or nothing at all.

It was expected that private firms would be anxious to maximise profits and one way to do this might have been to push workloads up. Equally plausible was the notion that the many non-profit agencies would seek to maintain a philanthropic approach and would therefore keep low caseloads. The figures showed a strong, statistically significant relationship between type of agency and case load level, but not in the direction expected.

The highest case loads were in the government owned agency and these far exceeded those of private contractors. Even more surprising were the loads in the private sector which were the smallest of all, throw-

Table 6.3   Australia: Type of agency and case loads (%)

	Up to 50	51 to 100	101 to 150	151 and above
Public	1.5	14	40	44
Non-Profit	8.7	57	21	13
For-Profit	4.3	55	30	10
Number of Advisers	17	142	109	86

ing doubt on the idea that labour-saving strategies would distinguish market from non-market players.

Obviously these figures tell us little about what actual work was being carried out and signal only broad-gauge differences. The treatment of job seekers also reflected the way case managers allocated their time between job seekers, employers and administrative tasks. The networks they used can be assessed by looking at the frequency of contact they reported with welfare organisations, training agencies, educational institutions and other relevant actors. If case management was to meet even its most basic ideals it is reasonable to expect that the case managers would be extensively involved with a variety of other services and not simply fixed in a job seeker processing role similar to that found in the CES.

For 80 per cent of case managers, up to two-thirds of their week was spent in direct contact with job seekers. Employer time accounted for only 10 per cent of their total effort and time spent with other service providers was also extremely low, most spending less than 10 per cent of their time on such work. Although the public, for-profit and non-profit agencies reported similarly high rates of job seeker contact, as well as equally low contact rates with other agencies, there were important differences in their relationships with employers. Private firms were much more likely to spend over 10 per cent of their time working with employers. Thirteen per cent of them devoted over one quarter of their time to employers, while the average in the system as a whole was 5 per cent.[5]

In an effort to gauge whether these patterns of contact represented a different kind of intensity in the patterns of work, the frequency of contact with a range of associations thought to be most relevant to the case management process was also examined. These included various other government organisations, other offices of their own organisations and providers training. The figures for intensity of contact with employers matched those already discussed for the amount of time spent each week on employer-related activity. Here the differences between public and non-government services follow the expected pattern. Only 28 per cent of the public case managers had daily contact with employers, while the comparable figure for both for-profit and non-profit staff was 50 per cent.

When the range of other possible networks was identified some further differences emerged and for the most part these supported the idea that using different types of contractor would produce different effects at the service delivery level. For example, when asked about their intensity of contact with government departments other than the CES, public case managers had significantly higher rates of contact than did either for-profit or non-profits. Some 74 per cent of the public staff had either daily or weekly involvement with government agencies, while the comparable figure for the contractors was 55 per cent. The public case managers were also more likely to have regular contact with welfare organisations, indicating that although their loads were higher they were attending more closely to the ideal of providing at least some of their clients with a range of interventions.

The contractors had higher rates of contact with employers and also spent more time with local service clubs such as Lions and Rotary and more time with local schools, colleges and universities, where both jobs and training placements could presumably be found. In short there were important differences between the way the three different agencies approached the task of developing networks in the service delivery field. While for the most part they concentrated on managing large lists of job seekers, time spent with employers also rated as important for the non-government agencies. The government officials appeared more hamstrung by high workloads and more likely to use existing contacts with other government agencies than were the two types of private contractor. The next chapter discusses this networking issue and the implications of these patterns for the governance models and strategy types. The present point is that these Australian agencies were very different.

Aside from the frequency and the intensity of contact between case managers and job seekers it was also anticipated that the level of expectation regarding 'reciprocal obligations' would vary between agencies. While the government had not published targets for sanctioning, they had certainly made the penalty system more exacting by allowing a graduated system of benefit reductions to be imposed for failures to come to interviews or to seek work. As noted, they also gave authority and responsibility for recommending sanctions or 'breaches' to the new private contractors. While contractors did not earn any direct income from sanctioning their clients, they could use this as a means to 'clean the rolls' of job seekers they saw as unlikely to succeed at training or work. This in turn would free a place for the agency to gain another applicant from the CES roll. In other words the incentives were

Table 6.4 Australian agencies and sanctioning rates, 1996 (%)

	No Sanctions	1 to 3	4 or more
Public (EAA)	12	68	20
Non-Profits	65	32	3
For-Profits	47	47	7

certainly in the direction of encouraging sanctioning, though not very strongly so.

The sanctioning issue is clearly complex. The front-line staff in these organisations do not control the number of clients who actually get breached, only the numbers recommended for sanctioning.[6] Simple rates of breaching provide a baseline for comparing different case management organisations. However it is also important to seek to understand whether or not the front-line staff assess their clients as complying with their obligations. Comparing the estimated rate of compliance with the numbers the case managers say they have tried to breach gives a realistic sense of how tough or tender the system is, and how differences between agencies play out. The expectation of commentators and participants was that for-profit contractors would be least sympathetic to job seekers, followed by the public agency and that non-profits would be reluctant to sanction any but the most blatant cases.

When asked how many on their own case list 'were not complying with the terms of their activity agreement' or of the social security obligations, more than two-thirds of the case managers estimated the non-compliance rate at 20 per cent or less. That is, one job seeker in five. This estimate in 1996 did not vary in any significant degree between public, non-profit and for-profit agencies.[7] Having asked about the rate of compliance, case managers were then questioned about the numbers they had reported for sanctioning during the past two weeks. Forty-three per cent had not sanctioned anyone and the majority had reported only one or two of their large list of clients. The differences between agencies were pronounced but quite different to what had been expected. As Table 6.4 indicates, the private contractors were unlikely to have sanctioned their clients at all and were least likely to have sanctioned more than one, two or three clients in the previous fortnight. The public agency, EAA, accounted for most of the disciplinary action taking place during this period.

Numerous explanations were offered when it became obvious to the government that the contractors were not performing as intended. During 1994 and 1995 their low rates were excused as start-up problems which showed a lack of confidence and expertise. This was how DEETYA presented the problem in its interim evaluation. But by mid-1996 the contractors were commencing their second year of work and could hardly be viewed as innocent of the regulations and procedures.

It was more likely that sanctioning played no strong role in the incentive system and therefore could be ignored. Added to this, contractors reported in interview that they did not want to get a reputation for toughness because this might stop job seekers choosing them for service. And even a malingering client earned the contractor a commencement fee.

From a policy maker's perspective these characteristics of the new 'market' were both interesting and somewhat worrying. Certainly the workload data showed that variation would indeed follow the breakup of the public service system. However the fact that the loads overall were so high undermined confidence that the system would result in individually tailored programs for each client. The different networks used by the three types of agency also engendered hope that the 'market' might create innovation in the way job seekers were treated. But here again the time spent on anything more than job seeker registrations, repeat interviews and submissions to job interviews, was very small and hardly large enough to qualify as integrated case management.

And if there were 'reciprocal obligations' between the government and the job seekers, these were only evident in the work of the public office. Although all the agencies reported the same level of compliance, only EAA was willing to sanction more than a handful of those regarded as breaching their agreements. Although this study does not attempt to evaluate the economic performance of these agencies it is also worth noting that the ESRA data showed the contractors to be the weaker performers overall. In the period September to November 1996 the public agency had most of its offices performing in the high volume or medium level where 10 to 30 per cent of job seekers found work or training. A few private contractors had spectacularly high outcomes but many more were also in the lowest performance grade. In other words contracting created the same pattern of performance variation as was evident in other aspects of the service, while the public agency continued along a steady, median path.[8] By 1999 this had changed dramatically and Employment National (EN) was on the verge of closure as a result of its very poor performance as a private sector mimic.

Job Network – From Model to Practice

The effectiveness of the Working Nation training programs would remain a political issue and both sides drew comfort from the equivocal evaluations done at the time. These showed that for the most popular programs such as the Landcare and Environmental Action Program (LEAP) the rate of entry into open employment was 32 per cent after three months and 41 per cent after twelve months. Job Clubs were a little better but not much. The best programs were those involving apprenticeships and subsidised employment in a real workplace. In these cases the employment levels rose to 60 per cent (DEETYA, 1996, p. 5). The problem, of course, had been that programs like LEAP were quick and easy to administer and so it was these which DEETYA pushed most energetically in its own struggle to meet the government's performance objectives for *Working Nation.*

Whether 32 per cent was a good number or a bad one would be the subject of heated debate throughout the policy sector for the years that followed. Critics claimed it was not much more than the rate at which unemployed people found jobs under their own steam and was thus an expensive exercise in 'deadweight loss'. Supporters argued that very long-term unemployed people had much poorer chances of getting work under their own steam and that moving one third of them off benefits was a very significant achievement. For its part the Coalition preferred the arguments of the critics. They provided political ammunition against Labor and they opened a path to major budget cuts.

Between its election in March 1996 and May 1998 the Coalition implemented a $1.7 billion tender for new contractors. It appointed 300 or so new providers of 'intensive assistance', 'job brokerage' and 'job club' services. Far fewer job seekers qualified for the new intensive assistance part of the service than were eligible for case management. Yet this drop in numbers did not result in more intensive service for those eligible for it. Instead workloads increased significantly. In 1996 the average load across all agency types had been 133 clients per case manager. When the final survey of all sectors was completed in January 1999 the case loads had increased dramatically to an average of 184 clients per front-line staff member.[9]

The large increase in numbers signified a dramatic shift in the intervention strategies of front-line staff and of their organisations. Cost saving strategies led most organisations to reduce the effort devoted to placing more difficult clients. Instead of the abbreviated form of case management practised under Working Nation, it was now clear that staff were selecting the most job-ready in their case load and moving them quickly into job search activity. Since no training programs were available there was little need to spend time assessing the job seeker's skill development needs and the pressures for a fast throughput of clients appeared to make health and welfare interventions too expensive to warrant an investment of time by front-line staff. In interviews the

Table 6.5   Australian advisers' allocation of time in an average week, 1996–99 (%)

	Job seekers	Employers	Others	Admin.
Working Nation	53	11	10	26
Vanstone	47	13	12	29
Job Network	46	19	5	30

intensive assistance consultants confirmed a picture of high pressure and rapid processing:

> We try to get them to do more for themselves. Our philosophy is that if they do their own search and find their own job it's good for them and its good for us.
>
> All the assessment stuff we used to do (under case management) has pretty much gone by the board now . . . We are really only able to add a bit of polish with things like résumé preparation and motivation . . .
>
> Out method is to give them weekly interviews for about three weeks just to see if they have the 'get up and go' . . . then it's back to one a month or just a phone call to check that they are still going for job interviews an' stuff like that.
>
> To be honest we can't really tell why some get jobs and others don't so we just try to keep them all moving along and hope about a third will do something.

The work patterns also reflected a greater attempt by front-line staff to reach out to employers in order to find job vacancies. Many agencies reported using staff to do both job seeker interviews and employer contact work, although the advent of call centres also meant a shift of some work away from consultants or advisers and towards lower skilled workers following a standard script.

When asked about the amount of their time spent with job seekers, employers, agencies such as welfare or health organisations and the amount spent on administration these changes were striking. In the first survey during Working Nation, two-thirds of case managers spent most of their time working with job seekers. By 1999 this had dropped to 49 per cent of staff. In the earlier period 52 per cent of case managers had 'parked' approximately one third of their caseload. By 1999 this figure had risen to 66 per cent.[10]

The shift from working with job seekers was achieved by devoting more time to seeking job vacancies from employers and by increases in administration. In 1996 the numbers of case managers spending more than 5 per cent of their time with employers was 62 per cent but by 1999 this had risen to 73 per cent. As Table 6.5 indicates, the average time spent with employers rose steadily from 11 per cent in 1996, to 13 per cent in 1998 and up to 19 per cent in 1999. At the same time the front-line staff were spending less time consulting other agencies such as education, welfare or health organisations, indicating that the focus of the work was now almost entirely upon job search and was not at all concerned with addressing the job seeker's barriers to employment.

The biggest drop in time allocated to job seekers occurred after the introduction of the Vanstone reforms that saw training programs removed. Because these data only include responses from public service case managers it is wise to be cautious. However it appears highly likely that it was the removal of training programs which signalled the end of job seeker-focused work at the front line, and not the later introduction of the job-matching activity. This latter function helps explain a further decrease in the time advisers were spending with other agencies and this was significant, but the decline in time spent with job seekers had already begun to take place by this point. This would suggest that it was not a simple matter of the front-line staff having to choose between working with the job seeker or working with employers. Rather the shift was in how they worked with job seekers and the clearest signal that this had changed was found in the fall in consultative activity involving other agencies. The steady increase in administrative work also gives pause to those wishing to promote quasi-markets as a less regulated, less costly alternative to bureaucracy.

These evident changes in strategy affected government, profit and non-profit organisations in different ways, underlying the earlier point that agency type had a major influence on the way job seekers and others were treated. As Table 6.6 shows, public advisers had the highest loads and these increased rapidly to the point where more than half were in the highest category by 1999.

The for-profits had much lower loads both under Working Nation and under Job Network, although they were also increasing rapidly. Three times as many of their advisers had loads in the highest category by 1999 and their average workload had moved from fewer than 100 job seekers to well over 100. But the most significant changes took place among non-profit agencies where the average workload jumped from fewer than 100 job seekers per adviser to over 150. By 1999 this sector had similar workloads to the public sector where loads had traditionally been much higher.

When viewed over time this trend indicates a convergence in front-line work across the industry. Why should this be the case? There appear to be several forces at work here. First of all the shift which took place at the time of the Job Network tender made it necessary for all agencies to cost their services in a similar fashion. For the first time

Table 6.6   Australian advisers' case loads, 1996–99 (% of total load)

	Up to 50		51 to 100		101 to 150		over 150	
	1996	1999	1996	1999	1996	1999	1996	1999
Government	1	6	14	16	40	25	44	53
Non-Profit	9	7	57	24	21	15	13	54
For-Profit	4	8	55	12	30	50	10	29

the public agency was subject to a similar incentive structure to the contractors.

Second, unlike the ESRA tender where loads were rationed with a workload formula per case manager, under Job Network no assumptions or stipulations were included in the guidelines provided to contractors. The convergence was also consistent with the political signal that 'intensive assistance' could now only refer to 'polishing' and other job search preparations of a low cost nature. The withdrawal of training programs sent a strong material and symbolic message to all contractors to focus their efforts on rapid, low-cost movements of clients into job search. With the new requirement to find vacancies, this shift was all but obligatory. Faced with stronger competitive pressures, the logical way for agencies to plan their front-line strategy was to economise. This involved lifting the numbers managed by each adviser, reducing the effort expended on each case and then becoming selective in the use of even the most basic interventions (regular interviews, training etc.).

The other side of the job search relationship concerned compliance and sanctioning. As noted, under Working Nation the government had increased the penalties for mis-behaviour by job seekers and had strengthened the requirements for case managers to monitor and report any failure by the job seeker to meet the terms of their contract. The existence of the training programs had provided the government side of this 'reciprocal obligation' regime and was intended to further strengthen the willingness of advisers to insist upon compliance.

Under Job Network the government side of the relationship was defined simply as the provision of income support, in return for which the job seeker's 'mutual obligation' was to oblige their chosen contractor with attendance at interviews, job search activities and other requirements included in the activity agreement. As under Working Nation, there was a weak response to these tougher demands on the part of contractors. They seemed little interested in the policy objectives espoused by government and were indifferent to that part of their own contract which required them to sanction all mis-behaviour, even those consisting only of administrative breaches for such things as failure to attend a case management interview.

During the first Job Network period the estimated rate of noncompliance increased. Asked how many of their clients 'did not comply with their obligations', in 1996 the reported average was 22 per cent and by 1999 25 per cent. Of course it needs to be stressed that these are the perceptions of advisers, not figures on the actual number of job seekers in breach of their contracts. We can interpret the compliance estimate as a reflection both of the actual behaviour of job seekers and the degree of heightened awareness on the part of the adviser to notice and register forms of noncompliance. Since the objective elements of the system were apparently becoming more severe so far as compliance was concerned, increased reporting by advisers might reflect the changed policy environment as well as difficulties job seekers were experiencing in meeting tougher 'mutual obligations' standards.

Sanction rates followed this upward trend and confirmed the view that job seekers now faced a significantly tougher regime. The average number of sanctions meted out by advisers in 1996 was one a fortnight and by 1999 this had grown to three a fortnight.[11] Significant changes took place among the three types of agency, however. Most non-profits only sought to sanction up to three clients in 1996, but by 1999 they had grown much more severe. There was a 20 per cent growth in the number of non-profit advisers sanctioning four or more job seekers a fortnight. The for-profits had an even steeper trend towards severity.

In 1996 some 96 per cent of the private sector advisers sanctioned at the rate of zero to three, almost the same figure as for the non-profits. By 1999 this level of leniency had dropped to 59 per cent and the numbers sanctioning more than four job seekers per fortnight were consequently over 40 per cent. The increases for the public agency were much less spectacular because they came off a higher base. That is, the public advisers were already sanctioning at a higher rate in 1996. They increased this rate with a 12 per cent rise in the numbers who reported sanctioning more than four clients a fortnight. By 1999 the 'league table' so far as reported sanctioning was concerned had seen a significant change. Most severe now were the for-profit agencies, followed by the public advisers and then the non-profits. As well as indicating how the market acted as an upward pressure towards convergence, these figures help explain why advisers reported spending more time on administration and less time working with job seekers.

By 1999 normative orientations and assumptions had also changed. Attitudes to advocacy were significantly more equivocal. Significantly more advisers either disagreed with the idea that they were 'advocates of the client's rights', or held no opinion. Although still the majority view, the advocacy approach had dropped from 78 per cent agreement to 59 per cent agreement. By the time Job Network was in place the front-line staff were also more aware of the priority to 'shift the maximum number of clients off benefits'. Only 46 per cent saw this as the objective of their work in 1996 but three years later some 72 per cent agreed that this was a prime motivation. This transformation of the system into one focused exclusively upon the immediate economic outcomes defined by current government priorities was also reflected in attitudes to whether or not it was advisable to organise one's own work mostly according to 'those actions with clients which will generate a payable outcome'. Only 17 per cent of staff thought this described their strategy in 1996 but by 1999 this was the preferred approach of 78 per cent of front-line staff.

Given that staff were less likely to follow the government's sanctioning priorities, even if their own rate of compliance with policy did increase over time, why were they more attentive to this part of the scheme? Plainly the power of the new Welfare-to-Work ideology is not enough on its own and it can be assumed that those policies which directly affected the agency's incentive system were powerful. All of these incentives drove advisers towards quick, superficial interactions with job seekers and toward strategies which maximised the agency's short-term financial performance. If this had been less true of non-profit contractors under Working Nation, it was now standard practice throughout the system.

Conclusions

Paradoxically, then, the hybrid-market system appeared even more open to direct political manipulation by senior bureaucrats, provided that these interventions carried strong, immediate financial payoffs. Policy intentions which affected quality or ethical issues, such as client rights or sanctions, appeared far less open to influence from above than under procedural and corporate governance regimes where staff were often equipped with mandated programs and clients had basic entitlements which could not be deleted.

The Australian officials were plainly the least procedural of all four cases. This showed through in their lower use of diagnostic instruments and their reduced reliance upon computer technology to manage interactions with job seekers. But beyond this general point about their divergence from the older norm, no single generalisation is capable of defining this mix of agencies. Instead organisation type becomes a more powerful explanation of governance strategies and norms.

The Australian for-profit agencies emerged as those who spent large amounts of time working with employers, but less time than most others on welfare or training-related work. Their advisers were older than elsewhere and significantly less likely to be unionised. Even though they did not network with other service providers they did attend outside meetings of other officials, perhaps reflecting their need to size up the competition. In interviews they complained that such 'network' gatherings were a waste of time, yet they also said that it was important to have someone from their office attend. It was expected that these would be the officials most motivated by the need to generate income for their agency and the Australian for-profit agencies certainly rated this value more highly than most others in the study. But they were not the most income-conscious, this distinction going to the Australian non-profits. These were the least likely of any group to use their computer system to order interactions with job seekers and they also made less use of classification methods than most others.

The Australian non-profit met the expected standard of co-operative activity, reporting the highest overall commitment to helping other advisers with such things as computer problems. But while this distinguished them from government officials, it did not put them in a different category to Australian for-profits who also revealed co-operative norms. In fact the two non-government agency types were significantly different to the government office with regard to sanctioning (lower) and time spent with employers (higher).

Yet the convergence in methods evident after 1997 showed how dependent these agencies were upon the pricing system manipulated by the Department. At each new tender stage the for-profits and non-profits struggled to find a stable, minimal regime of services which would keep them in business. While all were attracted to a similar regime of minimal inputs, there were differences and these showed through in the second tender round when performance in placing Flex Three, or very disadvantaged job seekers, became most telling.[12]

Employment National's spectacular failure, like the poor performance of a number of the private recruitment agencies such as Drake, resulted from their inability to place the most disadvantaged job seekers into jobs. EN went out of its way to style itself as an aggressive profit-making agency and this included a determination by senior management to rid itself of any suggestion that this was (or ever had been) a public service organisation with a public interest commitment. Instead EN courted non-government contracts and described its Job Network strategy as one in which the 'damaged fruit' would simply be slipped into the barrel with ordinary job seekers destined for normal recruitment contracts. Despite regular warnings that its performance was slipping and its strategy totally wrong-headed, the EN leadership took just two years to turn a 40 per cent share of the 'market' and a government investment of A$150 million into one of the worst failures in the history of the Australian public sector. It was the church and community owned agencies which were most successful in the second tender round because it was they who had the best rapport with very disadvantaged job seekers, yet remained open to the legitimate concerns of employers.

A general reduction in attention to the needs of job seekers was the central paradox and criticism of a system that had promised 'market' responsiveness as an alternative to bureaucratic inflexibility. As the next chapter shows, far from conforming to the simple dictates of a market logic, the Australian agencies developed a preference for networking, albeit a form of networking which reflected major differences between agency types. This suggested not one governance strategy but three, with each finding a distinctive path towards self-enterprise for front-line staff and job seekers.

Notes

1 While no official name was given to this amended scheme, it was largely associated in the public mind with the minister responsible, Senator Amanda Vanstone.

2 The Howard Government continued this regime through 1996 and 1997 but had foreshadowed a further development of this market to commence in 1998. This is known as the 'Flex program' and imposes further change upon the various participants. The government announced it would close down its own Commonwealth Employment Service and merge these functions with the social security office, now to operate as a service delivery agency (called CentreLink) for all recipients of income assistance. This new bureaucracy would undertake the basic registration and referral functions found in all public employment agencies. Those deemed likely to benefit (and subject to available funds) would then be referred to three levels of assistance (Flex One, Two and Three) to be provided by either the new public agency, or by one of the contracted agencies.

3 CentreLink was to be one of many Australian innovations which confounded theorists of public administration. As a service delivery agency it was 'owned' by no department and instead had its own clients sitting on its Board. Within months of establishing the new agency the Board began a savage restructure which saw significant job losses and cuts to the quality of service offered to job seekers and others.

4 Twenty-two interviews were conducted with eleven for-profit and eleven non-profit managers from Victoria and NSW. They were asked, 'How would you rate the Flex One arrangements now that you have had a chance to see them in operation? Generally good? Mixed? Generally bad? Further comment?'

5 Eighty-two per cent of public case managers spent less than 10% of their week on employers. Seventy-six per cent of non-profits spent only this low

amount. Sixty-three per cent of firms devoted 10% or less, with the rest spending up to 40%.

6 The recommended sanction is passed to the CES where a senior officer decides whether to recommend to the Department of Social Security (DSS) that benefits be reduced or stopped. At this point the job seeker may use the Social Security Appeals Tribunal to appeal the DSS action.

7 Although there were important differences over the three surveys with the contractors eventually reporting higher rates of non-compliance than the public agency.

8 ESRA (1997) *Partnership for Work*, Melbourne, p. 31.

9 By this point it was difficult to assess how many staff were actually performing intensive assistance and how many were simply conducting job matching interviews. But those asked to complete the questionnaire were staff who devoted at least a part of their time to intensive assistance, indicating that the case loads undoubtedly referred to their intensive assistance clients rather than to the other clients who would not normally be regarded as part of any particular staff member's case list.

10 The question was, 'In an average week, what proportion of your time do you spend in direct contact with job seekers, working with other service providers, working with employers, and on general administration?'.

11 The question was, 'How many clients have you recommended for sanctioning in the past two weeks?' In 1996 the mean was 1.189 and in 1999 it was 2.904.

12 Although details of actual performance remain secret, with the government only being prepared to list agencies in a 'star rating' schedule.

CHAPTER 7

Taking the Measure of 'New Governance'

WITH JENNY M. LEWIS

For social theorists the central problem of governance is neatly defined and awkwardly positioned by the traditions pioneered by Foucault and Habermas. Both find their starting point in the critique of liberalism and each seeks a path away from the dominion of economic modes of organisation, be that the siren call of efficiency or the politics of programmed social change. Central to these two different accounts is a concern with individual freedom and the state. True, Foucault and his inheritors remain suspicious of the very idea of escape paths and counter-programs. All prescriptive acts threaten to concede control to agents of the gulag. Instead the way out is found in an 'aesthetics of existence' which avoids any possibility of control by logics of social order or the imperatives of a concerted consensus (Bell, 1996, p. 84). And for Habermas too the risk of colonisation is deeply inscribed in the manifold gestures of modern bureaucratic politics. His alternative is found in a distinction between 'life world' and 'system' in which the former promises to prioritise the unique and authentic possibilities of normative work and which imagines a new 'communicative action' as the means for fashioning a legitimised politics (Habermas, 1988).

The primary puzzle for students of governance is precisely this pernicious, unresolved tension between contending expectations about the relationships between people and institutions. For present purposes a feasible track though this impasse is to recognise that relations between officialdom and its subjects ultimately inhere within some discernible field of micro-relations between state organisations and their clients. Neither officials nor citizens may any longer be defined in theory or principle as the embodiment of some settled status or other. Both have become agents of a new social practice which is 'made up' in a cultural project of individuation. Actions, programs, benefits and entitlements

144

now carry a new code which calls upon actors to self-construct their use of public resources and values in order to succeed in what Beck (2000, p. 164) has called 'a life on the run'.

The examination of Welfare-to-Work institutions in these four different advanced systems has sought to view this new, contingent world by looking at the way certain images and expectations of governance are played out at the front line of government. This encounter between reform strategies and actual programs produces both confirmation of new models and surprises concerning their implementation. The enterprising ideal certainly defines a new form of program flexibility for officials and a strong imperative for them to generate specific performances for their superiors and a new 'pliability' among their clients. Standard pathways are not altogether abandoned but are everywhere hinged to cultural strategies which exchange official support for private acts of reinvention. This is not so much a revolutionary change in paradigms of assistance as one in which a single path is continually split and redefined as one of several possible trajectories, all of which require trade-offs, brokered options and temporary adjustments to new requirements.

The next chapter discusses this new solicitude. The focus of this chapter is on the ways in which these changes describe differences in the four systems and thus in governance as a more or less unified field. As already recounted, stereotypes of neo-liberalism and reinvented forms of social democracy prove to be, at best, a partial explanation of what really goes on at the front line. Surprises are as numerous as confirmations. While this says something about the inadequacy of even a reasonably comprehensive method of inquiry, it also tells us that ten years of radical change have produced no single model of new governance, even among rather similar, liberal-democractic states. Instead, the world of the official and the public contractor is shot-through with hybridity, boundary crossing and institutional experimentation. Interestingly research in other sectors suggests that this new form of public–private sector hybridisation is fast becoming a recognisable feature of innovation and system renewal more generally (Breschi & Malerba, 1997; Marceau, 1994).

In each of the four countries there is a pattern of major, radical change in the governance arrangements affecting unemployed people and those involved in what can broadly be called Welfare-to-Work institutions. In two countries this involved the restructure and de-coupling of a single public service system and in Australia and the Netherlands the reform strategy included the creation of a 'mixed economy' of public and private agencies. In all four the pressures for change came from a crisis of confidence in previous social security arrangements which were seen as too relaxed about return-to-work obligations, too willing to ignore the problem of long-term unemployment and too quick to hand the welfare issue back to policy makers as just another claim for higher expenditure on benefits.

In finding a path towards more active, individualised service, these four countries provide us with unique opportunities to see how new forms of governance are invented at ground level. Comparisons between the four have so far concentrated on a few core issues such as the way relations at the front line are defined, the workloads of advisers and the approach to key issues such as networking and sanctioning.[1] These confirm significant differences between the countries and also challenge some of the assumptions linking each country with certain standard images or models of reform. So, for instance, while more procedural than the others, the UK was nevertheless well advanced in its pursuit of a stronger corporate governance system. There were few indications that Thatcherism had led to much interest in market-type methods inside the public service or to privatisation of core welfare functions. In New Zealand the neo-liberal zeal was also something short of systemic. Radical change there had paid close attention to a thin panic about increasing poverty in the early 1990s which, in turn, resulted in stronger corporate control but with greater commitment to empowering advisers to help the most disadvantaged job seekers. The Dutch approach was less willing to release the state from its social commitments, but more than willing to open the borders of the state to private methods of intervention. Yet the process of neo-corporatist negotiation obviously creates less interest in competition as a method for selecting potential partners. And while more committed to markets for service delivery, the Australians actually did least to inspire multiplicity and variation among the hundreds of agencies contracted to serve the state.

The analysis to this point suggests highly adaptive, even innovative forms of central control by states seeking alternatives to single-path programs and mass entitlement benefits. Now is an opportune time to turn from recounting difference and surprising achievements to discussing what the states have in common. Chapter 2 described a possible logic of reinvention by defining the enterprise project as a turn away from an older model called proceduralism, towards one of three styles of reform. The three new models were taken from the rhetoric and promise of reformers and the management theorists they favoured. Like every attempt to reduce complexity to theoretical constructs, these four were never going to be any better than convenient generalisations. And as such the sharp borders of a four-by-four table were always open to the risks of over-simplification.

This chapter re-examines these orderly expectations. It reveals that the work of the reformers, polemicists and reinventers has not gone for nothing. Much of their effort has indeed created a new set of expectations and norms for the way the state's work is done. Those who choose to believe that large, expensive bureaucracies carry forward a power structure which resists executive control and holds its own line against the times will be disappointed. Instead there is also successful breaking open and highly effective engineering from above. But the results of this contrived reform play out with a subtlety which suggests a new kind of perpetual motion, of flux and process, not the settling of a new, resolved model of post-bureaucratic power.

The processes which the new models share is a similar enterprising interest in transition, in phase-shifting and in mixing the public and private spheres. In each of the four cases this is seen in new instruments of central control, tighter mandates to empower them to co-ordinate other agencies more tightly and tougher, more selective approaches to job seekers. But did this broad interest in reform result in the emergence of any more systematic view of governance to replace the classic standard of the procedural regime? To what extent did those three alternative regimes identified in Chapter 2 actually appear in the work of these new institutional ensembles? And if the new pattern is for no single pattern of public or private organisation to dominate, can we see any strong forms of hybridisation inside these blurring boundaries, and some new structural tendencies within the new commitment to process and flow?

In assessing the impact of these enterprising dynamics on the ordinary work of government Chapter 2 identified four governance types. The central proposition was that the established bureaucratic norms and structures defined as 'rule by procedure and supervisory control' were in rapid, perhaps terminal, decline and that this procedural governance was being replaced by three other ideals of good governance. The first, the corporate governance type, often described as 'managerialism', asserted the importance of strong corporate control as a means for improving general efficiency and the political responsiveness of public organisations. A second, termed market governance, proposed dividing state services into myriad competing businesses and contractors. Finally, network governance sought effectiveness through inter-organisational collaboration, joint action and greater empowerment of local agents.

In the individual country studies the corporate type comes closest to defining the formal pattern of reform enacted in the UK, the Netherlands and New Zealand. Australia comes closest to the 'market' type. Both the Netherlands and Australia might be seen as more 'networked' than the other two, at least so far as the overall map or grid of governance relations is concerned. However it is not enough to define these systems simply as a political economy of treatments, targets and contracts. The study's purpose has been to show that these practical arrangements exist within larger normative systems which seek to re-imagine the logic and process of governance, not just its formal structures. How then do front-line staff define and explain the work they do? This is less a matter of opinion than of perception and evaluation.

The forty governance items in the survey were refined into twenty-eight items of simple, colloquial statements about the way officials approached core aspects of their work. These normative statements were derived from the interview transcripts. Officials were asked whether they agreed with these statements and if so, how strong their commitments were. They were then asked to choose between four 'core' statements which aimed to summarise the attraction each model of governance held for them. It needs noting that the process of extracting a long list of governance survey items from in-depth interviews and reducing the list to forced-choice statements is risky. In attempting to contain those risks, great care was taken in defining terms and in checking that the phrases and concepts made sense. As well, care was taken to ensure that in their responses to the supposed appeal of a particular model, officials were referring to their own work at that point, and not according to some preferred model. Fortunately, these officials were a highly articulate and sensitive group. Their whole working life is concerned with making assessments, filling in forms and choosing between strategies. This fact, as much as the method, underlies the reliability of the results.

The original intention in developing the normative statements about governance was to create a set of scales or indices for each of the four types defined in Chapter 2. What follows is a brief description of the factor analysis, designed for the general reader. The footnotes contain more detail, as does the Statistical Appendix. The use of factor analysis as the primary tool of investigation signals the exploratory nature of this part of the study. This was viewed as a reasonable strategy given that these changes herald complex shifts in both work and normative orientations of officials and have only recently been put to the test. The aim was to investigate which items formed coherent and sensible dimensions, and then to test these against the governance types derived from policy statements, public management plans and organisation theory. Since these sources might express both whimsical ideas about actual reforms and real claims about their core orientations, the exploratory approach required several implementations and refinements.

First, a process called principal components analysis was used on the twenty-eight items to identify the underlying or latent dimensions of each governance regime type.[2] The use of a procedure called varimax (orthogonal) rotation aimed to determine each dimension with its own subset of non-overlapping indicators. Reliability analysis was then used to test how well the dimensions (or models) formed into subgroups,[3] and correlation and reliability of difference coefficients were then calculated to determine the 'separateness' of these governance models.[4] These allowed answers to two centrally important questions: Are the models really the expected combinations of the items we thought would be important? And, are the four, as anticipated, significantly different from one another?

Three Governance Strategies not Four

The factor analysis showed that the central argument of the book holds true – governance now works as a set of different conceptions of authority and organisation and these are both coherent and robust. However, the normative basis of this reform process shows that there are three not four dominant discourses. The study shows a successful three-factor solution that is reproduced in the Statistical Appendix. The first factor, called 'corporate-market', combines or hybridises some key elements of both the 'corporate' and 'market' governance models. Re-testing in the Australian case only served to strengthen this conclusion. This indicates that these two governance orientations, derived from the reform literature and previous research, are a single strategy. Officials do not distinguish them as alternate approaches, rather they successfully synthesise them into a new form.

This 'corporate-market' orientation combines key norms from both the original types defined in Chapter 2. The 'corporate' elements include statements that recognise the organisation's emphasis on output and its interest in targets for priority clients. The 'market' elements include the officials' willingness to maximise financial outcomes and to take note of actions that help create 'payable' outcomes for the organisation or staff member.

An earlier analysis of the results from the first Australian survey in 1996 showed the existence of the corporate-market type in that country (Considine & Lewis, 1999).[5] Given that the Australian public sector was then in the midst of its first radical pro-market reform process, this might have been regarded as an aberrant case. However the results for the combined data from the four countries, spread over four years, supports the conclusion that the 'corporate-market' model is both meaningful and powerful. Applying these same tests to each of the four country samples, the same result showed through. This indicates that officials in enterprising states blend or synthesise corporate goals and targets with some competitive, quasi-market techniques for achieving them, and that this hybrid governance strategy is evident across systems and, in one case at least, across time.

The second dimension defined through the factor analysis was the 'procedural' type. This was the position often represented in the literature as the Weberian or classical bureaucratic type. As predicted, it was composed of those items concerning strong forms of supervision, expert supervision and the preference for treating clients as part of a universal service. In other words, it was composed of the expected elements or norms.

The third model was the 'network' type. As earlier acknowledged, this was the most difficult to specify precisely. It contained sentiments and norms which favoured a range of fuzzy networking attributes, including 'joined-up government' and the breaking down of so-called 'silo organisations', as well as various forms of case management and increased discretion for officials. An important finding in the study is that this network type forms a coherent dimension. Using material from interviews and site observations, the survey items selected for this type were those which expressed a commitment to inter-agency relationship building and brokerage. It also included the desire to gain the trust of clients, a recognition that outcomes were a joint effort, and a willingness to help other agencies with problems.

Having identified three models or dimensions through factor analysis, three corresponding scales were then constructed and their reliability was analysed using Cronbach's alpha coefficient. The items included in each scale (Tables 7.1, 7.2 and 7.3) were derived from a combination of the expected location of items on the different governance scales, as well as from the three-factor solution.[6] While none of these three scales achieved very high alpha scores, they certainly meet the standard of reasonable internal reliability required of newly constructed scales (Nunnally, 1978). The corporate-market scale had the highest alpha coefficient at .65, followed by the network scale at .51, and the procedural also at .51.

It can be said, then, that the corporate-market model is clearly the most impressive of the governance dimensions to be identified in practical terms. It is clear that items concerning both the centrality of targets and the front-line responsibility for financial outcomes have been concentrated within this scale. The corporate-market dimension first found in the initial Australian study contained all of the nine items included here, plus two additional market items and one network item, none of which contributed to the scale when examined within the entire sample. The alpha coefficient for this scale in the earlier study was .67, and the reliability of the scale for the whole study, with three fewer items, was only marginally lower (.65).

Table 7.1   Corporate–Market Regime Scale (n=1066, alpha=.65)

Scale items	Alpha if item deleted
15. In my job I am NOT influenced by numerical targets (reversed)	.64
17. Our organisation has targets for certain types of client	.63
27. I often remind clients of the sanctioning power to get them to pay attention	.63
28. My job is determined by goals set elsewhere	.61
30. More and more the objective in this job is to maximise the organisation's financial outcomes	.60
31. I think the objective in this job is to shift the maximum number of clients off benefits	.60
32. I use our information technology to track priority clients	.63
33. I do tend to take note of those actions with clients that will generate a payable outcome for the office	.63
38. In my job clients are organised into formal and informal priority groups	.64

Table 7.2   Procedural Regime Scale (n=1150, alpha=.51)

Scale items	Alpha if item deleted
6. The lines of authority are not clear in my work (reversed)	.55
10. My supervisor knows a lot about the work I do day-to-day	.32
19. When I come across something not covered by the procedure guide I refer it to my supervisor	.35

Table 7.3   Network Regime Scale (n=1119, alpha=.51)

Scale items	Alpha if item deleted
9. When it comes to day-to-day work I am free to decide for myself what I will do with each client	.49
12. The really important rules in this job are the ones to do with obtaining assistance from other organisations	.46
16. The main thing you have to do in this job is gain the trust of the client	.44
24. I like to keep my own records and files on clients and programs	.45
26. When you get good results with clients it's usually a team effort by yourself, trainers and the employer	.49
37. If an official from another employment organisation asked for help in using the computer I would help them	.46

The procedural scale contains only three items, all of which relate to aspects of hierarchy or supervision. As such, this scale, and the dimension it represents, expressed the predicted and much discussed path of bureaucratic standardisation.

Other than the fact that the dimension did in fact emerge, what is most interesting is its weakness, with an alpha of .51. Clearly this dimension has only a limited capacity to explain the norms of front-line officials, a fact which helps confirm the destruction of older forms of governance by enterprising reinventions. In particular it is evident that core bureaucratic attributes which concern co-ordination and control methods have a very weak influence on the norms regularly used by officials.

The network scale began as the most exploratory and ended as the most theoretically challenging. This set of ideas had been less precisely articulated in the literature than the other governance types. This lack of clarity in articulation may reflect policy-maker unease with a system of co-ordination that does not emphasise the fashionable role of strong managers, hierarchies or markets.[7] Or it may be that this is simply the most recent in the evolution of new governance strategies.

Yet the results do show the emergence of this new style of governance and indicate that it has many of the predicted attributes.[8] These include the willingness of officials to define their day-to-day work as based upon the development of trusting relationships with other agencies, officials' high levels of practitioner autonomy and willingness to co-operate with other agencies: these all signal a quite distinctive approach.

It is also interesting to note that the network governance model appears to combine two different elements of organisational practice. The first may be described as forms of inter-organisational collaboration. The second involves forms of autonomy, flexible work and discretion among officials. Greater collaboration might be seen to need these higher levels of independence in order to succeed, but until now they have been treated as different dimensions of work in complex systems. It is therefore helpful to know that, so far as these officials are concerned, the two form part of a single approach to meeting the expectations driving their current jobs.

Obviously there are many individual items and norms within these different models that might be considered attractive by almost any official. It is therefore of some importance that, so far as practitioners are concerned, the three different models or approaches are in fact quite separate. To determine the associations between these dimensions, the three scales were constructed by summing the items for each scale (Tables 7.1, 7.2 and 7.3). The information in Table 7.4 indicates that there is little overlap between the three governance dimensions, with

Table 7.4   Correlations, reliabilities and reliability of difference coefficients for the three governance scales

	Corporate-Market	Procedural	Network
Corporate-Market	.65	.07	−.18
Procedural	.55	.51	−.04
Network	.64	.53	.51

Note: This table contains reliability scores (alpha coefficients) on the diagonal, correlation coefficients above the diagonal, and reliability of difference coefficients below the diagonal. Hence, the alpha coefficient for the market-corporate dimension is .65, its correlation with the procedural dimension is .07, and the reliability of difference coefficient for these two dimensions is .65.

Table 7.5   Means and standard deviations for the three governance scales

	N	Mean	Std Dev
Corporate-Market	1066	67.4	10.9
Procedural	1150	67.4	15.8
Network	1119	71.5	10.7

the correlations between the scales all being relatively small, and the reliability of different coefficients all larger than .5.[9]

The study expected to find four quite different governance strategies at the front line. These data show that there are three, not four, dimensions or orientations. These dimensions have been successfully measured using three scales constructed from observed variables, and these scales were reasonably reliable. The relationships between these scales indicate that they do indeed constitute separate dimensions. Next, to determine the relative salience of the three orientations, the three scales were converted to percentages and treated pro rata. This means that the highest possible score for each scale corresponds to a score of 100 per cent. Treating the pro rata scores allows comparisons since the number of items in each scale has been taken into account.

As shown in Table 7.5, the highest mean rating was for the network scale, followed by the corporate-market scale and the procedural scales which had the lower mean scores. Reading these scores as indicators of the salience of each of these scales to the respondents (in relative terms) leads to some surprising findings. The network scale, which is the least well developed in the research literature, appears to be the most salient for our officials in the four systems. The procedural scale, representing a long tradition of bureaucratic work, is of the same order as the corporate-management scale.

Table 7.6   Means and standard deviations for the three governance scales by
country

	Corporate-Market		Procedural		Network	
	N	Mean (SD)	N	Mean (SD)	N	Mean (SD)
Australia	570	64.7 (11.1)	599	65.9 (16.9)	584	76.3 (9.2)
Netherlands	229	68.2 (8.9)	269	65.7 (13.5)	264	67.2 (9.1)
New Zealand	122	70.2 (10.6)	130	75.8 (12.8)	122	69.9 (8.5)
United Kingdom	144	74.7 (9.7)	151	68.9 (15.3)	148	61.7 (10.4)

The Governance Types in Context

In sum, the governance models or types make sense, can be measured
and are clearly separate from each other. It is relevant now to see
whether these models are related to other aspects of the organisation of
these services. Do different countries favour one type over another? Are
the backgrounds of advisers an important indicator of why some deploy
one strategy rather than another?

(1) Country

The most important question posed by the study was 'what difference
does country make?'. The design of the comparative approach was
based on the idea that different institutional histories, expressed in variations in the benefit systems and in the organisation of service delivery
responsibilities, would see each of the four countries positioned differently within the broader field of enterprise reinventions.[10]

The results derived from the scale development process show that the
UK was the country with the strongest commitment to the corporate-
market type, with a mean score of 74.7. The strong emphasis upon
targets (Chapter 3) made this a predictable outcome. However Australia
was significantly lower than all the other countries on the corporate-
market scale, with a mean score of 64.7. This was interesting. Evidently
the break-up of that system into a diverse range of contractors weakened
the corporate elements. But the market norms failed to grip these
participants with sufficient force to allow this model to become a new
source of coherence. There was no significant difference between New
Zealand and the Netherlands so far as the corporate-market scale was
concerned.

Analysis of the results for the procedural scale showed New Zealand
to be significantly different from the other three countries. This system
had the strongest commitment to the traditional procedural governance
model. The high mean score for New Zealand (75.8) was significantly

different to the others. Next came the UK (68.9). It was significantly higher than the means for both Australia and the Netherlands. The scores were not significantly different between Australia and the Netherlands. The study's original hypothesis had not anticipated this. The analysis of the institutional features of the UK system, together with the review of its Conservative government's statements about its reform intentions, had led to the expectation that it would rate high on the procedural scale.

It is important to note, however, that the results confirm the expected differences between the UK and New Zealand on one hand, and the two mixed-economy cases (Australia and the Netherlands) on the other, so far as attachment to more traditional norms is concerned. The chapter later discusses the effects of agency ownership upon different governance systems.

On the network scale each of the four countries was significantly different. Australia emerged as the most committed to network norms and orientations. It had the highest mean score (76.3), followed by New Zealand and the Netherlands (69.9 and 67.2), with the UK having the lowest mean score (61.7). Again, this was different to the expectations built upon an analysis of documents and institutional histories. Although its reform rhetoric was loud in its affection for market behaviour, the front-line officials in Australia were more strongly oriented to norms that are consistent with the network type. This is both a consequence of the market type failing to emerge as a distinct type in its own right, and is a likely result of the Australian system generating high levels of insecurity among its large retinue of contractors. As later discussion shows, these contractors do not often collaborate with one another, rather they develop different networking styles depending on whether they are in the government, non-profit or for-profit sectors.

(2) Ownership

Like country, the position of respondents on the three scales was associated with the ownership structure (privatisation etc.) of agencies. For the corporate-market type the important differences were between the government services and those run by both non-profit and for-profit agencies. The government-only services rated highest of all on the corporate-market scale (70.7), as might be expected. There were no significant differences between the two non-government types of agency. This is interesting in that it might be expected that the profit-taking firms would register significantly higher on this scale, given their pro-market elements. One likely reason is that non-profits have converged in their basic approach to this work as a result of the systemic

Table 7.7   Means and standard deviations for the three governance scales by ownership

	Corporate-Market		Procedural		Network	
	N	Mean (SD)	N	Mean (SD)	N	Mean (SD)
Government	657	70.7 (9.8)	691	68.2 (14.9)	672	69.3 (10.4)
For-profit	193	62.2 (9.8)	226	67.3 (15.0)	223	72.0 (10.4)
Non-profit	179	61.5 (11.1)	195	63.7 (18.4)	188	78.3 (9.2)

incentives and opportunities provided by the overall governance structures established by policy makers.

For the procedural governance scale the government services also rated highest with a mean score of 68.2, but this was not statistically significantly different to those working in for-profit agencies. The non-profit agencies rated significantly lower (63.7) than their government colleagues on the procedural scale. This represented a change from the first Australia-only study, where the non-profits did rate more strongly on procedural items. This too confirms the claim that the procedural regime had weakened over this period and that as it weakened the non-profits became more and more like their colleagues in for-profit agencies.

So far as ownership was concerned, the network scale proved to be the most discriminating of all. It shows significant differences between government, non-profit and for-profit agencies. The scores also followed in the expected direction, with non-profit agencies having the highest mean scores for networking (78.3), then for-profit (72.0) and the lowest scores for government officials (69.3).

Drawing the Threads Together

The corporate-market scale has the highest reliability, and is strongly associated with country and ownership in the expected ways. The procedural scale is by far the weaker, despite early expectations and some first round results. The network scale just meets an adequate reliability level and clearly requires further development, experimentation with further items and so on. However it appears to be a highly salient concept to the officials surveyed, and it provides a very successful means for discriminating between different normative aspects of governance within these Welfare-to-Work systems.

There is a strong and expected association between network orientation and ownership. Non-profits are more strongly committed to this set of norms than for-profits. Both are more committed to it than government officials. The country differences are also consistent with this pattern. Australia's multi-agency system provokes the strongest commitment to network norms. The UK is the least network-oriented and this is consistent with its single focus on a universal service.

The fact that the network scale successfully discriminates between each of the countries and ownership types provides evidence of an important, emerging alternative to what is clearly the now dominant governance strategy – the corporate-market model.[11] The procedural dimension, while it did exist, formed a somewhat weaker scale than the other two. Declining support for this model is not surprising, but the lack of a coherent set of norms is. This lack of coherence in the relatively low scores for this scale indicates the decline of traditional bureaucratic ideals as the core orientation of officials working in these public programs. This is all the more compelling given the fact that public servants constituted a majority of the sample and were the monopoly providers in two of the four countries. This provides support for the idea that the 'enterprising spirit' is associated with the 'end of bureaucracy'.

Viewed from this perspective it is tempting to conclude that economic-rational principles (corporate-market governance) have become dominant everywhere. However the emergence of the network type indicates that the corporate-market form may itself be subject to important counter tendencies. It is therefore worth spending a little more time on the network type to define its dynamics and to understand who views this as the normative structure which best explains their work.

'Basic', 'Public' and 'Civic' Networking

First, however, do those who see themselves as 'networkers' also behave as such? Do they actually spend more time negotiating with others, moving between organisations, developing new solutions to problems or brokering deals between different parts of the public and private systems? Are these networking strategies linked to differences in countries and in organisations?

The governance types as normative structures exist as models and cognitive maps of the way officials understand their work; as evaluations of their own roles; as statements of their official priorities; and as summaries of the way they interact with other key actors, including their colleagues and managers. A sceptic might well point out that there are apt to be differences between the way people present themselves in interviews and surveys and their actual behaviour or priorities in day-to-day work. So 'Do networkers actually network?'. The short answer to this question is that indeed they do. All officials exhibited a regular pattern of interactions with some outside agencies, that is, agencies beyond their

Table 7.8   Frequency distributions for networking items

Frequency of contact with:	Never	Quarterly or less	Monthly	Weekly	Daily
Other parts of Own Organisation	1.5	2.6	12.4	42.5	40.9
(Other) Government Departments	12.6	21.6	26.5	25.3	14.1
Local Government	25.5	41.3	21.5	9.0	2.6
Welfare Agencies	14.4	37.7	26.5	15.3	6.2
Employers	2.6	8.8	17.5	34.1	36.8
Training Agencies	2.6	18.8	31.0	36.6	12.1
Advisers in other Agencies	8.1	23.5	28.7	30.2	9.5
Local service clubs (e.g. Rotary)	31.6	36.1	20.5	9.6	2.1
Schools and universities	20.0	39.5	23.8	13.3	3.4
Local media	52.6	29.5	9.9	7.0	1.0

own door. But from here the picture becomes more complex. Three significantly different networking strategies were evident, ranging from an elementary or 'basic networking' type which was minimal in its scope or reach, an intermediate type, called 'public networking', and a more elaborate type, called 'civic networking'. The officials from different countries, from different ownership groups and with different background characteristics varied significantly in their use of these three networking sub-strategies.

(1) Networks as Patterns of Contact

To understand how these officials in different national systems and organisations actually related to or connected with one another they were asked to define their frequency of contact with a range of likely agencies in their environments. These were first defined through interviews as being the key contributors to the service sector as a whole. This contact matrix included frequency of contact with officials from their own organisations located at other sites; officials from (other) government departments; and contact with a range of separate organisations including local government, welfare agencies, employers, training providers, other employment agencies and local service clubs such as Rotary, schools and universities and the local media.

Each official was asked to score their own frequency of contact with each of these ten agencies on a six-point scale from 'daily contact' to 'never contacted'.[12] The frequency of contact with different agencies is shown in Table 7.8. Most of the officials reported high levels of contact on two of these items – contact with other parts of their own organisation and contact with employers. More than 80 per cent of officials were

Table 7.9 Networking items and factor loadings from three factor solution

Frequency of contact with:	Public	Civic	Basic
Other parts of Own Organisation			.77
(Other) Government Departments	.75		
Local Government	.49		
Welfare Agencies	.64		
Employers			.75
Training Agencies	.72		
Advisers in other Agencies	.44	.49	
Local service clubs (e.g. Rotary)		.70	
Schools and universities		.72	
Local media		.67	

Note: This table shows the varimax rotated solution. Only factor loadings with a magnitude of .40 and greater are shown here, for ease of interpretation.

in either daily or weekly contact with others in their own organisation, and over 70 per cent were in daily or weekly contact with employers. At the other end of the scale, many officials reported rather low levels of contact with the local media, local service clubs, local government and schools and universities.

Factor analysis was again employed to estimate how well these three formed separate, reliable types. The ten networking items in Table 7.8 were analysed using principal components analysis in order to identify underlying networking alignments. Three factors emerged which had eigenvalues greater than one. Factor loadings for these are shown in Table 7.9. The first factor, 'public networking', indicated a pattern in which officials mostly interacted with government organisations, municipal institutions, welfare agencies and training groups. The second, 'civic networking' type, involved frequent contacts with officials and advisers in other organisations, service clubs, schools and universities and the local media.

The third 'basic networking' strategy saw contacts confined to just two groups – advisers from the official's own organisation and employers. This factor has been labelled 'basic' because the two individual items which load on this factor represent the most elementary and routine forms of interaction which we would expect even the most single-minded official to have. Consequently it is no surprise to see very high scores for this type within the whole group of officials surveyed. The frequencies shown in Table 7.8 indicated an almost universal subscription to this kind of contact at daily, weekly or monthly intervals.

The frequency distributions and the factor analysis of the ten contact variables indicated the existence of a basic network that almost

Table 7.10   Types of agency and networking factor scores

	N	Public	Civic	Basic
Government	635	.18	−.20	−.04
For-profit	210	−.63	.29	.29
Non-profit	172	.10	.33	−.17

everybody involved in this work used regularly. The other two networks of public and civic contacts can now be considered to be additional to this core network. In this sense these networks are cumulative, most using a basic network, and some officials using either or both of the other networks. The question of interest then becomes focused on the location of the officials who undertake 'extra' or more elaborate forms of networking.

One-way analysis of variance[13] showed significant differences between the three networking styles for government, for-profit and non-profit organisations. Regression factor scores for each network type and each agency are reported in Table 7.10. These are standardised scores which have a mean score of zero and a variance of one. Hence any score above zero indicates a higher than average score, while a score below zero indicates a lower than average score.

Table 7.10 shows that officials in for-profit agencies are significantly less likely to engage in 'public networking' than either government or non-profit agencies. Both for-profits and non-profits employ 'civic networking' significantly more than government officials, who register a lower than average use of this style. Officials in for-profit agencies are significantly more likely to engage only in 'basic networking'. Given the cumulative nature of these different networks, it appears that for-profit officials spend their time on routine contacts, neglecting the public network. Interestingly, both the non-profit and for-profit officials make higher than average use of civic networking. Government officials use public and basic networking in line with their non-profit colleagues, but make below average use of civic networking.

Networking also varied significantly by country (see Table 7.11). New Zealand had the highest score on public networking, followed by the United Kingdom, then Australia, while only the Netherlands had a below average score. Each country differed significantly on this aspect of networking. New Zealand also had the highest score on civic networking, followed by Australia, then the Netherlands, which was very close to the average, while the United Kingdom scored lowest on civic networking. New Zealand was significantly higher and the United Kingdom was significantly lower than all the other countries.

Table 7.11   Country and networking factor scores

	N	Public	Civic	Basic
Australia	552	.10	.14	−.22
Netherlands	245	−.75	−.04	.42
New Zealand	109	.62	.46	.00
United Kingdom	145	.40	−.81	.13

For the basic networking style, the Netherlands had the highest score, followed by the United Kingdom. Advisers in New Zealand made more use of public and civic networking than their counterparts in other countries. Australian advisers used public and civic networks moderately, and basic networks less than the average. UK advisers made greater use of public networks and less use of civic networks. While officials in the Netherlands reported lower than average use of public networks and average use of civic networks, they made much more use of the basic networks than did the other countries.

Did advisers who expressed a stronger network orientation (the normative network governance type) actually spend more time negotiating with others, moving between organisations, developing new solutions to problems or brokering deals between different parts of the public and private service delivery systems? The answer is yes. Correlation coefficients between the three governance orientations and the networking scores indicate that the highest correlation is between the network orientation and civic networking (at .27). The correlation between networking and the normative corporate-market orientation is also strong, but negative (−.18). This is to be expected. Those who professed a network orientation on the normative scale also engaged more often in the most elaborate network activities and relationships, and those working with corporate-market norms network less.

(2) Networks and the Use of Time

As a second test of the strength of the different normative orientations (or governance models) the analysis examined the way officials actually divided their time between their work with job seekers, employers, other agencies and administration. By allocating their own time between these core activities the officials showed how they deploy the main resource at their disposal. The network orientation was positively correlated with percentage of time spent with other agencies (.17), but not with any of the other time commitments (with job seekers, employers or on administration).

This makes sense. Work with job seekers, employers and on administration can be regarded as mandatory functions which all officials must
perform to some extent. Work with a wider range of other agencies
offers an opportunity for the exercise of more discretion and implies
greater potential choice for the individual adviser and for the local
agency. It is therefore consistent with the other findings that the frequency of adviser attendance at regular meetings outside their own
organisation was also strongly correlated with the network orientation
(.34).

These findings indicate that officials who had a stronger normative
orientation to networking also engaged more often in discretionary
networking behaviour. They reported more contact with the public and
civic networks (that is, networking beyond the basic tasks that virtually
all officials do), they spent more time working with other service
providers and they more frequently attended regular meetings outside
their own organisations. In light of this, it can be concluded that the
underlying normative structure of the network type is consistent with
what officials actually do in their normal work roles.

Who are the Networkers?

Having established the distinctions between three types of networking,
and the association between a network orientation and networking
behaviour, it makes sense to examine which background factors are
associated with a networker type.

Table 7.12 shows bivariate analyses of each of the three networking
types against a number of important work and personal characteristics.[14]

As noted, 'basic networking' was common to all groups and represents the core features of this role. The main hallmark of those advisers
who used only this basic approach was that they were more likely to use
a client classification instrument and likely to be somewhat younger
than the rest.

The level of 'public networking' was significantly higher for advisers
who work in an organisation which targets particular groups; make less
use of the client classification tool; have only worked in the one organisation; are union members; and are older than the other two groups.
Significantly higher levels of 'civic networking' were found among those
who had not worked in a single organisation, were not union members
and were male. In other words, the extent of networking was positively
associated with adviser profiles which diverged significantly from the
background of the traditional career bureaucrat.

While some of these background features are suggestive, it was
nevertheless very clear that organisational characteristics were more

Table 7.12 Work and personal characteristics and networking factor scores

	N	Public	Civic	Basic
Work in an organisation that targets particular groups?				
Yes	582	.13	.02	.00
No	462	−.16	−.03	−.01
Use client classification tool in dealing with jobseekers?				
Yes	492	−.09	.04	.19
No	498	.11	−.06	−.22
Only worked in this organisation?				
Yes	397	.07	−.23	−.03
No	645	−.05	.14	.01
Union membership?				
Yes	465	.22	−.17	−.04
No	573	−.18	.14	.03
Age group:				
Up to 24 years	45	−.45	.24	.15
25–34	365	−.22	.01	.19
35–44	348	.19	.03	−.13
45–54	236	.13	−.10	−.10
55 and over	44	.28	−.15	−.32
Gender:				
Male	373	.04	.08	.05
Female	667	−.02	−.05	−.03

important than biographical attributes. For example, the tendency for public networkers to have worked in only one organisation, to be union members and to be older was undoubtedly because this form of networking was the one most often found in government organisations (Table 7.10).

Conclusions

This part of the study confirms a number of hypotheses concerning enterprising reinventions within these Welfare-to-Work institutions. The four expected models resolved into three dimensions, with the corporate-market type emerging as the dominant image or model of front-line governance across all four systems. The classical or procedural type was in decline, now commanding significantly less support than would be predicted using Weberian definitions or other accepted administrative models. A new type – the network model – attracted significant support, even if the scale itself requires further strengthening and refinement.

Although country differences indicated stable, path-dependent qualities in each case, country generalisations did not always follow the pattern that might be expected given the reform rhetoric and political values of each system. There is certainly no simple extension of neo-liberal precepts into these institutions, even though the inclusion of the UK and New Zealand provided the two best documented models of this governance type. This suggests a weakness in the literature rather than confusion in practice. It may be that too much has been made, here and elsewhere, of the neo-liberal attributes of some of these countries and too little consideration given to the process of hybridisation which occurs when an indigenous institutional ensemble comes to terms with imported techniques. New Zealand rated highest on the procedural scale. Plainly their use of a Re-engineering strategy had produced a more procedure-oriented system than one simply based on targets or markets. The UK did not emerge as the most procedural. Instead its very strong attention to targets helped put it at the top of the new corporate-market index. And the Netherlands, far from emerging as a network type, was weaker on this than expected. It was the Australian advisers who were most attracted to the network model, but here the internal variation was so great that the type of agency overrode country attributes.

The normative and practical aspects of network governance were closely related, providing important insights into this emerging form of governance. This also allows us to re-assess the question of coherence within governance strategies. Plainly the enterprising process does not create an infinite diversity of models and paths: the corporate-market type is clearly dominant. Space for alternatives is clearly limited but networking emerges as a major alternative model and one which has great potential to explain the variable impact of structural changes such as increased privatisation and the greater use of flexibility within programs.

Just how these changes influence the purpose and impact of Welfare-to-Work systems and what this might say about the nature of the new pathways created by these enterprising states is the subject of the concluding chapter.

Notes

1 The discriminant analysis was used to determine which descriptive variables took prominence in this mapping process. See Statistical Appendix.
2 Principal components analysis was used to extract factors from the governance scale items. Using a scree plot of the eigenvalues as a guide to the appropriate number of factors, three, four and five factor solutions were generated with varimax rotation. From these models, three credible factors appeared to exist, with the fourth and fifth factors containing sets of items

which were not strongly related to any of the hypothesised governance orientations.

3 Nunnally, 1978.

4 Cohen & Cohen, 1983.

5 Considine and Lewis, 1999, op. cit.

6 Note that the direction of some items has been reversed when undertaking the reliability analysis, based on the direction of the relationship between the factor loadings and the relevant factor.

7 Walter J. M. Kickert, E. H. Klijn & J. F. M. Koppenjan (eds) *Managing Complex Networks: Strategies for the Public Sector*, London, Sage, 1997.

8 These items capture the overlapping nature of meanings in some of these dimensions. For example, item 9 could be read as an indication of an orientation that was simply not procedural, rather than being specifically a market orientation. Items 24 and 37, which indicate flexibility with technology and opportunities for input to innovation respectively, could arguably represent either a network or a market-corporate orientation.

9 The reliability of difference coefficients indicated that there is a reasonable level of separation between the scales. All of these coefficients are larger than the recommended .50 that is taken as indicating that separate dimensions are being measured (Cohen & Cohen, 1983).

10 Using bivariate analyses, significant relationships between the scales and other key aspects of these services were investigated. In other words, the governance types identified were investigated for associations with contextual variables. This provides a concrete method for estimating the extent to which bureaucratic or post-bureaucratic orientations can be attributed to key institutional influences. All the differences reported in the following analyses were significant at the .05 level. One-way ANOVA was used to determine significant differences between the scales for each of the independent variables. The post hoc pair-wise comparisons reported are based on Tamhane tests, as in many cases the assumption of homogeneity of variance was violated.

11 More research is also needed to strengthen the network scale. It is possible that the present items measure two different, but related aspects of networking – inter-organisational brokerage and intra-organisational autonomy. Some of these elements may be program specific, such as the desire to maintain one's own records. If so, it seems likely that in other programs different measures of autonomy will be more salient. Since the best items are those which concern inter-organisational values (trust, joint responsibility) it is likely that the scale could be strengthened by adding new items which express knowledge, skill and positive interest in dealing with other organisations.

12 Question 14 in the survey read 'Excluding contacts associated with assisting a particular job seeker to obtain a job interview, how often would you have some form of contact (including telephone) with the following: Another official from your organisation, official from other government department, local government, welfare agencies, employers, training providers, advisers in other agencies, local service clubs, schools or universities, local media?'. The options included: daily, weekly, monthly, quarterly, less than quarterly, never.

13 With post hoc pair-wise comparisons using Tamhane tests.

14 T-tests were used to establish whether significant differences existed between groups (with p=.05) for all except age groups, where one-way ANOVA was used.

CHAPTER 8

Conclusion:
De-Coupling, Contracting
and Self-Enterprise

Perhaps there was a time when the primary purpose of governance was not hedged by prefixes or held aloft within inverted commas. Post-industrial, postmodern, post-bureaucratic, reinvented government, post-Fordist and their kin speak to us of nothing so much as our profound uncertainty. Evidently we are more sure of what has been lost than of what might have been gained. Some theorists have ventured beyond this conditional state. But here the tendency has been to meet the contemporary ferment with contempt. It is easy then to overestimate the uniformity of the 'new governance' reform movement and to find within it only a malevolent purpose. Rose (1996, p. 37), for example, identifies an 'economic machine' which acts by 'implanting modes of economic calculation' throughout advanced societies. While this certainly helps draw attention to particular technical features of the new performance culture in advanced liberal systems, it risks asserting only the elements of control or regulation and closing off access to the subtle dynamics of invigoration which attend many of these reinvention strategies.

The development of the reflexive idea of 'enterprising states' and the 'enterprising of states' in this study has been, in part, an attempt to move beyond both the pitfalls of prefixes and the risks of reductionism. But now it is important to restate the primary theoretical argument of the book and address some of the implications of these more general findings. The new strategies of governance at ground level are most definitely phenomena which raise profound issues about the larger significance of public programs and of the very nature of the public sphere in this new era of detraditionalisation and 'sheer flux' (Sennett, 1998, p. 19). No one can doubt that the radical transformation of established methods for positioning the state shapes the path that might be taken towards both imagining and securing a common future.

Others have used the enterprise idea to nail the lid on these so-called 'post-Fordist' changes in contemporary forms of organisation. For instance in the work of du Gay (1993) and du Gay and Salaman (1996) the idea of enterprise is used to define a general shift away from bureaucracy, or even an opposition between the norms of the old public sector and this new world of complex, hybrid forms of governance. But for these other theorists the enterprised state is typically described as a single, resolved alternative to the standardised, hierarchical state system that came before. An overwhelming suspicion of a new corporate determinism too easily rolls flat the more permeable, perhaps fragmented, and path-dependent character of the reform process.

The strategy in this study has been to identify the subtlety of the cultural project that seems to distinguish mass, standardised public organisations from the new forms of agency in which selectivity and hybridity abound. As part of this structural shift the normative basis of public organisation certainly undergoes a major challenge. In championing a new set of ideals, reformers and reinventers have contributed to a coalition against public bureaucracy. In large part this has led to a series of methodological and theoretical slides and elisions which have also turned the reasonable complaints about bureaucratic and governmental rigidity into a more general attack on the very idea of the public sphere itself.

It is surely one of the most remarkable cultural changes in contemporary political life that this convergence of critiques of state-delivered services has so far been competent to unite libertarians, neo-classical economists, public choice theorists, feminists, postmodernists and communitarians. But perhaps this is always the way major social institutions are forced to capitulate. They do not surrender to any solitary assault, but are mobbed by a Lilliputian coalition of both venal and long-suffering local interests.

In this general assault a reduced confidence in government services has been articulated as a rejection of standardisation and inflexibility. Barely concealed within this critique of bureaucracy is a rejection of the role of unions, professions, administrators and other so-called 'rent-seekers'. All forms of collective organisation are then rendered suspect. This allegedly results in a left–right concord to reduce the state role as a precondition for either the revival of a micro-cultural politics, or one based on the triumph of markets. Or so it would seem from a reading of the critiques. At ground level a different picture emerges.

Interestingly this flawed dichotomy between the lock-step world of the bureaucrat and the endlessly flexible realm of the entrepreneur had been used in all four countries to engineer and market a number of very different governance strategies. It was simply not possible to describe case management, re-engineering and quasi-markets as birds of one feather. Some of the outcomes have been similar, but others remained remarkably different. Nor were the differences merely the inevitable residue of local custom. They expressed important general adaptations and new forms of robust re-organisation of the state itself.

The book's central purpose was to capture both the turn away from simple hierarchy and to express the common interest in hybridity or boundary-shifting within the new transformation agenda. These enterprising reformers share a loss of faith in the state's capacity to answer social problems with universal programs. Instead they all want the state's role hinged to something else. But while the book's title deliberately invokes a corporate world, it does so in the form of actions which are yet unfinished and which may yet prove reflexive. The verb does not always require the noun: One might be enterprising without becoming an enterprise. Ashby's (1960) law of requisite variety suggests that the enterprise can also be explained as a dexterous mirroring of exactly the forms of social change which have dealt these states a problem hand which cannot be played or arranged according to former principles of hierarchy, specialisation or subordination.

These enterprising states are involved in new forms of conduct that act simultaneously both upon the idea of government and upon the character of those whom governments seek to organise. While they gesture to a corporate world far beyond the public sphere, and although the contemporary forms of privatisation are real enough, the most challenging changes are actually those which maintain a public role in a new form. Those who prefer the prefix game will recognise this as the politics of 'reinvention' (Beck, 1992; Osborne & Gaebler, 1992; Culpitt, 1999).

At the empirical level this enterprising spirit and motive creates new models of governmental power which are neither simply private nor public, neither market nor bureaucracy. The models in question are in fact new strategies of public organisation in which certain corporate and market techniques and norms are suffused within quite new, even more powerful, public programs. These remain public institutions and this shows through in the way officials value and arrange their own duties and commitments. In some cases these blended public–private arrangements generate significantly greater transformative authority over other institutions of governance than either markets or bureaucracies could ever have imagined. In other cases the hybrid form appears to reach a genetic dead end. The Australian attempt to put a public employment office into direct competition with hundreds of private recruitment agencies was a model with this kind of terminal redundancy, and during the life of the study this public agency went from the monopoly provider to the largest contractor and then to the most futile and feeble of all the agencies studied here.

Once understood as neither bureaucracy nor market, these new governance systems can be better defined by their hybrid vigour. This is not only a critique of the ideal-type formulations that have motivated much organisational theory, it is also a practical rejection of the notion that the state any longer owns one particular mode of organising itself in a complex society. The idea of the great divide between politics and markets (Lindblom, 1977) or markets and hierarchies (Williamson, 1975) is probably now even less helpful than at any time in the history of liberal capitalist systems. Structural distinctions are less important than processes of governance. In a theoretical sense process is therefore far more important than structure.

And this is not the only change in our thinking about the basic architecture of governance required by these findings. Traditional distinctions between market, state and civic associations have assumed fundamentally different rationales for action and affiliation for the three. Money defined the decision making of the private firm. Law determined action by the state. Group identity gave the civic association a way to order its activity. Luhmann (1995) has argued that it is in the establishment of such clear forms of identity as binary codes (legal/ illegal, profitable/not profitable, member/non-member) that any system becomes 'open by being closed'. That is, by having a distinctive means, or rationale, through which to define what is within and what lies outside its scope, a system achieves its functional autonomy from others. A measure of functional autonomy is, in turn, a key determinant of the capacity to contribute some distinctive value to other systems. In other words autonomy or distinctiveness is a prerequisite for differentiating the activities of different systems. Piaget (1955) argued much the same thing about the self-directed nature of personality with the observation that 'intelligence organises the world by organising itself'.

In the 'new governance' models of these four Welfare-to-Work states, there were still important differences between the operational strategies of state, private and civic association. But they were not necessarily divided in the manner expected. State organisations within 'mixed economy' systems adopted more market-type norms. And while for-profit and non-profit agencies were different to state agencies in these cases, they were not all that different to one another. Civic and market agencies both adopted entrepreneurial standards and tools with evident dexterity.

In all four countries there was a decisive turn away from legal-rational institutions, and from law as the guiding rationale for public action. Front-line staff did not consider rules to be much help in determining their work and neither did their managers. This was not simply a matter of their needing more discretion, since discretion might simply imply power to vary the implementation of still standard rules (Hawkins, 1992, p. 29). Instead there was a shift towards forms of intervention that involved quite different decisions for people with otherwise similar needs. Citizens attending different agencies received different programs, those attending the same office were granted variable opportunities, and the same person attending the same bureau was often treated differently each time.

Nor did those being paid as agents of the state operate according to the principles of economic exchange. Nowhere did private participation lead to the formation of actual markets. Markets served mainly as a kind of institutional paternity for creating a new generation of hybrid offspring. What the different forms of private participation mostly achieved was not the production of markets but a new contractualism. The competitive element of this system was entirely episodic, occurring once and only at certain tender moments. In Australia agencies were in blind competition for a few weeks while officials decided who was to receive contracts, or for a few moments while job seekers considered whether they would deal with private agencies. After that the system closed back towards a defined, mandatory path. Mead (1997) has rightly defined this as a 'new paternalism' and its narrow solicitude should not be mistaken for either choice or empowerment for consumer-citizens. Instead a carefully prescribed moment of choice was primarily used as a spur to mobility along a route heavily fortified by new conditions and expectations of specific performance on the part of job seekers and advisers. From this point these agencies operated by managerial, non-market strategies, filling orders, meeting targets, shaving costs. All this without having to worry whether their clients might take their business elsewhere. Although this was certainly a money economy it was hardly based on prices or on the search for breakthrough innovations. Newly empowered senior bureaucrats defined the terms of this 'specific performance' and sat alone in the judgement of outcomes.

Even though a variety of non-profit agencies were given a stake in the new governance strategies identified in the book, their civic virtues seemed not to be their primary value to decision makers. Governments acted strategically in appreciating that they might benefit from having elaborate, formal relationships with public clients, but the same governments were at best ambivalent about whether this should result in any tangible form of service innovation from below. This remained public money and the idea of large profits being made from unemployment programs was still dangerous, as was the thought that intensive assistance might lead job seekers to make stronger demands upon the state or upon employers.

Incentive Management

As noted in Chapter 7, the most compelling type of the three enter-prising strategies proved to be the corporate-market model. It replaced procedural bureaucracy as the dominant means for organising public sector work. It is a hybrid model of governance in which powerful cen-tralising norms coexist with requirements for officials to monitor and act upon their own local economic output. Often these officials resembled nothing so much as a new class of franchisees. Their methods and goals were carefully prescribed, yet their routines and methods were kept open and flexible to allow for the possible effects of their own self-enterprising efforts.

The most significant alternative to this strategy was provided by the 'network governance' model. While the corporate-market strategy was plainly driven by strong internal organisational requirements, the network model was the type most clearly associated with inter-agency activity. Newer and less popular than the corporate-market type, network governance is nevertheless a coherent answer to the questions raised by enterprising reformers. Performance improvement is linked to teamwork with other agencies who have an influence on the job seeker's chances of success. Getting the client's trust is more important than using sanctions. And even quite sensitive corporate resources such as the IT system are more apt to be shared with others.

Within the network strategy it was also possible to identify three prac-tical sub-strategies being used by front-line staff. These showed that the normative dimensions do provide a solid, reliable basis for understand-ing real actions. While most officials engaged in some form of basic networking, only those with stronger affiliations to the network method were found engaged in the more sophisticated networking strategies. Not surprisingly these were also the people who were more likely to attend outside meetings. Having a network orientation was thus strongly associated with being a networker, especially if this involved extending one's range of interests and contacts beyond the basic, mandated requirements of the job.

While country remained the most important source of difference overall, there were surprises. Initial assumptions derived from the case studies of the four systems did not always accurately predict the emerg-ing strategies. The UK was not the most procedural, although its history predicted that. The Netherlands was not the most 'network' oriented, even though its consensualism and neo-corporatist commitments suggested it would be. More reassuring perhaps was the fact that there were major differences between the public service systems and the two 'mixed economy' types. But the method used to discern the governance types did provoke important questions not available in the individual case studies. For example, the UK affection for the corporate-market orientation was much stronger than expected. This can only mean that the target setting and measurement system enacted as part of the JSA reforms had been far more effective at moving that system away from traditional procedural strategies than was previously thought. Whether one believes this to be the best arrangement from a job seeker's perspective or not, it is clear that it is the mode of governance most likely to empower senior bureaucrats and politicians in periods when the call for active reinvention was strongest. Provided policy goals could be reduced to operational targets this de-coupled regime was plainly extremely robust.

In the Netherlands case the expectation that networking would be at its strongest had been based on that system's long commitment to building neo-corporatist institutions. The commitment to 'social partnership' looked very much like a commitment to inter-agency joint ventures. The contract with the two temporary work firms supported this assumption. However, as noted, the Dutch officials were less enamoured with networking than anyone except UK officials. Instead the Dutch maintained very strong corporate affiliations which limited the potential for variation and experimentation at the front line. Perhaps the incorporation of employers and unions into the running of these institutions had increased their conservatism by multiplying the points at which riskier strategies and alternative alliances could be vetoed? Certainly it showed how such formal consensus building could inhibit more radical experimentation in the short run.

On the other hand, New Zealand showed the predicted affection for the corporate-market approach yet also managed a high level of commitment to networking norms and activities. The re-engineering strategy and the Task Force that sponsored it help to explain this. Strong corporate-market norms strengthened internal control and upward responsiveness. But the New Zealanders plainly also wanted a system which would be inclusive so far as employers and other 'opportunity providers' were concerned. They therefore created a normative system that valued inter-organisational negotiation and brokerage. No doubt the small and pliable New Zealand political system made it easier to embrace thoroughgoing reform, and thus to choose a strategy which accommodated neo-liberal norms without making them the basis of fundamental change.

Australia was almost the reverse of the New Zealand case. Both its two major reform waves challenged the line management system within employment services. First the public agency was subjected to outside competition, then its monopoly was abolished altogether. Although the

Australian government chose to call its new arrangements a 'Jobs Network' this was far less than a unified corporate identity. Instead a collection of competitive agencies undertook their own efforts to meet their private performance targets. Not surprisingly this resulted in Australian officials having weak affiliation to norms of corporate governance.

More surprising was that their affection for competition did not strengthen the 'market' side of this regime. In fact the Australians rated these values very highly but this was not sufficient to make this their strongest governance strategy. Instead they were much more likely to rate networking norms as the most important. In a system so radically de-coupled as this one every agency was required to maintain good relationships with any group that might conceivably offer a means to assisting the agency to win scarce resources.

Each of these enterprising strategies enacted by central departments and their consultants must be regarded as highly successful in instrumental terms. That is, each has been highly influential in changing the systems they set out to reform. And these cannot be regarded as especially pliable institutions, easily manipulated by policy makers. Just the reverse. The mix of income support entitlements, job search requirements and large-scale operations certainly generate as much inertia as one could expect to find in any state sector. So these large systemic changes must rate as a considerable achievement by these central policy-makers, whatever one thinks of the outcomes.

Common Ground

Although different in styles and effect, these four countries nonetheless demonstrated some interesting common conditions. Central to each was a process of organisational de-coupling. To reform a traditional bureaucracy it seems one first has to detach it from the policy-making arm of the system and thus from traditional forms of support and defence. In each country central agency bureaucrats and politicians were happy to see a large part of their organisational empire handed over to others to run.

The paradox in this strategy was that de-coupling was strongly associated with increased dependency. In the UK the agency arrangements and annual targets gave Whitehall ample opportunity to fix the activities of the Employment Service, making it a more efficient deliverer of standard services than before. The Dutch de-coupling had much the same effect, making it easier for the Ministry to cut budgets and raise output requirements. Although, in this case, the creation of tripartite boards of management initially provided the Arbeids Voorziening with a useful buffer against central agency pressure for the reasons described above. New Zealand followed the UK model, with agency annual contracts becoming a very powerful means for controlling the more autonomous NZES than previous internal bureaucratic tools had allowed. And obviously in the Australian case the quasi-market made both public and private agencies totally dependent upon 'purchaser' funds and thus on central government program objectives. Virtually all other slack and alternative values were quickly removed.

The use of contracts between agencies, governments and clients was a second theme in these four reinvention stories. These contracting strategies reflected an interesting coincidence of values. On one hand the contract was quite obviously a means for tying organisational actors to more precise behaviours. In this regard the contracting process reflected a desire to limit cheating, gaming and the displacement of goals. Coincidentally, the process of engaging actors in the contracting process was also the occasion for a number of self-enterprising norms to be articulated. To sign a contract one has first to assert some level of autonomy and have one's identity as an independent agent acknowledged. Of course these normative gestures may count for nothing if the contract is exploitative and self-enterprise may quickly dissolve into self-censure. But even here, in those cases where exploitation was strongest, before such actors could be drawn into a new form of mandated activity, they had first to be willing to define themselves as self-enterprising agents.

This process can be seen at two levels. The public agencies 'contracted' to deliver employment services in each country were all required to re-identify as companies or enterprises in response to central ministry demands. For example the UK's Employment Service quickly established itself with new office furniture, uniforms and new corporate personnel practices. The new *esprit de corps* motivated managers and staff to imagine a future that was now in their own hands to a far greater extent than before. While this may have been exaggerated it was not completely untrue. The fact that the annual contracts offered to the ES, and the informal controls established by Whitehall, made it difficult for the ES to enjoy its new status should not blind us to the fact that the agency achieved a new practical authority over its own work. When the ES management boasted that their staff had consistently achieved the higher targets set for them they were pointing to the greater leverage which this new identity gave them to motivate the front line in ways not available in the traditional bureaucracy. And if this did little to free up relationships with clients, it certainly made it more difficult for critics in government ranks to press forward with greater levels of privatisation.

In the Australian case the fate of the public agency was also affected by this new contracting strategy. First as Employment Assistance

Australia (EAA), then as Employment National, the public service agency steadily became more aggressive about its self-enterprising purpose. The EAA management complained that their staff were not sufficiently distinct from the rest of the public service. They sought and gained an autonomous status as Employment National and then used this status to separate themselves from any form of 'public identity'. In communications with the outside world they referred to themselves as 'the company' and spoke downwards to their local managers with the new authority as 'the Board', even when that only meant the senior management committee. Their contract with the purchaser provided them with a means for completely reshaping their obligation to taxpayers and citizens, effectively eliminating both these interests in favour of management's own preferences. But this overcommitment to market norms did not succeed and the failure to develop a hybrid identity based on a real mixing of public and private sector strengths helps explain why this agency soon tumbled headlong towards the brink of collapse.

These forms of contracting between purchasers and agents created new organisational identities in these systems, identities that were not easily reconciled with the public interest. Indeed, one reason for their enactment seems to have been to deny these organisations any independent claim on the public interest and to reserve this role for ministers and central agency purchasers. The Dutch found this a troublesome arrangement, especially when regional boards composed of employers and unions successfully asserted parochial interests which overruled government policy. The New Zealanders attempted to resolve this dilemma by dividing the path towards the public interest in two. The quasi-independent NZES would supply outputs and the minister would take responsibility for outcomes. As one senior bureaucrat put it, this preserved the statutory right of politicians to 'choose their own road to hell'.

De-coupling and contracting these agencies helped policy makers specify precise targets. It also gave the agencies more control over their own identity and they used this successfully to mobilise their own staff according to the new enterprising motive that they wished to convey to clients. But it also encouraged these agencies to define their roles in instrumental terms, leaving public interest problems unresolved. Strategies like 'creaming', 'parking', 'herding' and target manipulation were more attractive to organisations whose charter increased the distance between them and the policy values of their parliaments and ministers. In this sense the new system for the production of contracted outputs also proved to be a powerful buffer.

At the other end of these systems, the service delivery end, we see contracting emerge as the instrument of choice for managing interactions between front-line staff and job seekers. In each system the reinvention process involved the creation of new requirements for job seekers and advisers to 'choose' their interactions rather than have these standardised. At its most basic this involved the UK system recasting the payment of income support from one of entitlement to a contract in which the job seeker agreed to specified conditions in return for continued payment of benefits. The regular re-testing of the job seeker's side of this bargain showed this contract to be highly conditional and often coercive.

In New Zealand the same process was established through the signing of a contract which included specified plans for the return to work. Australia developed much the same strategy, only in this case the signing by the job seeker also triggered the first payment to the agency so the one signature actually involved a double obligation. Mendicant agencies soon learned which of the two was more likely to ensure survival.

Clearly the formal contracts with job seekers were always likely to be highly unequal and perhaps exploitative encounters. Since payment of income support was at stake, one could expect clients to sign almost anything. In this regard the job seekers were in a position somewhat reminiscent of the plight of the contracted agencies. Entitlement and certainty had been replaced by conditional, temporary commitments. The purchasing ministry was also able to call the tune on most matters. While it is true that these were most unequal bargains they were not without subtlety, however. They underscored the new need to step past the formal status of the client as a claimant and to entertain new imperatives for engaging with their personal problems and likely strategies of resistance.

The Self-Enterprising Client

In all four systems a significant effort was put into drawing up and enacting these agreements. If the power relations between these parties were so asymmetrical, why would this two-way engagement be needed in the first place? The answer seems to be that self-enterprising behaviour demanded the creation of a different relationship between these parties. Simple command and control systems had proven inadequate. Dragging unwilling job seekers through programs and interview schedules could easily result in evasion by some and poor performance by many. This was plainly less desirable and more expensive than mobilising them to create an active commitment to new, flexible and more contingent labour market conditions.

While they rarely gave job seekers the choices they desired, these agreements and counselling strategies did involve an open acknowledgement of risk and selectivity, precisely the conditions to be found outside the agency's doors in the less regulated economy.[1] It made the process of choice by the adviser more visible to the job seeker and being more visible it also became more contingent and more obviously a product of any relationship the two might develop. Being more contingent such choices were far more decisive than those embedded in routine. And contracts could express potential threats as well as rewards. The writing of the contract and its occasional amendment provided opportunities to remove any sense of certainty the job seeker might have about the nature of continued support, including income support. While this was apt to be terrifying, it could also be presented as a form of rescue. Once the full weight of the newly precarious situation was evident, the adviser could show a path to safety. The greater scarcity of places in training programs and forms of assisted employment underlined the consequences of being relegated to the ever growing 'parking' lot. Advisers often interpreted their 'tough love' interactions with job seekers as a necessary facsimile of contemporary interactions between the job seeker and an employer. The risks and contingencies of the job search contract were used to mirror the same hazards to be found in the unprotected labour markets to which these clients were returning.

The contract with the job seeker was not often based on his or her preferences and seldom did the contract aim to improve substantive skills or address major job barriers. The Dutch system and the first Australian system (Working Nation) did involve a substantial list of possibilities which advisers could use. But these remained driven by supply. Job seekers responded to options put to them. In all the other cases the choice element of the contract was minimal. The heavy investment in contract negotiations is therefore best understood as a strategy of self-enterprise in which the job seeker was asked to take over and run his or her own job-finding endeavour, to become, in effect, a self-employed contractor building their job future in the manner of a one-person small business.

Critics complained that these contracts were largely devised to punish and exclude job seekers from the welfare system. By forcing them to sign more and more demanding agreements it was felt they would provide the agencies with greater opportunity to identify opportunities to sanction and dismiss claims. And even if they were not formally sanctioned, many job seekers would find this contracting system so oppressive that they would become discouraged and leave the formal labour market altogether. This study cannot settle such issues since to do so would require close examination of the strategies adopted by job seekers. But based on what has been learned from the advisers and their local managers, it is certainly possible to draw some provisional conclusions.

The advisers acknowledged that they used these sanctioning procedures to 'work' the clients and to force them to either submit to a new flexibility or leave. The willingness to sanction for 'administrative' breaches was evidence of a more punitive strategy. But advisers were remarkably selective in the use of these sanctions. In each system the rate of sanctioning was a good deal lower than the estimate of non-compliance. Advisers chose two strategies to fill their quota of sanctions. First, unless they perceived a risk of violent retaliation, they routinely sanctioned those whose behaviour was flagrant. Such violence seemed more likely in routinised systems like the UK and rather minimal in the most flexible regimes. And even here the officials devised their own highly inventive safeguards against violence which frequently meant sanctions fell short of the more coercive options available. The second strategy was to use both the threat of sanction and sanctions themselves to motivate tardy clients. In these cases the advisers often sought to adjust the threat to fit their own sense of the individual's personal circumstances. For example the New Zealanders would not lightly sanction someone with children. The Australians were more harsh on young people, while in the UK there was greater interest in whether or not the job seeker was earning income on the 'black market' or had access to one of the better local labour markets.

Sanctioning therefore had less to do with a general commitment to punish and was more often a part of the struggle to define ways to circumvent defiance and to 'activate' dormant or lethargic clients. It was therefore predictable that the effort put into sanctioning was related to whether or not the adviser believed there was a job available for a particular client, regardless of official policy. This explained why the Dutch sanctioning rates were higher. More plentiful jobs meant more choices for job seekers and thus fewer excuses for inactivity. This pressure might have been even stronger had the Dutch insurance system not given many job seekers the 'right' to claim a certain period on benefits before coming under stronger pressure to take any available job.

These actions by advisers and the complex strategies devised by their employing agencies pointed to the formation of a different kind of civic persona. The decline of entitlement as a defined right to assistance, the more contingent nature of this contracting process, and the different pressures now placed on officials all point towards the systematic encouragement of a more calculating disposition. Each job seeker was encouraged to confront and assess the new costs of coming to the employment agency for help. These costs included the prospect of being 'worked', 'parked', 'herded' or 'creamed' and they were more visible because the agencies were required to make such transactions much more transparent to their clients. The more these agencies struggled to

Table 8.1   Country comparison: 'We pick the best job seekers and give the best service' (%)

	Agree	Neither agree/disagree	Disagree
Australia	43	15	43
Netherlands	39	11	50
New Zealand	17	9	74
United Kingdom	12	17	71

make costs and benefits a part of the personal transaction with the job seeker, the more obvious it became to these clients that their own behaviour would influence whether scarce opportunities were offered to them or a taxing regime of minor demands would be exacted as the price of income support.

Looked at from the governance perspective, this new citizenship is not entirely a bad thing, or perhaps, more accurately, not only a bad thing. The advisers rightly saw a motivated and mobile job seeker as someone less likely to fall into, or stay in a condition of, long-term dependence. But in order to make that outcome more attractive they colluded with opponents of welfare by making receipt of income support a more stigmatised condition. The longer one 'depends' on that support, the faster one loses credibility as an independent agent. The irony is plain to see. Successfully gaining and continuing to receive income support in these countries is far harder than before. To do so involves being very disadvantaged and yet ever more resilient, competent and resourceful. Some unemployed people have these attributes but a large number do not.

For the public officials who carry the burden of these new expectations the pressures are profound. As noted, the performance requirements were more exacting and more transparent than ever. Secure work in a public service career has given way to limited term employment in agencies with uncertain futures. The pressures which officials were required to put on clients were the same ones they had to negotiate in their own workplaces. In place of clearly supervised and defined roles they often had front-line responsibilities which involved them 'making up' their own strategies. The new forms of intensive assistance required advisers to mobilise their own personalities as a way of motivating, cajoling, engaging, reviving and disciplining job seekers. These clients sometimes suffered great disadvantage and were burdened by the most serious problems. Rarely were the advisers trained to diagnose or treat such problems. Yet, in order to attempt to create a major shift in capabilities, they had to enter the world of the person with serious drug problems, mental illness, or a history of crime and incarceration.

The purpose of the relationship was to create 'openness' or 'willingness' in the client and typically this meant advisers had to share or extend their own positive outlook and energy with their clients. They said in interview that they were now brokers in self-esteem. Their own personalities, skills at interaction and capacity to project an extrovert's faculty for engendering enthusiasm became paramount. Just as the job seeker had to be taught to project a very positive, engaged style to the prospective employer, so too the adviser had to train herself to both nurture and extol. It is not surprising that these agencies favour mainly women as the front-line staff for advisers needed permission from adult, male clients to allow this level of interaction concerning their own personal outlook and prospects.

Agency leaders were well aware that the new performance culture of their organisations had swung decisively towards the mobilisation of personality as the primary resource for both job seekers and advisers. The head of one of the larger non-profit organisations in Australia dismissed an offer to participate in a project to identify the training needs of advisers with the summation, 'We have looked at every aspect of what we do and I think the whole business now depends on just one critical variable – the personality of the staff member.'

While prey to manipulation and increased insecurity, for the advisers this new set of practices also represented their own emergence as a more valued group in the agency's strategy. Their flexibility to manage their own clients, to negotiate with them and thus to be free of lock-step rules and programs was a direct source of their increased commitment and higher levels of job satisfaction. Their managers knew less about the work their staff did than before, and their own personal capabilities had become a major criterion by which local strategies by the agencies were selected.

These changes in local strategy and micro-relationships reflect the larger process the book describes as the creation of an enterprising state. There are important links between the processes of state reform across these four different systems. These include the de-coupling of policy and service delivery, the use of performance contracts, the use of targets and quotas, the involvement of private agencies, the greater demand for job seekers to 'earn' or even 'co-produce' their service, and a far greater emphasis on the personal or cultural capital of advisers and job seekers than upon the supply of jobs or training.

These changes impose complex choices on all these participants. The more centralised systems such as that of the UK appeared to lack flexibility and integration into the wider social environment. The most decentralised system, the Australian quasi-market, lacked central coherence, even though private agencies were better networked than elsewhere. But most important of all, these new forms of state action offer major choices regarding the civic virtues or norms that are to form the foundation of the new welfare state. While no one can seriously doubt the value of greater self-reliance, the self-enterprising emphasis has a flaccid and failing interest in the material side of the welfare equation. As one adviser in the UK put it, 'they can't pull themselves up by their boot laces if you don't have a shoe subsidy to start with'. Even the most sophisticated of the 'intensive service' models the study identified were very weak in their attention to material support for these clients. Income support remained the only consistent form of assistance and it was rarely open to more flexible forms of deployment. Training and in-work subsidies were the two forms of support that almost every adviser regarded as vital to the chances of returning the most disadvantaged to the workforce, yet these were in short supply. They were also seen as an old solution and one that created too many rigidities.

Client-Centred Service

Plainly the further enterprising of states and their agencies will need to graduate from the focus upon the most simple, cultural aspects of such treatments and begin to identify the stronger aspects of hybrid organisation that are most likely to assist the seriously disadvantaged. For example, this might involve the re-coupling of agencies into organisational clusters and chains with common performance payments. This might be a better way of blending private participation with public responsibility. Clustered or linked contracts might also provide a vehicle for agencies to embrace the investment side of the welfare problem by using schooling, child care and health resources where people have major barriers to employment. At present the emergence of a new diversity of agents acts as a disincentive to any one taking a longer view of the client's needs. This can only result in 'dumbing down' the service. Stronger, performance-linked networks are one alternative.

Linked to this issue of reattaching all agencies to a core social purpose is the question of what to do about government-owned agencies that have been de-coupled. At present they risk a total identity crisis or eventual privatisation. The enterprising emphasis upon arm's length distance between purchasing departments and contracted public agencies disables the public interest role for these agencies and creates the false impression that they are no more than instruments. Rather than duplicating the same roles for public and private agents, reformers need to consider greater specialisation, perhaps in the Dutch manner although with greater variety than was permitted there.

Finally it needs recognising that the plight of job seekers has become more varied and risky under the pressures exerted by these enterprising states. The attention to greater levels of activity and mobility provide positive support for those already able to take the jobs available. The new rhetoric of client choice opens the door to eventual empowerment of those job seekers able to select and defend the service option best suited to them. And even the new emphasis upon 'reciprocal obligation' offers clearer pathways than were available in more routinised services. But, and it is a large 'but', these normative moves or strategies are not currently attached to real material opportunities. If they do not soon offer real returns they will rightly be consigned into history as among the most manipulative and cynical welfare reforms ever adopted by governments. An enterprising spirit that looks no further than the dumping of these already demoralised clients into the worst, most dangerous and unrewarding posts is bound to earn contempt.

In the end the form of self-enterprise most likely to succeed is one where stronger pressures to perform are buttressed and enhanced by a far more subtle mix of opportunities and with a wider sharing of risks. But governments will need to resist the strong temptation to inject coherence into such systems by re-standardising work at the front line or keeping control by limiting pathways for clients. The evidence from successful micro-level reform is that 'no two persons take exactly the same route out of welfare' (Schorr, 1997, p. 171). The governance regime most likely to achieve this will undoubtedly involve both multi-agency co-operation and the exacting of forms of strong performance which raise the condition of the least advantaged, though the imperilled ideal of public service found in all four systems does cast doubt upon the immediate prospects for such a renaissance. However, the fact that these state systems are now more pliable and more committed to continuous experimentation at least promises an increase in the number of vantage points from which better policy might be launched, vantage points which include those at the front line where governance remains most decisive in the lives of ordinary citizens.

Note

1 This helps explain why the Netherlands was less strong in its use of these contracts. Their labour markets had avoided the resort to a low-wage, contract form of employment for job seekers returning to the workforce.

Statistical Appendix:
Questionnaire and Further Statistics

As Chapter 2 noted the method for this study involved surveys of front-line staff in four countries. In Australia this was complicated by the fact that there were three different sectors (government, for-profit and non-profit) to investigate as well as three reform stages (Working Nation, Vanstone and Job Network). In the Netherlands the survey was administered to the public agency and to one of the two private organisations involved in delivering services to public clients. A copy of the Questionnaire is provided below.

The country chapters provide a range of descriptive statistics, all of which are significant at least to the .05 level. The selection of the variables for the country comparisons reflects, in large part, the results of the discriminant analysis described below. In addition the governance scales developed from the model provided in Table 2.1 were derived from a factor analysis and the loadings for the three factor solution are also provided here.

(UK version)
A. Questionnaire

Please read each question carefully, then circle one number to mark your response. Some questions may have more than one response. For these questions, tick all that apply.

1. Approximately how many people work at your office at THIS location?
2. Does your organisation have a specialist responsibility for services to a particular target group (e.g. youth, disabled)?

   Yes 1
   No 2

3. Other than serving INDIVIDUAL unemployed clients, does your organisation offer any other services for job seekers, employers , etc. (e.g. training programs, job clubs)?

Yes 1

No 2

If 'yes' please specify . . . .

. . . .

4. What would you estimate your own current case load to be? If you do not have a case load as such, how many clients would you see in an average day?

                      Case load? . . . . .OR

                      Average number of clients per day . . . .

5. Using 1 as 'easier to place' and 4 as 'difficult to place', what proportion of your clients would you place in these four categories:

        (easier to place)   1 . . . .%

                       2 . . . .%

                       3 . . . .%

      (difficult to place)   4 . . . .%

6. What is your best estimate (in percentages) of the number of job seekers on your current case load who:

- have NOT signed a Job Seeker's Agreement? . . . .%
- have completed a Restart Course? . . . .%
- are participating in an activity (e.g. a training course, job club, job plan seminar, etc.)? . . . .%
- are classified as currently looking for employment? . . . .%
- are in Post Placement Support? . . . .%
- are not doing any of the above? . . . .%

7. Do you use the answers to any standard CLIENT CLASSIFICATION tool or checklist when deciding what to put into the agreement with the job seeker (JSAG, CMAA, etc.)?

Yes 1

No 2

Your Work

8. How influential are the following factors in determining what activities are recorded in the formal Agreement you make with a job seeker?

(Circle one response for each item.)

		not at all	some-what	quite	very
a.	answers to a standard set of assessment questions	1	2	3	4
b.	other assessment results	1	2	3	4
c.	my own judgement	1	2	3	4
d.	job seeker's preference for activities	1	2	3	4

e.	labour market demand for job seeker's stated employment goal	1	2	3	4
f.	availability of labour market program vacancies	1	2	3	4
g.	access to funds for special assistance	1	2	3	4
h.	need to substantiate a case for sanctioning	1	2	3	4
i.	need to get an outcome quickly	1	2	3	4

9. What proportion (if any) of your referrals to labour market programs or training activities have been rejected by the service provider?

..................................%

10. To what extent are the following factors a barrier to using computer information technology to assist job seekers?
(Circle one response for each item.)

	not a barrier	a minor barrier	a major barrier
The cost of access to computers	1	2	3
Insufficient training on how to use the system	1	2	3
Insufficient documentation on the system	1	2	3
Accuracy of information on the system	1	2	3
Temporary system failures and breakdowns	1	2	3

Other *(please specify)* ....

....

11. In an average week, what proportion of your time do you spend?
(Please give your best estimate.)

In direct contact with job seekers ....%

Working with other service providers ....%

Working with employers ....%

On general administration ....%

12. Generally, how often do you contact job seekers to discuss their progress? For job seekers who are:
(Circle one response for each item.)

	weekly	monthly	6-weekly	quarterly	less than quarterly
Job searching	1	2	3	4	5
Attending a course or undertaking training	1	2	3	4	5
Employed in subsidised employment	1	2	3	4	5
Under post placement support	1	2	3	4	5

Awaiting program commencement	1	2	3	4	5
Receiving your assistance only	1	2	3	4	5
Receiving assistance from another agency	1	2	3	4	5
Unable to be assisted	1	2	3	4	5

13. Generally, how often would you have some form of contact (including telephone) with the following: *(Circle one response for each item.)*

	daily	weekly	monthly	quarterly	less than quarterly	never
A government employment office (other than your own)	1	2	3	4	5	6
Official from other gov't depts	1	2	3	4	5	6
Local government	1	2	3	4	5	6
Welfare agencies	1	2	3	4	5	6
Employers	1	2	3	4	5	6
Training providers	1	2	3	4	5	6
Employment advisers in other agencies	1	2	3	4	5	6
Local service clubs	1	2	3	4	5	6
Schools and universities	1	2	3	4	5	6
Local media	1	2	3	4	5	6

14. EXCLUDING contracts associated with assisting a PARTICULAR JOB SEEKER to obtain information or a job interview, how often would you have some form of contact (including telephone) with the following:
(Circle one response for each item.)

	daily	weekly	monthly	quarterly	less than quarterly	never
A gov't employment office	1	2	3	4	5	6
Official from other gov't depts	1	2	3	4	5	6
Local government	1	2	3	4	5	6
Welfare agencies	1	2	3	4	5	6
Employers	1	2	3	4	5	6
Training providers	1	2	3	4	5	6
Case managers in other agencies	1	2	3	4	5	6
Local service clubs	1	2	3	4	5	6

Schools and						
universities	1	2	3	4	5	6
Local media	1	2	3	4	5	6

14A. In a typical week, how many meetings (if any) would you conduct with your clients outside your office?

Number of outside meetings ....

14B. Among the clients you currently assist, what percentage do you:

Follow closely ....%
Follow somewhat ....%
Follow little or not at all ....%

100%

15. If you had more time, which of the following would you choose to spend more time on?

(Number the seven items from 1–7, with 1 as the highest preference.)

Spend more time developing my skills ....?
Spend more time with employers ....?
Spend more time planning my work ....?
Spend more time with each client ....?
Spend more time with harder-to-place clients ....?
Spend more time with program providers ....?
Spend more time on administration ....?

16. Are you involved in advising decision makers on which training courses, job clubs or other programs are offered to clients in your area?

Always 1
Most of the time 2
Sometimes 3
Never 4

17. Are you normally logged on and accessing your computer system when talking to job seekers?

Yes 1
No 2

18. What is your BEST ESTIMATE of the percentage of your job seekers who fail to comply with the terms of their job seeker agreement?

% of job seekers failing to comply: ....%

19. When would you recommend a job seeker be sanctioned?
    (Tick all that apply.)

	Yes	No
When they don't comply with their job seeker agreement	_	_
Job seeker refuses a suitable job offer	_	_
Job seeker fails to commence training course	_	_
Job seeker leaves training course	_	_
Job seeker fails to contact our office	_	_
Job seeker fails to attend job interview	_	_
Other *(please specify)*		
....		

20. Why might you decide NOT TO RECOMMEND that a client by sanctioned?
    (Tick all that apply.)

		Yes	No
a.	Can't substantiate the case	_	_
b.	Job seeker agreement not specific enough	_	_
c.	Fear for personal safety	_	_
d.	Sanctions are always overturned	_	_
e.	Sanctioning is not an incentive to compliance	_	_
f.	Don't want a reputation for being too tough	_	_
g.	This office does not encourage sanctioning	_	_
h.	Penalties are too harsh	_	_

21. What proportion of your clients would you recommend for sanctioning in an average week?

    Percentage referred ....%

22. On average, how many of the clients you refer for sanction would receive some penalty for non-compliance?

    Percentage of referrals who are penalised ....%

23. Where do you get information about the local labour market?
    (Tick all that apply.)

    A government support service ....

    My own experience in industry ....

    Newspapers ....

    Direct contact with employers ....

    From my fellow employment officers ....

    I have no such information ....

24. Please give a rating for each of the following:

	strongly agree	agree	neither	disagree	strongly disagree
I believe the current system of employment assistance is working very well	5	4	3	2	1
Many of our clients will never find regular jobs	5	4	3	2	1
I consider myself to be an advocate for the client's rights	5	4	3	2	1
Public servants have special responsibilities which are different from other service delivery staff	5	4	3	2	1

25. Which ONE of the following four statements BEST DESCRIBES the thing that determines the work priorities in your office? *(Tick one only.)*

    1. Knowing the RULES and official PROCEDURES ....
    OR
    2. Following the TARGETS set by management. ....

OR

3. COMPETING successfully with other service providers. . . . .

OR

4. Having the best possible SET OF CONTACTS outside the organisation. . . . .

26. We are interested in your opinion regarding the following items.

(Please read each statement carefully and circle the number which is closest to your view.)

	strongly disagree	disagree	neither	agree	strongly agree
I find using sanctions against clients can really damage our reputation with clients and others in the industry	1	2	3	4	5
The lines of authority are not all that clear in my work	1	2	3	4	5
In this job I find myself working for a number of superiors in different places	1	2	3	4	5
I do not like my competitors to know too much about how I go about getting my results	1	2	3	4	5
My job can be done by following a few basic rules	1	2	3	4	5
When it comes to day-to-day work I am free to decide for myself what I will do with each client	1	2	3	4	5
My supervisor knows a lot about the work I do day-to-day	1	2	3	4	5
I am often involved in discussions concerning ways we could improve our procedures	1	2	3	4	5
The really important rules in this job are the ones to do with relationships with other organisations	1	2	3	4	5
I regularly get involved in discussions about ways we could make things better for our clients	1	2	3	4	5

If I want to I can vary the service I provide to any client	1	2	3	4	5
I don't think there are any set rules for doing this job	1	2	3	4	5
In my job I am NOT influenced by numerical targets	1	2	3	4	5
I usually use my computer while interviewing clients	1	2	3	4	5
The main thing I have to do in this job is gain the trust of the client	1	2	3	4	5
Our organisation has a set method for dealing with clients	1	2	3	4	5
I understand that our organisation has special targets for certain types of client	1	2	3	4	5
My supervisor does not know much at all about the work I do on a day-to-day basis	1	2	3	4	5
When I come across something not covered by the procedure guide I refer it to my supervisor	1	2	3	4	5

27. Here are some more general questions which we would like you to respond to by using the same agree/disagree scale. (*Please circle the response which best describes your views.*)

	strongly disagree	disagree	neither	agree	strongly agree
The goal in this work is to find a middle ground between the needs of clients, trainers, employers and the social security system	1	2	3	4	5
I use a lot of personal judgement to decide what is best for each client	1	2	3	4	5
Before reporting a client for non-compliance I would always consider which					

target group they belonged to	1	2	3	4	5
If clients do not follow the rules I report them only if I'm sure I have a watertight case	1	2	3	4	5
I like to keep my own records and files on clients and programs	1	2	3	4	5
In the majority of cases our information technology systems tells us what steps to take and when to take them	1	2	3	4	5
When you get good results with a client it's usually a team effort by yourself, trainers and the employer	1	2	3	4	5
I think it is helpful to remind clients of the sanctioning power to get them to pay attention	1	2	3	4	5
My job is determined by goals set by others	1	2	3	4	5
My supervisor does not know very much about my day-to-day work	1	2	3	4	5
More and more the objective in this job is to maximise our financial outcomes	1	2	3	4	5
It is important to run an office set-up where everyone reinforces the same message with the client	1	2	3	4	5
I think the objective in this job is to shift the maximum number of clients	1	2	3	4	5
I use our information technology to track priority clients	1	2	3	4	5
I do tend to take note of those actions with clients that will generate a payable outcome for the office	1	2	3	4	5

All my clients receive a similar service	1	2	3	4	5
My work unit is sometimes asked to suggest ways to improve things	1	2	3	4	5
I am aware that my organisation pays attention to the funds I generate by placing clients	1	2	3	4	5
If an official from another organisation asked me for advice on how to help a client I would gladly help them	1	2	3	4	5
In my job clients are organised into formal and informal priority groups	1	2	3	4	5
It is not my job to think about ways to change this service	1	2	3	4	5
If an official from another employment organisation asked for help in using the computer I would help them	1	2	3	4	5
I have rules and procedures to guide me in most key decisions affecting this job	1	2	3	4	5

28. Gender:
    Male 1
    Female 2

29. Age:
    Up to 24 1
    25 to 34 2
    35 to 44 3
    45 to 54 4
    55 and over 5

30. What level is your current job according to your organisation's classification code?
    . . . .

31. Have you always worked in THIS employment organisation?
    Yes 1
    No 2

How long have you been employed here?

less than 1 year 1

1–5 years 2

more than 5 years 3

32. Do you have any formal qualifications?
   (*Please specify the qualifications and field of study.*)
   . . . .
   . . . .

33. What was your job before becoming an employment officer?
   . . . .
   . . . .

34. Are you a member of a trade union?

Yes 1

No 2

35. Do you attend any REGULAR meetings outside your own organisation of
   employment program providers, case managers and/or trainers from other
   organisations?

Yes 1

No 2

36. If yes, how often does this group or network meet?

Weekly 1

Monthly 2

Quarterly 3

Less than quarterly 4

Work in the Employment Sector

Please circle the relevant number.

37. To what degree do you feel PERSONALLY committed to the GOALS of your
   organisation?

| Very Committed | 1 | 2 | 3 | 4 | 5 | 6 | 7 | Not very committed |

38. To what degree do you feel personally committed to the VALUES of your
   organisation?

| Very committed | 1 | 2 | 3 | 4 | 5 | 6 | 7 | Not very committed |

39. To what extent would you be willing to exert considerable extra effort on
   behalf of your organisation?

| Very willing | 1 | 2 | 3 | 4 | 5 | 6 | 7 | Not very willing |

40. To what extent are you satisfied with your present conditions of work (pay,
   hours, promotion, etc.)?

| Very satisfied | 1 | 2 | 3 | 4 | 5 | 6 | 7 | Not very satisfied |

41. How much variety is there in the activities that make up your job?

| Little or no variety | 1 | 2 | 3 | 4 | 5 | 6 | 7 | A great deal of variety |

42. To what extent do you do the same things, in the same way, each day at work?

Almost totally the same each day	1	2	3	4	5	6	7	Almost totally different each day

43. To what extent are the activities that make up your job ROUTINE?

Very routine	1	2	3	4	5	6	7	Little or no routine

44. Here is a list of decisions which get made on the job. For each of the following decisions, please indicate HOW MUCH SAY YOU ACTUALLY HAVE in making these decisions.

(*Circle one for each decision.*)

		no say at all	some say	moderate say	a good deal of say	a very great deal of say
a.	How you do your job	1	2	3	4	5
b.	Sequence of your job	1	2	3	4	5
c.	Speed at which you work	1	2	3	4	5
d.	Changing how you do your job	1	2	3	4	5

45. How well INFORMED are you about each of the following aspects of your job.

(*Circle one for each aspect.*)

		very well informed	quite well in-formed	fairly well informed	somewhat informed	hardly at all informed
a.	What is to be done	1	2	3	4	5
b.	Policies and procedures	1	2	3	4	5
c.	Priority of work to be done	1	2	3	4	5
d.	How well the job is done	1	2	3	4	5
e.	Technical knowledge	1	2	3	4	5
f.	Nature of equipment used	1	2	3	4	5
g.	How you are supposed to do the job	1	2	3	4	5
h.	Dollar value of your interactions with each client	1	2	3	4	5

46. How often do you see people you work with in this organisation outside working hours in a social context (drinks, dinners, lunch, etc.)?

(*Please circle the most appropriate response.*)

Almost every day 6

Roughly between two and six times a week 5

About once a week 4

About every other week 3

About once a month 2

Less than once a month 1

No friends among fellow workers 9

47. How often would you see people you work with from other organisations in the employment field, in a social context (drinks, dinners, lunch, etc.)?

Almost every day 6

Roughly between two and six times a week 5

About once a week 4

About every other week 3

About once a month 2

Less than once a month 1

No friends among fellow workers 9

48. Which of the following statements most clearly reflects your feelings about your future in the employment sector?

Definitely will not leave 4

Probably will not leave 3

Uncertain 2

Probably will leave 1

Definitely will leave 0

49. Compared to the effort that you put into your job, how do you feel about the pay you receive?

Compared with the effort, my pay is very poor .0

Poor 1

About right 2

Good 1

Compared with the effort, my pay is very good .0

50. How much do you agree or disagree with each of the following statements about your job? *(Please circle one for each statement.)*

		strongly agree	agree	neither agree nor disagree	disagree	strongly disagree
a.	I find real enjoyment in my job	1	2	3	4	5
b.	I consider my job rather unpleasant	1	2	3	4	5
c.	I am often bored with my job	1	2	3	4	5
d.	I am fairly well satisfied with my job	1	2	3	4	5
e.	The most important things that happen to me involve my present job	1	2	3	4	5
f.	To me, my job is only a small part of who I am	1	2	3	4	5
g.	I live, eat and breathe my job	1	2	3	4	5

h. Most of my personal life
    goals are job-orientated   1   2   3   4   5
i. Usually I feel detached
    from my job   1   2   3   4   5

51. In your judgement how effective is the current employment service in help-
    ing clients find a job?

    Not effective   1   2   3   4   5   6   7   Very effective

52. In your judgement how effective is the current employment service in get-
    ting clients off welfare?

    Not effective   1   2   3   4   5   6   7   Very effective

53. The practice in my agency is to pick out the most capable welfare recipients
    and give them the best service.

                                                                    Strongly
    Strongly Agree   1   2   3   4   5   6   7   disagree

54. Based on the practices in your office today, what would you say IS the more
    important goal of your agency: to help clients get jobs as quickly as possible
    or to raise education or skill levels of clients so that they can get the job, in
    the future?

    To get   To raise
    job quickly   1   2   3   4   5   6   7   skill levels

55. After a short time attending your service, an average job seeker is offered a
    low-skill, low-paying job that would make him or her better off financially.
    Assume he or she has two choices: either to take the job and leave welfare
    OR to stay on welfare and wait for a better opportunity. If you were asked,
    what would your personal advice to this client be?

                                                            Stay on welfare
    Take the job and   and wait for a
    leave welfare   1   2   3   4   5   6   7 better opportunity

56. What advice would your supervisor give to a client of this type?

    Take the job   Stay on welfare
    and leave   and wait for a
    welfare   1   2   3   4   5   6   7 better opportunity

57. In your opinion, which is more often to blame if a person is on welfare: lack
    of effort on their part, or circumstances beyond their control?

                                                              Circumstance
    Lack of effort   beyond their
    on their part   1   2   3   4   5   6   7   control

58. In your opinion, approximately what percentage of people who apply for
    welfare would rather be on welfare than work to support themselves and
    their families?

    . . . . %

59. How much does your agency emphasise giving clients more choice about
    the services they receive?

    None   1   2   3   4   5   6   7   A great deal

60. To what extent are the decisions you make about your clients determined by the central program rules and regulations?

Very little   1   2   3   4   5   6   7   A great deal

61. How much leeway do you have in deciding which program or activity the client should be assigned to?

| Very little | | | | | | | | A great deal |

Very little
leeway   1   2   3   4   5   6   7   of leeway

62. Does your office encourage staff not to be lenient or to be lenient in the use of sanctions?

Not to be lenient 1   2   3   4   5   6   7   To be lenient

63. In your role as an employment adviser, how much time do you spend on the following tasks?

		very little						a great deal
a.	Client assessment	1	2	3	4	5	6	7
b.	Employability plan	1	2	3	4	5	6	7
c.	Planning and case review	1	2	3	4	5	6	7
d.	Referral to programs	1	2	3	4	5	6	7
e.	Referral to job interviews	1	2	3	4	5	6	7
f.	Referral to other services (counselling, drug abuse treatment, etc.)	1	2	3	4	5	6	7
g.	Monitoring and checking on clients	1	2	3	4	5	6	7
h.	Involvement in sanctioning	1	2	3	4	5	6	7
i.	Advocacy for clients	1	2	3	4	5	6	7
j.	Help clients with self esteem	1	2	3	4	5	6	7
k.	Counsel clients for personal, family and other issues	1	2	3	4	5	6	7
l.	Case conferences with other service providers	1	2	3	4	5	6	7
m.	Explaining your actions to supervisors/ management	1	2	3	4	5	6	7

64. Suppose a client has been assigned to an activity outside your office but STOPS ATTENDING AFTER THE FIRST SESSION. How long, on average, would it take for the staff person monitoring this client to learn about this situation from the service provider?

One week or less 1
Two weeks 2
Three weeks 3
Four weeks 4
Five weeks or more 5
Not usual to find out 6

65. Suppose a client has missed more than one interview or more than one session of a program activity they had been assigned to giving emotional problems as a reason. Below is a list of actions you might take. Please put a '1' next to the action you are most likely to take. Put a '2' next to the second most likely action and continue to do so until you have rated all of them.
    - Inform the client that they will be referred for sanctioning.
    - Provide or refer the client to counselling.
    - See if there is a way to withdraw or exempt the client from the activity.
    - Assign the client to another interview or activity.
    - Point out the importance of this activity to getting a decent job.
    - Give the client a motivational talk.
    - Other *(please specify)* . . . .
      . . . .
      . . . .

66. In your opinion, does the employment assistance process allow too few or too many 'second chances' for clients?

    Too few   1   2   3   4   5   6   7   Too many

67. In your opinion, are sanctions an effective or ineffective tool for improving client compliance?

    Very ineffective   1   2   3   4   5   6   7   Very effective

68. In your opinion does the use of sanctions make it harder or easier to get a client into a job?

    Harder   1   2   3   4   5   6   7   Easier

69. If you have any other comments or suggestions about services provided for the unemployed, or about this survey please write them in the space below.

B. Normative Basis of the Four Governance Models

1. Proceduralists were defined as having a strong orientation to rules. Statements such as 'I have rules and procedures to guide me in the work I do' were used to test commitment to this idea. This scale also contained variables testing 'knowledgeable supervision', 'standardised service to clients', and low interest in the role of output measurements.

2. Corporate Managers were defined as less interested in rules and more clearly motivated by targets and plans for specified client groups. Major interest was seen to reside in the need for officials to service target groups who were valued in policy and program plans. Approaches to the use of sanctions and special treatments were presumed to follow recognition of such group prioritisation.

3. Marketeers were defined by items which measured responsiveness to the costs and prices for different services and different clients. A high consciousness of the need to beat one's competitors was also included. Objectives were viewed as less a matter of goals and plans, and more clearly defined by 'payable outcomes'.

4. Networkers were defined as those who saw their work as based upon the co-production of results using brokerage and negotiation. A high value was

presumed to be placed on trust and maintaining good contacts with clients and other service providers, including competitors. Advisers using this approach were presumed to be the most likely to say 'when you get good results with clients it's usually a joint effort by yourself, the training person, the employer etc.'.

C. The Three Factor Solution

Table A1   The three factor solution

	Corporate/ Market	Network	Procedural
5. I find using sanctions against clients can really damage your reputation with clients and others in the industry			−.23
6. The lines of authority are not clear in my work			−.61
7. I do not like my competitors to know how I go about getting my results			−.41
8. My job can be done by following a few basic rules			
9. When it comes to day-to-day work I am free to decide for myself what I will do with each client		.36	
10. My supervisor knows a lot about the work I do day-to-day			.53
12. The really important rules in this job are the ones to do with obtaining assistance from other organisations		.57	
15. In my job I am NOT influenced by numerical targets	−.36	.27	.23
16. The main thing I have to do in this job is gain the trust of the client		.51	
17. Our organisation has targets for certain types of client	.40		
19. When I come across something not covered by the procedure guide I refer it to my supervisor	.28		.50
20. The goal in this work is to find a middle ground between the needs of clients, employers and the social security system	.29		
21. I use a lot of personal judgement to decide what is best for each client	.28		
22. Before reporting a client for non-compliance I would always consider which target group they belong to	.28		
24. I like to keep my own records and files on clients and programs		.47	
25. Our computer system tells me what steps to take with clients and when to take them	.34		
26. When you get good results with clients it's usually a team effort by yourself, trainers and the employer		.49	
27. I often remind clients of the sanctioning power to get them to pay attention	.46		
28. My job is determined by goals set elsewhere	.54		

Table A1   (cont.)

	Corporate/ Market	Network	Procedural
30. More and more the objective in this job is to maximise the organisation's financial outcomes	.56		–.40
31. I think the objective in this job is to shift the maximum number of clients off benefits	.58		
32. I use our information technology to track priority clients	.48		.35
33. I do tend to take note of those actions with clients that will generate a payable outcome for the office	.46	–.22	
34. All my clients receive a similar service			
35. I am often asked to suggest ways to improve things		.28	.29
36. I am aware that my organisation pays attention to the income I generate by placing clients			–.33
37. If an official from another employment organisation asked for help in using the computer I would help them		.48	
38. In my job clients are organised into formal and informal priority groups	.40		

Note: To simplify this table, only factor loadings with a magnitude of .20 and greater are shown

D. Discriminant Analysis

The purpose of this procedure is to choose which variables best discriminate between country and organisation types, or, to phrase it another way, to determine which variables account for the underlying differences between these groups. It is difficult to separate out the independent effects of country and ownership as not all countries have all ownership types. Consequently, the data have been grouped according to country AND organisation type and discrimination made between these groupings. The resulting seven groups are listed below:

1. Australia – government
2. Australia – private for-profit
3. Australia – private non-profit
4. New Zealand – government
5. United Kingdom – government
6. Netherlands – government
7. Netherlands – private for-profit

Because this procedure is highly sensitive to missing data (the whole case is deleted if a single variable contains missing data) the model used was based upon the surveys conducted after the 1996 Australian study. The 1996 Australian questionnaire contained a number of different items which were later deleted or amended. A second model was developed for the total of all survey groups including 1996 and this showed substantial overlap with the model presented below.

In descriptive discriminant analysis (DDA) we are basically looking for a 'definable and interpretable structure underlying group differences'.[1] We do this by forming linear combinations of the 'independent' variables to help us discriminate between the groups. These linear combinations are used for assigning cases into groups. Essentially, the linear equations are used to give discriminant scores. The equation coefficients are estimated to give the greatest separation between groups – based on the discriminant scores. The grouping factor can be thought of as the independent variable and the response variables as the outcome variables. The criterion used to 'maximise' differences is called Wilks' lambda. In order to maximise differences between the groups we need to minimise Wilks' lambda.

It is usually recommended that variables be screened, whether for theoretical or practical reasons. It may also be helpful to screen variables based on statistical tests – the most obvious being multiple one-way analyses of variance (ANOVAs) based on the grouping variable. In order to avoid excluding cases, however, a build-up approach had to be taken. This was difficult with so many variables. Variables of most interest were ranked priority 'A' or priority 'B' based on the research hypotheses of the study described above. The final model was therefore developed in the following manner:

(1) Stepwise selection was applied to variables with at least 800 cases and the resulting discriminating variables found.

(2) Stepwise selection was applied to variables considered to have an 'A' priority and the resulting discriminating variables found.

(3) Stepwise selection was applied to variables with at least 700 cases and the resulting discriminating variables found.

(4) From Steps (1) to (3), an initial core group of variables was selected by choosing the resulting discriminant variables common to at least two of the above steps.

(5) The model was built up by adding every other variable, one at a time, to the initial core group of variables from Step (4) and then selecting only those variables that increased the percentage of cases correctly classified by 1% using the discriminant rules (i.e. the resulting linear equations). These variables were then included in the stepwise modelling process.

(6) Once the final model was nearly established, some of the variables that were on the borderline of being included were tried in and out of the model in order to try and obtain the best model. The best model was judged as the model with the highest percentage of cases correctly classified when using the discriminant equations.

After the final model was resolved, the resulting Wilks' lambda was determined for each variable if that particular variable were to be left out of the model. As Wilks' lambda is minimised when the groups have the greatest separation, the variable that makes Wilks' lambda the lowest will be the variable that contributes most to group separation. Hence, using this approach implies that variables may

Table A2 Number of cases analysed (excluding Australia 1996)

Group	Number in final model	Number of potential cases	Percentage of cases
Australia – government	112	139	81
Australia – for profit	17	26	65
Australia – non-profit	55	86	64
Netherlands – government	123	153	80
Netherlands – for-profit	94	112	84
NZ – government	82	132	62
UK – government	116	153	76
Total	599	808	74

Table A3 Potential order of importance of the discriminant variables based on Wilks' lambda and the F Test (variable number)

1	Network with Welfare (13)	13	Targets priority clients (17)
2	Specialist? (2)	14	Other services? (2)
3	Time with job seekers (11)	15	ES gets people off welfare? (52)
4	Staff numbers (1)	16	Goal to get job or raise skills? (54)
5	Not reveal methods (26–4)	17	ES help find job? (51)
6	Union member (34)	18	Use breaching power (27–8)
7	Dollar Value (27–18)	19	Tech (45 e)
8	Logged-on (17)	20	Reinforce message (27–12)
9	Time in job (31)	21	Network with Media (13)
10	Speed (44 c)	22	Breaching reputation (26–1)
11	Network (31)	23	Age of adviser (29)
12	Use CCL (7)	24	Network with Other Gov (13)

Note: Numbers in parentheses indicate position in questionnaire (see above).

be ranked in order of 'importance' (greatest group separation) by ranking the Wilks' lambdas when each in turn is left out of the model.

Analysis

The numbers of cases in the final model are given in Table A2. Overall about 74% of possible cases were included. The minimum per cent of cases used in any group was 62% in the New Zealand group and the maximum was 84% in the Netherland for profit group.

There were 24 variables included in the final discriminant analysis. The tests for equality of group means were statistically significant for all 24 variables. The pooled within-groups correlation matrix showed little correlation between any of the variables. The strongest correlation was r=.55 between 'ES help find job?' and 'ES gets people off welfare'. The majority of correlations were between –.1 and +.1. As expected, Box's Test for equal population covariance matrices was highly significant (p=.001). The potential ordering of variables based on group separation is given in Table A3.

Table A4 The variables that correlate the most highly with the discriminant equations

		Equation			
1	2	3	4	5	6
Would not reveal methods	Staff numbers	Goal to get job or raise skills?	Time spent in job	Is Union member	Thinks ES helps find jobs?
Networks with other Govt	Never worked elsewhere	Specialist Provider?	Breaching reputation	Time spent with job seekers	Uses breaching power
	Networks with Media	Networks with welfare	Age of adviser	Dollar values	Logged-on
	Has targets for priority clients	Provides other services?	Technical knowledge		Uses CCL
		Speed of work			ES gets people off welfare?
		Reinforce same message			

The pairwise group comparisons of the mean vectors of the discriminant variables showed statistically significant differences between all of the groups except the two Australian private groups – 'Australian for-profit' and 'Australian non-profit'. This suggests not only differences between countries but also differences between government and privately owned employment services. However the number of Australian for-profits in this comparison is small.

The eigenvalues represent the variance within the 24 variable system of the final discriminant model. Eighty-five per cent of the variation between the seven groups is represented by the first three discriminant equations; 48% from the first, 24% from the second and 13% from the third. The tests of the six discriminant equations show that the first five equations significantly contribute to interpreting the differences between the groups and the last equation does not. Table A3 shows which variables are most strongly correlated with these discriminant equations.

The variables correlating with equation 1 are about how often the employees contact and network with officials from other departments and engage in sharing information with competitors (about getting client results). The variables correlating with equation 2 are related to the number of staff in the employee's office; the types of clients seen, including clients perceived as never likely to get regular work; and whether the organisation had targets for certain types of clients. The amount of contact with local media is also correlated with this equation. The variables correlated with equation 3 seem to be about how the employment services are run – the goals of the service, programs offered by the service, consistent messages within the service and the speed at which employees are able to deliver services.

The cross-validated classification rates provide a measure of how good the discriminant model is. The overall percentage of cases correctly classified was

82%. If cases were correctly classified according to the prior probabilities only (and not the model), you would expect 14% to be correctly classified. If cases were correctly classified by chance only, according to the proportion of cases within each group you would expect 17% to be correctly classified. This suggests the model is useful in defining underlying differences between the groups.

With the exception of the Australian private agencies the classification rates range from 80% to 93%. The classification rates in the Australian for-profit group and the Australian non-profit groups are 47% and 67% respectively. The mistakes in classifications come from being incorrectly classified as each other, showing it is more difficult to separate these two groups than any of the others in the study on the basis of country and ownership.

Note

1 C.J. Huberty (1994) *Applied Discriminant Analysis*, New York, John Wiley and Sons.

Bibliography

Aberbach, Joel D., Robert D. Putnam & Bert A. Rockman (1981) *Bureaucrats and Politicians in Western Democracies*, Cambridge, Mass., Harvard University Press.

Alford, J. & M. Considine (1994) 'Public Sector Employment Contracts', in John Alford & Deirdre O'Neill (eds) *The Contract State: Public Management and the Kennett Government*, Geelong, Deakin University Press.

Allen, R. (1992) *Purchasing and Providing Social Services in the 1990s: Drawing the Line*, London, Policy Studies Institute.

Almond, Phillip & Jill Rubery (2000) 'Deregulation and Societal Systems', in Marc Maurice & Arndt Sorge (eds) *Embedding Organisations: Societal Analysis of Actors, Organisations and Socio-Economic Context*, Amsterdam, John Benjamins Publishing, pp. 277–95.

Amin, Ash (1994) *Post-Fordism: A Reader*, Oxford, Blackwell.

Anderton, Bob (1997) *UK Labour Market Reforms and Sectoral Wage Formation*, National Institute of Economic and Social Research, Discussion Paper No. 121, July.

Ashby, R. W. (1957) *An Introduction to Cybernetics*, New York, Wiley & Sons.

Ashby, R. W. (1960) *Design for a Brain*, London, Chapman & Hall.

Aucoin, Peter (1990) 'Administrative Reform in Public Management: Paradigms, Principles, Paradoxes and Pendulums', *Governance*, 3 (2) April, pp. 115–37.

Austin, C. D. (1993) 'Developing Case Management: A Systems Perspective', *Journal of Contemporary Human Services*, October, pp. 451–9.

Barney, Jay B. & William G. Ouchi (eds) (1986) *Organizational Economics*, San Francisco, Jossey-Bass.

Bartlett, Will & Lyn Harrison (1993) 'Quasi-Markets and the National Health Service Reforms', in Le Grand & Bartlett, op. cit., pp. 68–92.

Barzeley, M. (1992) *Breaking Through Bureaucracy: A New Vision for Managing in Government*, Berkeley, University of California Press.

Beck, Ulrich (1986) *Risikogesellschaft*, Frankfurt a. M., Suhrkamp.

Beck, Ulrich (1992) *Risk Society: Towards a New Modernity*, Trans. Mark Ritter, London, Sage.

Beck, Ulrich (2000) 'Living Your Own Life in a Runaway World: Individualisation, Globalisation and Politics', in Will Hutton & Anthony Giddens (eds) *On the Edge: Living with Global Capitalism*, London, Jonathan Cape, pp. 164–74.

Becker, F. W. & A. J. Mackelprang (1990) 'Attitudes of State Legislators towards Contracting for Public Services', *American Review of Public Administration*, 29 (3), pp. 175–89.

Becker, Uwe (1999) 'The Dutch Delta Model: Employment Growth in a Still Generous Welfare System'. Paper presented to the Department of Political Science, University of Melbourne, 26 March.

Beer, Samuel (1970) 'The Strengths of Liberal Democracy', in William S. Livingston (ed.) *A Prospect of Liberal Democracy*, Austin, University of Texas Press, pp. 215–29.

Beilharz, Peter, Mark Considine & Rob Watts (1992) *Arguing About the Welfare State: The Australian Experience*, Sydney, Allen & Unwin.

Bell, Vicki (1996) 'The promise of Liberalism and the Performance of Freedom', in Andrew Barry, Thomas Osborne & Nikolas Rose (eds) *Foucault and Political Reason: Liberalism, Neo-Liberalism and Rationalities of Government*, London, UCL Press.

Bendix, R. (1968) 'Bureaucracy', in D. L. Sills (ed.) *International Encyclopedia of the Social Sciences*, New York, Macmillan, pp. 206–19.

Blau, Peter M. (1956) *Bureaucracy in Modern Society*, New York, Random House.

Boston, J., John Martin, June Pallot & Pat Walsh (eds) (1991) *Reshaping the State: New Zealand's Bureaucratic Revolution*, Auckland, Oxford University Press.

Boston, Jonathon, John Martin, June Pallot & Pat Walsh (1996) *Public Management: The New Zealand Model*, Auckland, Oxford University Press.

Bourdieu, P. (1991) *Language and Symbolic Power*, London, Polity Press.

Breschi, S. & F. Malerba (1997) 'Sectoral Innovation Systems, Technological Regimes, Schumpeterian Dynamics and Spatial Boundaries', in C. Edquist (ed.) *Systems of Innovation: Technologies, Institutions and Organisations*, London, Pinter, pp. 130–56.

Brudney, J. & R. England (1983) 'Toward a Definition of the Co-Production Concept', *Public Administration Review*, 43 (1), pp. 59–71.

Burrows, Roger & Brian Loader (eds) (1994) *Towards a Post-Fordist Welfare State?*, London, Routledge.

Caiden, Gerald E. & Heinrich Seidentopf (eds) (1982) *Strategies for Administrative Reform*, Lexington, Mass., Lexington Books.

Cameron, D. (1992) 'Institutional Management: How should the Government and Management of Universities in Canada Accommodate Changing Circumstances?', in J. Cutt & R. Dobell (eds) *Public Purse, Public Purpose: Autonomy and Accountability in the Groves of Academe*, Halifax, Institute for Research on Public Policy.

Capling, Ann, Mark Considine & Michael Crozier (1998) *Australian Politics in the Global Era*, Longman, Melbourne.

Carter, Jan (1998) *The Policy Process and Unemployment Reform*, Deakin Human Services Australia, Working Paper, Melbourne.

Castells, Manuel (1996) *The Rise of Network Society*, Vol. I, Malden Mass., Blackwell.

Castles, Francis & Ian Shirley (1996) 'Labour and Social Policy: Gravediggers or Refurbishers of the Welfare State', in Castles et al. *The Great Experiment*, op. cit., pp. 88–100.

Castles, Francis, Rolf Gerritsen & Jack Vowles (eds) (1996) *The Great Experiment: Labour Parties and Public Transformation in Australia and New Zealand*, Sydney, Allen & Unwin.

Chandler, Alfred D. (1977) *The Visible Hand: The Managerial Revolution in American Business*, Cambridge, Mass., Belnap Press.

Chandler, Alfred D. (1990) 'The Enduring Logic of Industrial Success', *Harvard Business Review*, 68 March–April, pp. 130–40.

Chapman, Bruce (1993) *Long Term Unemployment in Australia: Causes, Consequences and Policy Responses*. A Report Prepared for the Department of Employment, Education and Training, December, 95 pp.

Christiansen, Peter Munk (1998) 'A Prescription Rejected: Market Solutions to Problems of Public Sector Governance', *Governance*, 11 (3) July, pp. 273–97.

Ciborra, Claudio U. (1996) *Teams, Markets and Systems: Business Innovation and Information Technology*, Cambridge, Cambridge University Press.

Cohen, J. & P. Cohen (1983) *Applied Multiple Regression/Correlation Analysis for the Behavioral Sciences*, 2nd Edn, Hillsdale, NJ, Lawrence Erlbaum.

Colmar Brunton Research (1995) New Zealand Employment Service Consultant's Report, Wellington, 28 pp.

Commonwealth of Australia (1994) *Working Nation: Policies and Programs*, Government White Paper, Canberra, Australian Government Publishing Service.

Connor, S. (1992) *Theory and Cultural Value*, Oxford, Blackwell.

Considine, Mark (1990) 'Managerialism Strikes Out', *Australian Journal of Public Administration*, 49 (2), pp. 166–78.

Considine, Mark (1994) *Public Policy: A Critical Approach*, Melbourne, Macmillan.

Considine, Mark (1996) 'Market Bureaucracy? Exploring the Contending Rationalities of Contemporary Administrative Regimes', *Labour and Industry*, 7, (1) June, pp. 1–27.

Considine, Mark (1999) 'Markets, Networks and the New Welfare State: Employment Assistance Reforms in Australia', *Journal of Social Policy*, 28 (2), pp. 183–203.

Considine, Mark (2000) 'Selling the Unemployed: The Performance of Bureaucracies, Firms and Non-Profits in the new Australian "market" for Unemployment Assistance', *Social Policy and Administration*, 34 (3), pp. 27–95.

Considine, Mark & Jenny M. Lewis (1999) 'Governance at Ground Level: The Front-line Bureaucrat in the Age of Markets and Networks', *Public Administration Review*, 59 (6), pp. 467–80.

Considine, Mark & Martin Painter (1997) 'Introduction', in Considine & Painter (eds) *Managerialism: The Great Debate*, Melbourne, Melbourne University Press.

Cox, Robert Henry (1998) 'Review of "A Dutch Miracle"', *Journal of Public Policy*, 18 (2), May–August, pp. 209–11.

Craig, J. J. (1996) *The Contract State: Administrative Law Revisited*, Colloque International, Secteur Public et Contractualisation dans Les Pays Industrialisés, Fondation Nationale des Sciences Politiques, Paris.

Culpitt, Ian (1999) *Social Policy and Risk*, London, Sage Publications.

Department of Employment Education and Training (DEET) (1993) *National Survey of Jobseeker CES Satisfaction February/March 1993*, Evaluation and Monitoring Branch, EMB Report 9/93, Canberra.

Department of Employment, Education, Training and Youth Affairs (1996) *12 Month Post-Program Monitoring Survey: Summary Report*, September, Canberra, DEETYA.

Department of Employment, Education, Training and Youth Affairs (1996) *Working Nation: Evaluation of the Employment, Education and Training Elements*, Evaluation and Monitoring Branch Report 2/96, Canberra, DEETYA.

Department of Labour (1995) *Evaluation of Job Action*, Wellington, New Zealand, August.

Department of Labour (1997) *Corporate Plan 1997/98*, Wellington, New Zealand.

Dolowitz, David (1997) 'British Employment Policy in the 1980s: Learning from the American Experience', *Governance*, 10 (1) January, pp. 23–42.

Donaldson, Lex (1995) *American Anti-Management Theories of Organisation: A Critique of Paradigm Proliferation*, Cambridge, Cambridge University Press.

Douglas, R. (1993) *Unfinished Business*, Auckland, Random House.

Drucker, Peter F. (1992) 'The New Society of Organisations', *Harvard Business Review*, 70 Sept–Oct, pp. 95–104.

du Gay, P. (1993) 'Entrepreneurial Management in the Public Sector', *Work, Employment & Society*, 7 (4), pp. 643–74.

du Gay, P. & Graeme Salaman (1996) 'The Cult(ure) of the Customer', *Journal of Management Studies*, 29 (5), pp. 615–33.

Easton, Brian (1996) *Does Free to Work Tell a True Story?*, Economic and Social Trust of New Zealand, Wellington.

Efficiency Unit (1988) *Improving Management in Government: The Next Steps*, London, HMSO.

Employment Services Regulatory Authority (ESRA) (1997) *Best Practice in Case Management*, Melbourne, ESRA.

Employment Services Regulatory Authority (ESRA) (1995) *Annual Report 1994–95*, Melbourne, ESRA.

Esping-Andersen, G. (1990) *Three Worlds of Welfare Capitalism*, Cambridge, Polity.

Etzioni, Amitai (1964) *Modern Organisations*, Englewood-Cliffs, New Jersey, Prentice Hall.

Feldman, Martha S. (1992) 'Social Limits to Discretion: An Organisational Perspective', in Keith Hawkins (ed.) *The Uses of Discretion*, Oxford, Clarendon Paperbacks.

Finn, Dan (1997) *Working Nation: Welfare Reform and the Australian Jobs Compact for the Long-Term Unemployed*, Darlinghurst, ACOSS.

Foster, Christopher D. & Francis J. Plowden (1996) *The State Under Stress: Can the Hollow State be Good Government?*, Buckingham, Open University Press.

Fournier, Valerie & Christopher Grey (1999) 'Too Much, Too Little and Too Often: A Critique of du Gay's Analysis of Enterprise', *Organisation*, 6 (1), pp. 107–28.

Fox, A. (1974) *Beyond Contract: Work, Power and Trust Relations*, London, Faber.

Fox, Charles & Hugh T. Miller (1995) *Postmodern Public Administration: Towards Discourse*, Thousand Oaks, CA, Sage.

Fulton Report, Committee on the Civil Service (1968) *Report of the Committee on the Civil Service*, Cmnd 3638, London, HMSO.

Gardener, M. R. & R. W. Ashby (1970) 'Connectance of Large Dynamic (Cybernetic) Systems: Critical Values for Stability', *Nature*, 228, p. 52–73.

Garrett, J. (1980) *Managing the Civil Service*, London, Heinemann.

Giddens, Anthony (1999) *The Third Way*, Polity Press, Cambridge.

Glennerster, Howard (1991) 'Quasi-Markets for Education', *The Economic Journal*, 101 September, pp. 1268–76.

Golembiewski, R. T. & Gerald Gabris (1995) 'Tomorrow's City Management: Guides for Avoiding Success-Becoming-Failure', *Public Administration Review*, May/June, 55 (3), pp. 177–91.

Gordon, C. (1991) 'Governmental Rationality: An Introduction', in G. Burchell, C. Gordon & P. Miller (eds) *The Foucault Effect: Studies in Governmentality*, Hemel Hempstead, Harvester Wheatsheaf, pp. 1–52.

Gore, Al (1993) *From Red Tape to Results: Creating a Government that Works Better and Costs Less*, Report of the National Performance Review, Washington, Times Books.

Grant, Judith & Peta Tancred (1992) 'A Feminist Perspective on State Bureaucracy', in Albert Mills & Peta Tancred (eds) *Gendering Organizational Analysis*, Newbury Park, CA, Sage, pp. 112–28.

Habermas, Jürgen (1988) *The Theory of Communicative Action*, 2 Vols, Boston, Beacon Press.

Hagan, Jan L. (1994) 'JOBS and Case Management: Developments in Ten States', *Social Work*, 39 (2), pp. 197–205.

Halligan, John & John Power (1992) *Political Management in the 1990s*, Melbourne, Oxford University Press.

Hamilton, Gayle & Thomas Brock (1994) *The JOBS Evaluation: Early Lessons from Seven Sites*, New York, Manpower Demonstration Research Corporation, December.

Hammond, Barbara (1997) *Foundations of Case Management*, Waurn Ponds, DHSA, Deakin University Press.

Handler, Joel (1995) *The Poverty of Welfare Reform*, New Haven, Yale University Press.

Handler, Joel (1996) *Down from Bureaucracy: The Ambiguity of Privatisation and Empowerment*, Princeton, NJ, Princeton University Press.

Handler, Joel & Yeheskel Hasenfeld (1997) *We the Poor People: Work, Poverty & Welfare*, New Haven, Yale University Press.

Hardin, G. (1978) 'Political Requirements for Preserving our Common Heritage', in H. P. Bokaw (ed.) *Wildlife and America*, Washington, DC, Council on Environmental Quality.

Hasenfeld, Yeheskel (1992) 'Theoretical Approaches to Human Service Organisations', in Hasenfeld (ed.) *Human Services as Complex Organisations*, Newbury Park, CA, Sage.

Hasenfeld, Yeheskel & Dale Weaver (1996) 'Enforcement, Compliance, and Disputes in Return-to-Work Programs', *Social Services Review*, June, pp. 235–56.

Hawkins, Keith (1992) 'The Use of Legal Discretion: Perspectives from Law and Social Science', in Hawkins (ed.) *The Uses of Discretion*, Oxford, Clarendon Press, pp. 11–46.

Hayek, F. A. (1982) *Law, Legislation and Liberty*, Chicago, Ill, Chicago University Press, Vol 2, Chapter 10.

Hemerijck, A. & K. van Kersbergen (1997) 'Explaining the New Politics of the Welfare State in the Netherlands', *Acta Politica*, 32, pp. 258–80.

Hennessy, P. (1990) *Whitehall*, London, Fontana Press.

(Hilmer Committee) Independent Committee of Inquiry (1993) *National Competition Policy*, Canberra, Australian Government Publishing Service.

Hirschmann, A. O. (1970) *Exit, Voice and Loyalty*, Cambridge, Mass., Harvard University Press.

Hood, C. (1991) 'A Public Administration For All Seasons?', *Public Administration*, 69 (1), pp. 3–19.

Hood, C. (1995) 'The "New Public Management" in the 1980s: Variations on a Theme', *Accounting Organisation and Society*, 20 (2/3), pp. 93–109.

Hughes, Barry (1993) 'Investing in Labour Market Efficiency'. Address to the Metal Trades Industry Association, Hyatt Hotel, Canberra, October.

Hutton, Will & Anthony Giddens (2000) Editor's Preface, *On the Edge: Living With Global Capitalism*, London, Jonathan Cape, pp. vii–xi.

Ingraham, P. (1996) 'The Reform Agenda for National Civil Service Systems: External Stress and Internal Strain', in H. A. G. M. Bekke, J. L. Perry & T. A. J. Toonen (eds) *Civil Service Systems*, Bloomington, Indiana University Press.

Jessop, B. (1991) 'Thatcherism and Flexibility: The White Heat of a Post-Fordist Revolution', in B. Jessop, H. Kasterdiek, K. Neilson & O. K. Pedersen (eds) *The Politics of Flexibility*, Aldershot, Edward Elgar, pp. 135–61.

Kasper, W. (1996) *Free to Work: The Liberalisation of New Zealand's Labour Market*, Sydney, Policy Monograph, Centre for Independent Study.

Kelsey, Jane (1995) *The New Zealand Experiment: A World Model for Structural Adjustment?*, Auckland, Auckland University Press.

Kemen, Hans (1999) 'Political Stability in Divided Societies: A Rational-Institutional Approach', *Australian Journal of Political Science*, 34 (2), pp. 249–86.

Kettl, D. (1994) *Reinventing Government? Appraising the National Performance Review*, Report of the Brookings Institution's Center for Public Management, Washington, DC, August.

Kettl, D. F. (1997) 'The Global Revolution in Public Management: Driving Themes, Missing Links', *Journal of Policy Analysis and Management*, 16 (3), pp. 446–62.

King, Desmond (1995) *Actively Seeking Work? The Politics of Unemployment and Welfare in the United States and Great Britain*, Chicago, University of Chicago Press.

Knegt, R. (1986) *Regels en redelijkheid in de bijstandsverlening*, Groningen, Wolters Noordhof.

Knott, J. H. & Gary J. Miller (1987) *Reforming Bureaucracy: The Politics of Institutional Choice*, Englewood Cliffs, NJ, Prentice-Hall.

Kooiman, J. (ed.) (1993) *Modern Governance: New Government-Society Interactions*, London, Sage.

Krasner, Stephen D. (1983) 'Structural Causes and Regime Consequences: Regimes as Intervening Variables', in Krasner (ed.) *International Regimes*, Ithaca, NY, Cornell University Press.

Lane, R. (1991) *The Market Experience*, Cambridge, Cambridge University Press.

Larner, Wendy (1997) 'The Legacy of the Social: Market Governance and the Consumer', *Economy and Society*, 26 (3) August, pp. 373–99.

Lash, S. & J. Urry (1987) *The End of Organised Capitalism*, Cambridge, Polity.

Laver, M. (1986) *Social Choice and Public Policy*, Oxford, Blackwell.

Le Grand, Julian & Will Bartlett (eds) (1993) *Quasi-Markets and Social Policy*, London, Macmillan.

Lijphart, A. (1968) *The Politics of Accommodation: Pluralism and Democracy in the Netherlands*, Berkeley, University of California Press.

Lindblom, Charles (1977) *Politics and Markets*, Basic Books, New York.

Lipsky, Michael (1980) *Street-Level Bureaucracy: Dilemmas of the Individual in Public Service*, New York, Russell-Sage.

Logan Report (1991) *Review of State Sector Reforms*, State Services Commission, Wellington.

Luhmann, N. (1995) *Social Systems*, Trans. by John Bednarz with Dirk Baecher, Stanford, CA, Stanford University Press.

Lundvall, B. A. (1988) 'Innovation as an Interactive Process: From User-Producer Interaction to the National System of Innovation', in G. Dosi et al. *Technical Change and Economic Theory*, London, Pinter Press.

Marceau, Jane (1994) 'Chains, Clusters and Complexes: Three Approaches to Innovation with a Public Policy Perspective', in R. Rothwell & M. Dodgson (eds) *Handbook of Industrial Innovation*, Aldershot, Edward Elgar, pp. 1–12.

March, J. G. & Johan P. Olsen (1983) 'Organising Political Life: What Administrative Reorganisation Tells us about Government', *American Political Science Review*, June, pp. 281–96.

March, J. G. & Johan P. Olsen (1989) *Rediscovering Institutions: The Organisational Basis of Politics*, New York, Free Press.

Martin, John E. (1991) *Glimpses of the Past: The First Fifty Years of the Department of Labour*, Te Tari Mahi, Wellington, Department of Labour.

Martinson, Karen & Daniel Friedlander (1994) *GAIN, Basic Education in Welfare-to-Work Program*, New York, Manpower Demonstration Research Corporation.

McDonald, Paul & Ashwin Sharma (1994) 'Towards Work Teams Within A New Zealand Public Service Organisation'. Conference Paper, Graduate School of Business and Government Management, Victoria University of Wellington, September, 17 pp.

Mead, Lawrence (1986) *Beyond Entitlement: The Social Obligations of Citizenship*, New York, Free Press.

Mead, Lawrence (1989) 'The Logic of Workfare: The Underclass and Work Policy', *Annals of the American Academy of Political and Social Science*, 501, January, pp. 156–69.

Mead, Lawrence (1997) 'Welfare Employment', in Mead (ed.) *The New Paternalism*, Washington, DC, Brookings Institution.

Metcalf, L. & Sue Richards (1984) 'The Impact of the Efficiency Strategy: Political Clout or Cultural Change?', *Public Administration*, 62 (4), pp. 439–54.

Mintzberg, H. (1983) *Structure in Fives: Designing Effective Organisations*, Englewood Cliffs, NJ, Prentice Hall.

Moe, T. (1984) 'The New Economics of Organisation', *American Journal of Political Science*, 28, pp. 739–77.

Moldofsky, N. (1989) *Order – With or Without Design?*, London, Centre for Research into Communist Economics.

Morgan, C. & Stephen Murgatroyd (1994) *Total Quality Management in the Public Sector*, Buckingham, Open University Press.

Mulgan, Geoff (1997) *Life After Politics: New Thinking for the Twenty-First Century*, London, Fontana.

Niskanen, W. A. (1979) 'Competition Among Government Agencies', *American Behavioral Scientist*, 22, pp. 517–24.

Nunnally, J. C. (1978) *Psychometric Theory*, 2nd Edn, New York, McGraw-Hill.

NZES (1995) *Operation Future: An Update*, Wellington, 24 November.

NZES (1996) *Operation Future: Introduction: Detailed Design*, Wellington, 10 April.

Oakland, J. (1989) *Total Quality Management*, London, Butterworth.

O'Connor, Ian (1998) *Rethinking Social Work and the Human Services in Australia: An Introduction.* Paper presented to the Academy of Social Sciences in Australia Workshop, Brisbane, 10 August.

Organisation for Economic Co-operation and Development (1987) *The Control and Management of Government Expenditure,* Paris.

OECD (1992) *Performance Management in the Public Sector: Developments and Use in OECD Member Countries,* Paris, OECD, PUMA.

OECD, PUMA Public Management (1993) *Market-Type Mechanisms Series No. 6: Internal Markets,* Paris, OECD.

OECD (1995) *Governance In Transition,* Paris, OECD.

OECD (1996) *Employment Outlook 1996,* Paris (Organisation for Economic Cooperation and Development).

OECD (1999) *Implementing the OECD Jobs Strategy: Assessing Performance and Policy,* Paris, OECD.

Ormsby, Maurice J. (1998) 'The Provider/Purchaser Split: A Report from New Zealand', *Governance,* 11 (3) July, pp. 357–87.

Orr, Adrian (1995) 'New Zealand: The Results of Openness', *The OECD Observer,* No. 192, Feb/Mar, pp. 51–3.

Osborne, David & Ted Gaebler (1992) *Reinventing Government: How the Entrepreneurial Spirit is Transforming the Public Sector,* New York, Plume Books.

Ostrom, Elinor (1990) *Governing the Commons: The Evolution of Institutions of Collective Action,* Cambridge, Cambridge University Press.

O'Toole, Laurence J. (1997) 'Treating Networks Seriously: Practical and Research-based Agendas in Public Administration', *Public Administration Review,* 57 (1) Jan/Feb, pp. 45–51.

Peck, Jamie (1996) *Work-Place: The Social Regulation of Labor Markets,* New York, Guilford Press.

Pember Reeves, William (1902) *State Experiments in Australia and New Zealand,* London, Allen & Unwin.

Perri 6 (1997) 'Governing by Cultures', in Mulgan, op. cit., pp. 260–85.

Peters, B. Guy (1989) *The Politics of Bureaucracy,* 3rd Edn., New York, Longman.

Piaget, Jean (1955) *The Child's Construction of Reality,* London, Routledge & Paul.

Poggi, Gianfranco (1978) *The Development of the Modern State,* London, Hutchinson.

Polanyi, K. (1944) *The Great Transformation,* Boston, Beacon, reprint 1957.

Pollitt, C. (1990) *Managerialism and the Public Services: The Anglo-American Experiences,* Oxford, Basil Blackwell.

Powell, W. (1991) 'Neither Market nor Hierarchy: Network Forms of Organisation', *Research in Organisational Behaviour,* 12, pp. 295–336.

Prime Ministerial Task Force on Employment (1994) *Proposals for Action – Employment: Addressing New Zealand's Biggest Challenge. He Puanga Mahi Rau,* Wellington, New Zealand, November, 106 pp.

Pusey, M. (1991) *Economic Rationalism in Canberra: A Nation-Building State Changes Its Mind,* Cambridge, Cambridge University Press.

Putnam, R. (1993) *Making Democracy Work: Civic Traditions in Modern Italy,* Princeton, Princeton University Press.

Pyhrr, P. (1977) 'The Zero-Based Approach to Government Budgeting', *Public Administration Review,* pp. 371–8.

Reich, Robert (ed.) (1988) Introduction to *The Power of Public Ideas,* Cambridge, Mass., Ballinger Publishing Company.

Rhodes, Martin (1998) 'Globalisation, Labour Markets and Welfare States: A Future of Competitive Corporatism?', in M. Rhodes & Yves Meny (eds) *The Future of European Welfare: A New Social Contract?*, London, Macmillan.

Rhodes, Martin & Bastiaan van Apeldoorn (1998) 'Capitalism Unbound? The Transformation of European Corporate Governance?', *Journal of European Public Policy*, 5 (3), pp. 406–27.

Rhodes, R. A. W. (1990) 'Policy Networks: A British Perspective', *Journal of Theoretical Politics*, 2 (3), pp. 293–317.

Rhodes, R. A. W. & David Marsh (1995) 'Les Reseaux d'Action Publique en Grande Bretagne', in Patrick Le Gales & Mark Thatcher (eds) *Les Reseaux de Politique Publique: Debat autour des policy networks*, Paris, L'Harmattan.

Richardson, Ruth (1995) *Making a Difference*, Christchurch, Shoal Bay Press.

Robinson, Chris (1995) *Employment Case Management and Public Sector Reform*, Department of Prime Minister and Cabinet (PMC), 10 July, Canberra, PMC.

Rose, N. (1989) *Governing the Soul: The Shaping of the Private Self*, London, Routledge.

Rose, Nikolas (1996) 'Governing "Advanced" Liberal Democracies', in Andrew Barry, Thomas Osborne & Nikolas Rose (eds) *Foucault and Political Reason: Liberalism, Neo-Liberalism and Rationalities of Government*, London, UCL Press, pp. 37–65.

Ryan, William (1999) 'The New Landscape for Non-Profits', *Harvard Business Review*, 77 Jan–Feb, pp. 127–36.

Sabatier, Paul & Hank Jenkins-Smith (eds) (1993) *Policy Change and Learning: An Advocacy Coalition Approach*, Boulder, Colorado, Westview.

Sabel, C. (1994) 'Flexible Specialisation and the Re-emergence of Regional Economies', in P. Hirst & J. Zeitlin (eds) *Reversing Industrial Decline? Industrial Structure and Policy in Britain and her Competitors*, Oxford, Berg, 1989, pp. 17–70.

Salamon, Lester M. (ed.) (1989) *Beyond Privatisation: The Tools of Government Action*, Washington, DC, Urban Institute Press.

Sandel, M. J. (1988) 'The Political Theory of the Procedural Republic', in Robert Reich, op. cit., pp. 65–81.

Schick, Allen (1996) *The Spirit of Reform: Managing the New Zealand State Sector in a Time of Change*, Wellington, New Zealand State Services Commission and the New Zealand Treasury.

Schmitter, P. C. & J. R. Grohe (1997) 'Der korporatistische Sisyphus: Vergangenheit, Gegenwart und Zukunft', in *Politische Vierteljahres-schrift*, 38 (3).

Schokkaert, E. & L. Van Ootegem (1990) 'Sen's Concept of the Living Standard applied to the Belgian Unemployed', *Researches Economiques de Louvain*, 56 (3–4), pp. 429–45.

Schorr, Lisbeth R. (1997) *Common Purpose: Strengthening Families and Neighbourhoods to Rebuild America*, New York, Anchor Books.

SCP (1998) *Sociaal en Cultureel Rapport 1998*, Rijswijk, Sociaal en Cultureel Planbureau, Netherlands.

Sen, Amartya (1997) 'Inequality, unemployment and contemporary Europe', *International Labour Review*, 136 (2) Summer, pp. 155–72.

Sennett, Richard (1998) *The Corrosion of Character: The Personal Consequences of Work in the New Capitalism*, New York, W. W. Norton.

Shand, David (1996) 'Are We Reinventing Government?', in Glynn Davis & Patrick Weller (eds) *New Ideas, Better Government*, Sydney, Allen & Unwin, pp. 64–73.

Silverman, D. (1971) *The Theory of Organisations: A Sociological Framework*, New York, Basic Books.

Simon, Herbert (1957) *Administrative Behaviour*, New York, Macmillan.

Smith, Steven Rathgeb & Michael Lipsky (1993) *Nonprofits for Hire: The Welfare State in the Age of Contracting*, Cambridge, Mass., Harvard University Press.

Sociale Zaken en Werkgelegenheid (Ministry of Social Affairs and Employment) (1996–1997) *De Nederlandse verzorgingsstaat in internationaal en economisch perspectief*, The Hague.

Spinoza, B. (1677) 'Tractatus Politicus', in A. G. Wernham (ed.) (1958) *Spinoza: The Political Works*, Oxford, Clarendon Press.

St John, S. & A. Heyes (1994) 'The Welfare Mess', Policy Discussion Paper, Economics Department, University of Auckland, October, 22 pp.

Stein, R. M. (1990) 'The Budgetary Effects of Municipal Service Contracting: A Principal-Agent Explanation', *American Journal of Political Science*, 34, pp. 471–502.

Stone, Clarence (1983) 'Whither the Welfare State? Professionalisation, Bureaucracy and the Market Alternative?', *Ethics*, 93, April, pp. 588–95.

Stone, Alice B. & Donald C. Stone (1975) 'Early Development of Education in Public Administration', in Frederick C. Mosher (ed.) *American Public Administration: Past, Present, Future*, Tuscaloosa, University of Alabama Press.

Streeck, Wolfgang (1992) *Social Institutions and Economic Performance: Studies of Industrial Relations in Advanced Capitalist Economies*, London, Sage.

Streeck, Wolfgang & Phillipe Schmitter (1995) 'Community, Market, State and Associations?', in Streeck & Schmitter (eds) *Private Interest Government*, London, Sage.

Stromback, Thorsten, Michael Dockery & Wiwi Ying (1998) *Labour Market Programs and Labour Market Outcomes*, Australian Labour Market Research Workshop, Victoria University of Technology, 19–20 February.

Tabachnick, B. G. & L. S. Fidell (1983) *Using Multivariate Statistics*, New York, Harper & Row.

Thompson, Grahame, Jennifer Frances, Rosalind Levačić & Jeremy Mitchell (eds) (1991) *Markets, Hierarchies and Networks: The Coordination of Social Life*, London, Sage.

Toffler, A. (1971) *Future Shock*, London, Pan.

Touraine, Alain (1988) *The Return of the Actor: Social Theory in Postindustrial Society*, Minneapolis, University of Minnesota Press.

Treasury (New Zealand) (1990) *Briefing Papers*, Wellington, New Zealand.

U.S. General Accounting Office (1995) *Welfare to Work: Most AFDC Training Programs Not Emphasizing Job Placements*, Washington, DC, GAO.

van der Veen, Romke & Willem Trommel (1999) 'Managed Liberalisation of the Dutch Welfare State: A Review and Analysis of the Reform of the Dutch Social Security System, 1985–1998', *Governance*, 122 (3) July, pp. 289–310.

Vanstone, Senator Amanda (1997) 'Reforming Employment Services', Office of the Minister for Employment, Education and Training, Canberra, 31 pp.

Varian, Tom (1990) *Beyond the TQM Mystique: Real-World Perspectives on Total Quality Management*, Arlington, Va., American Defence Preparedness Association.

Veljanovski, C. (1987) *Selling the State: Privatisation in Britain*, London, Weidenfeld & Nicholson.

Visser, Jell & Anton Hemerijck (1997) *'A Dutch Miracle': Job Growth, Welfare Reform and Corporatism in the Netherlands*, Amsterdam, Amsterdam University Press.

Walsh, K. (1995) *Public Services and Market Mechanisms: Competition, Contracting and the New Public Management*, Basingstoke, Macmillan.

Walsh, Pat (1992) 'The Employment Contracts Act', in J. Boston & P. Dalziel (eds) *The Decent Society? Essays in Response to National's Economic and Social Policies*, Auckland, NZ, Oxford University.

Warner, W. (1984) *Organisations and Experiments: Designing Ways of Managing Work*, New York, John Wiley & Sons.

Warwick, D. P. (1975) *A Theory of Public Bureaucracy*, Cambridge, Mass., Harvard University Press.

Weaver, R. K. & Bert Rockman (eds) (1993) *Do Institutions Matter? Government Capacities in the United States and Abroad*, Washington, DC, The Brookings Institution.

Weber, Max (1947) *The Theory of Social and Economic Organisation*, Trans. A. M. Henderson & Talcott Parsons, New York, Oxford University Press.

Williamson, O. E. (1979) 'Transaction-Cost Economics: The Governance of Contractual Relations', *Journal of Law and Economics*, 22, pp. 233–62.

Williamson, Oliver (1975) *Markets, Hierarchies: Analysis and Antitrust Implications*, New York, The Free Press.

Wilson, Woodrow (1887) 'The Study of Public Administration', reprinted in Jay M. Shafritz & Albert C. Hyde (eds) *Classics of Public Administration*, Oak Park Ill., Moore Publishing, 1978.

Yeatman, Anna (1995) *Getting Real: Interim Report of the Review of the Commonwealth-State Disability Agreement*, Canberra, Australian Government Publishing Service.

Young, R. J. C. (1995) *Colonial Desire: Hybridity in Theory, Culture and Race*, London, Routledge.

Zifcak, S. (1994) *New Managerialism: Administrative Reform in Whitehall and Canberra*, Buckingham, Open University Press.

Index